Identity, Ignorance, Innovation

Matthew d'Ancona is an award-winning journalist and author. He is an Editor and Partner at *Tortoise Media*, and was previously Editor of *The Spectator*, lifting the magazine to record circulation. He has written columns for the *Evening Standard*, *Guardian*, *Daily* and *Sunday Telegraph*, *GQ*, and the *International New York Times*. He is a Visiting Research Fellow at Queen Mary University of London, and was elected a Fellow of All Souls College, Oxford, in 1989. He has two sons and lives in London.

Also by Matthew d'Ancona

Post-Truth
In It Together
Being British

Identity, Ignorance, Innovation

Matthew d'Ancona

HODDER

First published in Great Britain in 2021 by Hodder & Stoughton
An Hachette UK company

This paperback edition published in 2022

1

Copyright © Matthew d'Ancona 2021

The right of Matthew d'Ancona to be identified as the Author
of the Work has been asserted by Choose an item in accordance
with the Copyright, Designs and Patents Act 1988.

All rights reserved. No part of this publication may be reproduced, stored
in a retrieval system, or transmitted, in any form or by any means without
the prior written permission of the publisher, nor be otherwise circulated
in any form of binding or cover other than that in which it is published and
without a similar condition being imposed on the subsequent purchaser.

A CIP catalogue record for this title is available from the British Library

Paperback ISBN 9781529303988

Typeset in Sabon MT by Hewer Text UK Ltd, Edinburgh
Printed and bound in Great Britain by Clays Ltd, Elcograf S.p.A.

Hodder & Stoughton policy is to use papers that are natural, renewable
and recyclable products and made from wood grown in sustainable
forests. The logging and manufacturing processes are expected to
conform to the environmental regulations of the country of origin.

Hodder & Stoughton Ltd
Carmelite House
50 Victoria Embankment
London EC4Y 0DZ

www.hodder.co.uk

For Teddy and Zac
beloved sons

CONTENTS

INTRODUCTION
THE THREE 'I's

It is a joke in Britain to say that the War Office is always preparing for the last war.

Winston Churchill, 1948

I have a feeling, in a few years people are going to be doing what they always do when the economy tanks. They will be blaming immigrants and poor people.

Mark Baum (Steve Carrell), *The Big Short* (2015)

You know something is up when clichés start to regain their original meaning and impact. For as long as I can remember, it has been routine – practically orthodox, at some points – to claim that politics, or capitalism, or society, or the planet itself or all four are 'broken'. The familiar words of W.B. Yeats are rolled out on the trolley of commentary, especially 'Things fall apart' and 'the centre cannot hold'.

Their recitation feels like an incantation, a ritual to ward off the worst. As often as not, there is talk of a 'new politics', an ethical transformation of business, a systematic effort to help those who suffer the inequities of globalisation, and a green revolution. There are conferences, fretful speeches, editorials and documentaries, often legislation or new regulation. But what was declared to be an unignorable 'wake-up call' – war in the Balkans, 9/11, the financial crash – turns out to be nothing of the sort, and, after much agonising and a small dose of change, the train goes clattering on.

Yet – since the crash and especially since 2016 – these declarations of malfunction, pathology and failure have felt different, more substantial, less formulaic. As trust in institutions has collapsed, and polarisation deepened, so too we have seemed less competent as a species; less able to repair our institutions when they fail; less equipped to mend the tears in the social fabric; less resilient to the buffeting force of change. We prefer slogans to the heavy-lifting of collaboration; performance to practical reform; virtue-signalling (on left and right) to action.

For some years, I have been especially exasperated by a particular narrowing of analysis, and the extent to which all roads in British political debate have seemed to lead to the question of *immigration*, or one of its proxies.[1] This was most luridly apparent in the referendum battle over Brexit in 2016. Formally framed as a contest between two economic arguments – those who wanted the UK to pursue a buccaneering future in global trade, freed from the shackles of Brussels, versus those (like myself) who thought it was madness to cut Britain off from the largest single market in the world – the Brexit battle was, at its deepest level, uglier and more visceral.

In June 2017, a report compiled from the British Social Attitudes Survey showed that the most significant factor in the vote to leave the EU had been anxiety about the number of immigrants coming (or perceived to be coming) to the UK. Similar conclusions were drawn in a Nuffield College study published in April 2018. Yes, the campaign from Brexit had been won with a general invitation to 'Take Back Control'. But it was 'control' with one purpose above all others at its core – a purpose nastily symbolised by the poster unveiled during the referendum campaign by Nigel Farage, the then leader of the UK Independence Party, depicting a long queue of Syrian refugees under the inflammatory slogan: 'Breaking Point'.

The social media ads fired off by the official Vote Leave campaign had made much of the (remote) prospect – presented as a threat – of Turkey joining the EU, and of a consequent wave of Muslim migrants. Ending free movement within the bloc was always the non-negotiable demand of the Brexiteers.

An ugly nativism entered the blood of mainstream politics, rarely daring to speak its name explicitly but ever-present all the same. After the referendum, it became routine to hear Conservative ministers say that companies should keep lists of foreign workers, that employing non-British doctors denied British teenagers the opportunity to study medicine, even that foreign students ought not to aspire to settle in the UK. In August 2020, the home secretary, Priti Patel, let it be known that she was all for deploying the Navy to drive back migrants trying to cross the Channel.[2]

Such pledges came and went, not all implemented. But the foul taste of the rhetoric remained. Nor was it an accident that, in hardening his claim to the top job, Boris Johnson, the then former foreign secretary, chose in July 2018 the tactic of claiming that a Muslim woman wearing the niqab resembled 'a bank robber' and that it was 'absolutely ridiculous that people should choose to go around looking like letter boxes'.

All of this, of course, was a dilute but still depressing version of the brutally anti-immigrant strategy adopted by Donald Trump as candidate and president. On the very day that he entered the race, Trump had accused Mexico of sending 'rapists' to the US. One of his first actions as president was to sign an executive order banning foreign nationals from seven majority-Muslim countries for 90 days, suspending the admission of Syrian refugees indefinitely and prohibiting all other refugees from entering the US for 120 days. He would later describe unauthorised migrants as 'animals', mire himself in controversy by separating thousands of children from their parents or guardians at the Mexican border, and monstrously exaggerate the scale of a so-called 'caravan' of Central American immigrants in December 2018. He referred more than once to people coming from 'shithole countries'. So commonplace did such language become in presidential tweets and speeches that it took an effort of will to remember that this was the leader of the free world – holding the office once occupied by Abraham Lincoln, Franklin D. Roosevelt and John F. Kennedy – who was seeking to normalise the brutal slang of rednecks and white supremacists

Opposition to immigration (in all its forms) was the governing theme of the populist Right surge in the second decade of this century. Broadly speaking, the political ploy was always the same: to scapegoat migrants for the consequences of the financial crash, to blame them for economic insecurity and wage stagnation, and to implicate them in a supposedly historic struggle between native cultures and 'globalism'. As the British writer and broadcaster Afua Hirsch notes in her fine book on belonging, identity and race: 'It's hard to take out your frustration on declining international might, globalisation or the bureaucratisation of trade and regulation. The presence of large numbers of immigrants, on the other hand, is a tangible symptom of these changes, so naturally it gets the hit'.[3]

The most preposterous, outlandish and irresponsible version of this narrative was the white nationalist theory of the 'Great Replacement' (or *grand remplacement*), according to which European peoples were being progressively supplanted by non-European and predominantly Muslim incomers – mass immigration, falling birth rates among white Europeans and demographic growth among non-white populations conspiring to transform the very nature of the West.[4] But – for all its racist absurdity – this was the extreme version of an ideological force that burrowed deep into the heart of Western democracies. The core values of neo-nationalism and nativism had forced themselves into the mainstream and were seeking full decontamination. As Steve Bannon, Trump's former chief strategist, told members of Marine Le Pen's French National Front in March 2019: 'Let them call you racists, let them call you xenophobes, let them call you nativists, wear it as a badge of honour.'

I have always been in favour of immigration as a force of enrichment: cultural and social as well as economic. So – in common with most liberal commentators – I found this trend alarming, distasteful and profoundly irresponsible: around the world, populist Right movements, in and out of government, were fostering dissent, tribalism and ill feeling that, all too often, led to violence. The racist riots in Charlottesville, Virginia, in August 2017 – and Trump's extraordinary declaration that there had been 'very fine people' on both sides – fortified a more general fear that demons were being unleashed, atavisms awoken

4

and old crash barriers of civil discourse swept aside. Reason was losing out everywhere to furious emotion, turbocharged by social media and the broad decline of trust in institutions, experts and elites. And, though Trump was defeated in the presidential election of November 2020, it should never be forgotten that more than 73 million Americans voted to give him a second term: Trumpism survived the fall of the man Bannon called the 'very imperfect instrument'.

The wickedness of this new politics was, it seemed to me, grievously compounded by its fundamental dishonesty. The argument for sensibly managed border control had been allowed to escalate into a dangerously heated argument about the very nature and composition of nationhood. And the fraudulence at the heart of this argument was a simple fact: that the debate now being presented as long overdue and vividly of the moment had been conducted, and concluded, many years in the past.

The human story has been one of epic mobility, since the first explorers left Africa 80,000 years ago. Those who designed the modern international order, seeking a liberal market not only in goods but also in labour, did so fully aware of what they were doing: matching supply to demand, filling jobs that indigenous citizens would not take, seeking new workforces to meet new needs. The 72-year-old NHS is not only the institutional expression of the British belief in socialised medicine; it also – by its dependency upon migrant labour – enshrines a clear position on workforce mobility and the porousness of borders. For decades, whole sectors of the UK economy have relied upon the contribution of immigrants for their prosperity. Naturally, all advanced societies fine-tune and adjust their border management policies constantly, pragmatically and as a matter of course. But the populist Right's ascendancy has depended upon a total misconception about the structure of modern economies, and the very prosperity that funds our public services. It has long been the case that Britain – in common with many other Western nations – would collapse without newcomers: it is a collective dependency that should unite, rather than divide, us.[5]

In 2020, the onslaught of Covid-19 demonstrated the puny reality of this fierce debate about borders, immigration and supposedly reclaimed control. Yes, the nations of the world, with differing speed and severity, imposed their travel bans, their border closures and their quarantine periods for newcomers (patchily observed in many cases). But the virus was cunning in its evasion of all such restrictions, following trade and tourist routes, sneaking through the feeble barriers set up by its prey or reaching its destination before they were even imposed. It was not until 17 March 2020 that the UK Foreign Office advised British citizens against travel anywhere in the world – a full month after the school half-term – as a consequence of which, according to the government's scientific advisers, the most significant primary infections had taken place.

No less important was the interdependence that the pandemic quickly laid bare: never has the fragility of medical supply lines been so apparent and the reliance of individual countries upon access to each other's markets so clear. The scramble for protective equipment, testing supplies and ventilators was an object lesson in the interconnectedness of the 21st-Century world: in this case, a notable reliance upon Chinese supplies.

Not surprisingly, this prompted a discussion about the extent to which nation states could improve their resilience, planning more strategically for such 'high-impact, low-probability' events: shifting from a supply model based on the principle 'just in time' to the safer principle of 'just in case'. But only the most desperate nationalists argued for full-blown 'autarchy' or national self-sufficiency: one of the virus's many brutally administered lessons was that such propositions were nonsense in the modern context. Not even the world's two hyperpowers – the US and China – could generate all the resources that their respective populations required.

In this sense, Covid-19 was also an unambiguous rejoinder to the introspective nationalism of the populist Right. The pathogen was a planetary threat, a crisis, in the words of EU commissioner Thierry Breton, 'that knows no borders'. Like the climate emergency, the inequities of globalisation, fundamentalist terrorism, the challenge of human longevity and the technological revolution, it was a global phenomenon that demanded a global response – and, in the pitiful absence of truly coordinated international collaboration, continued its lethal sweep across the planet. The pandemic was not only a reminder of the fragility of human life; it also revealed desperate vulnerabilities at every level of political and governmental organisation.

All of which strengthened my conviction that political discourse needed to escape its fixation with immigration (a fixation that took many forms but sprang from a single, deeply embedded root: the fear of change). Furthermore, the quagmire of nationalism, nativism and fixation with population mobility seemed to me an emblem of a deeper torpor: an inability to speak meaningfully about the political challenges of the hour, a form of aphasia that could only make more probable the alarming submission-by-stages to creeping authoritarianism.[6] It is scarcely contested now that our politics is polarised, and that this rush to the extremes of the spectrum has been mobilised by social media. The greater question is what to do about it.

This book is an attempt to stimulate that debate. It is unashamedly polemical in tone, not least because I believe the urgency of the moment requires such interventions. Civilised disagreement should always be a hallmark of a decent society. But – to a perilous extent – we are shying away from difficulty, from tough terrain, from areas of discourse that will invite the telltale red laser dots of online snipers. Some of the themes in this book are extremely sensitive: discussion of them has become so toxic and so poisoned that (never officially, but in practice) they have been marked out as no-go zones except for tiny squadrons of authorised combatants on both sides.

The new mantra is to 'stay in your lane': to write only about your 'lived experience' and to steer clear of all else. It is important to recognise that this injunction usually has a benign purpose: to give those who lack a platform and a voice the opportunity to be heard, unimpeded by the obstructions of the powerful. It urges those with power not to trample on terrain of

7

which they know nothing, or to stifle the speech of those who are finding their feet in the public space.

The problem is that, in a pluralist, diverse society, there *are* no lanes: only an endless series of crossroads, junctions and contra-flows. All issues, challenges and problems interconnect. As I shall go on to argue, any respectable form of inquiry requires due diligence, accumulation of evidence and collection of testimony from those who know the subject best: it should be obvious that a white straight man cannot speak *for* a black queer woman. But that does not mean that he cannot speak *about* the issues that she raises or respond to the points that she might make.

To argue otherwise is a recipe for stultified silence, democratic disaggregation and a society of stockades, not common ground. Yes, and to an often shaming extent, there is much to be said and done about the position in democratic culture of the powerless and the disenfranchised: we often delude ourselves about the distribution of access to mainstream platforms and the comparative decibels that different groups can generate in public debate, and with what ease. But the *starting point* of such discussion cannot be a long list of prohibitions on who can speak about what. A society that conducted itself on this basis would barely be worthy of the name; it would certainly not be democratic in any meaningful sense.

My core premise is one that has long informed my political writing: namely, that there is no pendulum swinging conveniently back and forth between two positions, oscillating more or less predictably over the years. If this was ever so, it is certainly not today. Modern politics is *sequential*, rather than *adversarial*. Just as Tony Blair learned from Margaret Thatcher, so David Cameron learned from Blair. Trump's victory was not a restoration of what had preceded Barack Obama, but a right-wing populist response to his presidency. In his appeal to the disenfranchised voters of the US rust belt, the so-called 'left behind', Trump had more in common with Bernie Sanders than Obama's Republican predecessor in the White House, George W. Bush. In asking 'What comes next?' we must always resist the assumption that it will closely resemble what has gone before.

So – whatever Joe Biden achieves during his presidency – those who imagine that what follows the post-2016 populist Right ascendancy in global politics will necessarily be a patched-up version of the old liberal democratic order of the post-Second World War era are deluding themselves. That structure is dead or dying, its necrotic tissue all too visible. The pandemic showed how woefully ineffective its international institutions have become. At national and local level, public confidence in our institutions has plummeted, as has the belief in a widely honoured social contract; the notion of shared universal rights and responsibilities is mortally threatened in many places by a sense of futility and voicelessness.[7] The populist Right has prospered precisely because it has fanned the flames of this resentment and positioned itself as the enemy of supposedly unresponsive elites, real and imagined. The storming of the US Capitol in January 2021 was a shockingly violent illustration of what can happen when these flames ignite.

This book does not set out to provide an exhaustive guide to the new political landscape, not least because such a venture would buckle and groan under the weight of intellectual presumption. Except in the context of historical change and technological development, I have relatively little to say about the climate emergency, for instance, not because that issue is not a priority but precisely because it requires a book unto itself. This is a contemporary tract, not an all-encompassing medieval *summa*; its focus is practical and deliberate: the way in which we perceive the world, and the skills we need to do so. Its purpose is to shift attention from one 'I' – immigration – to three others: identity, ignorance and innovation.

Why these three themes?

IDENTITY

Though its roots are deep, the rise of identity politics as a driving force in modern political culture has been sudden, revolutionary and energetic. From the #MeToo movement, via trans activism, to Black Lives Matter – a movement that was globalised overnight by the horrific police killing of George Floyd in May 2020 – we have witnessed a fundamental reordering of political discourse around group and group affinity.

Those schooled in the tenets of mainstream liberal individualism, meritocracy and the Enlightenment have struggled with this phenomenon, temperamentally ill-equipped to deal with a form of political discourse that flows from group membership rather than individual rights and responsibilities.

The shift has also been intellectually traumatic for those who regard politics as a branch of economics and dismiss culture as a secondary force. For many of those born before the end of the Cold War – a decades-long struggle between different forms of global economic order – it is still hard to accept that identity, social narrative and tribal self-definition are now at least as important in shaping history as underlying socio-economic forces. For those who have grown up believing that every political question has an economic answer, the discovery that culture is now upstream from politics has been a painful and disorienting one. In this sense, identity politics is as challenging to the resurrected old Left, with its essentially Marxist class analysis, as it is for the classical economists and corporate leaders who regard Davos as the capital of the world.

It is my primary contention that this discomfort is healthy and should inspire those who experience it to reconsider their assumptions – instead of (as is often the case) rejecting identity politics *tout court* as either a fad, or a menace, or both. To approach the matter practically: identity politics is here to stay. And – in civil and ethical terms – we should welcome it as a fixture in political discourse. The more interesting question is how identity politics will and should evolve, given its new prominence, and how its high-octane activism might translate into measurable action and outcomes.

IGNORANCE

It is a central contention of this book that the younger generation – so-called Gen Z or iGen – deserves little if any of the opprobrium that is routinely heaped upon it in the media.[8] Consider their inheritance: climate emergency, diminishing chances of secure employment, unaffordable property, the pressures of social media, student debt, technological transformation, the prospect of looking after older relatives who will live much longer than their forebears, a society scarred by political dysfunction, low trust and extremism ... to dismiss those who confront this legacy as 'snowflakes' is as risible as it is insulting.

What *is* true is that this generation has been grievously betrayed by the education system through which it has passed: they are overqualified and undereducated. By this I mean that a hopelessly rigid and format-driven examination process has constricted their opportunity to acquire knowledge, schooling them instead in the sequenced regurgitation of information rather than intellectual development.

Lest there be the slightest misunderstanding: I am not impugning the *cleverness* of the young. Quite the opposite, in fact. To spend any time with under-30s at this moment in history is to realise why one should be optimistic about the future. If one may generalise, they tend to be brighter, more motivated and more ethically committed than their parents. Witness their intelligent and nimble activism: the survivors of the Parkland, Florida school shooting; the pupils inspired by the Extinction Rebellion movement to go on strike; and the remarkable youth wing of the UK People's Vote campaign that fought (unsuccessfully, but valiantly) for a fresh referendum on Boris Johnson's Brexit deal. It is no accident that the most famous political activist in the world is a teenage girl who describes her Asperger's as a 'superpower'.[9]

Yet it remains the case that this generation has been denied a true education – the imparting of wisdom, knowledge and the ability to think critically – by the factory-style schooling system through which they have passed, and an educational culture that values the rote techniques required to secure a 9 in GCSE (formerly an A*) more than it does, say, an imaginative, off-syllabus idea about George Eliot's *Middlemarch*, or a reference – inspired but unrelated to the rigid marking scheme – to the 1791 'Black Jacobin' uprising by the enslaved people of San Domingo. We have marched our children into a 13-year boot camp that – *by design* – discourages them from thinking outside the box of the syllabus and relegates such roaming to classes pitifully and euphemistically entitled 'Enrichment'.

So bombarded are young people today by the storm of online data, social media alerts and a rolling scroll of news, gossip and status updates that they struggle to keep pace with the present – let alone to relate it to a longer sequence of events, or the many entangled traditions of the past. For the generation reared on Instagram and TikTok, what happened a year ago is almost axiomatically irrelevant to the crushing digital demands of today. More than 40 per cent of Instagram users use the app on multiple occasions during the day.[10] Americans aged between 18 and 24 check their phones almost 200 times per day.[11] To imagine oneself embedded in a civic tradition or as a participant in an old and ongoing story is quite literally meaningless if your prime concern is whether your latest Instagram post has received more than 100 'Likes'.

This *compression of time* is an existential matter: it restricts access to all sorts of cultural and historical riches. It also nurtures the 'Year Zero' delusion: the misconception that all ideas worth considering, all movements worth following, all wisdom worth consulting, all texts worth reading are the product of very recent times. I have encountered extremely bright, often gifted twenty-somethings genuinely astonished to discover that James Baldwin was saying in the early Sixties most of what they themselves believe now about racial justice; and that Joan Didion was pioneering new ways of understanding the world a quarter-century before Sally Rooney was born. There are, of course, many exceptions to this trend – individuals who have become, in effect, autodidacts, schooling themselves broadly, eclectically and with a fearless interest in the cultural canons of the past. But that is what they are: exceptions.

Again, to be clear: this is the fault of *my* generation, not theirs. We have taught them to follow drills, not to think freely; to obsess over the approved interpretation of set texts, not to read widely and even eccentrically. We have crushed intellectual adventure, idiosyncrasy and creativity to suit the bureaucratic matrix of an exam system that reduces 'literacy' to a form of nationalised tick-box conformity. And – to cap it all – we have failed to teach them the *digital literacy* that will enable them to be masters rather than servants of the hyper-powered technology in their pockets.

But it need not be so.

INNOVATION

Every era is marked by profound technological disruption – one of the principal reasons why, as Karl Popper argued in *The Poverty of Historicism*,[12] all claims about the 'direction of history' are infantile, invalid and quickly rendered obsolete by the unknowable trajectory of scientific research.

There have been many technological revolutions that have profoundly altered the way in which we live. Most obviously: the proliferation of print in the 16th Century; the Industrial Revolution; the mass manufacture of the automobile; the shock-wave of television; and the commercially available contraceptive pill. One of the consequences of every such revolution is to divide society into the beneficiaries of the new technology or research, and those who are left behind.

Ours is the first era in which the technologically enabled face as many problems – albeit of a different character – as those who do not yet have access to the products of scientific innovation. In my last book, *Post-Truth*, I argued that digital literacy was the only effective form of immunisation against contemporary information overload. Unless tomorrow's citizens are taught from an early age how to sift, assess and filter what they are fed on social media and via search engines they will be paralysed within the digital instant.

But the Internet is not the only technological disruption that poses huge cultural, social and political challenges. Automation, for a start, will transform the world of work to an extent and with a speed that no political party is addressing with sufficient vigour. For the first time in history, it will be insufficient to ask: how can we keep the level of unemployment as low as possible? It will be: what gainful occupation or tolerable leisure activity can be found for the growing proportion of citizens who are not employable in the traditional sense – their jobs having already been taken by machines?

Far too little attention has also been paid to the radical disruptive potential of health tech. For instance: we are now, resources allowing, perhaps a decade away from a world in which incurable cancer will be a chronic rather a terminal illness. So quickly are immunotherapy and algorithmic protocols advancing that the old suite of chemotherapy, radiotherapy and resection will be remembered as analogue is now compared to digital.

The dramatic advance in medical technology, combined with the revolution in nutrition, will mark a fundamental change in what it means to be human. The conquest of disease, improvements in nutrition and increased longevity will rightly be hailed as a colossal achievement. But it will also pose challenges that – if not pre-empted by the political class now and culturally acknowledged by everyone else – will be profoundly destabilising.

To name but a few, from cradle to grave: the process of human reproduction has never been so open to manipulation. The now-familiar controversy over stem-cell research is only the prelude to a symphony of questions, whose main theme will be identifying the border between legitimate intervention and outright eugenics. The new century of health tech will increase the cost of medicine radically as innovative treatments pour on to the market. Yuval Noah Harari's vision of an algorithmically enhanced superclass, availing itself of advanced computerised medicine and detaching itself from the rest of humanity, is certainly arresting, and may prove at least partially correct.[13] But it takes insufficient account of the messiness of real-life politics.

Though such stratification of medical care is likely – even inevitable in some countries – the advance of medicine is also a Russian doll, in which multiple political and social arguments are waiting to be released. In particular, the shortcomings of social care for the elderly – horrifically exposed during the pandemic – will force a long-postponed recognition that the taxation of fixed assets is now essential, and that the principal question concerning 'wealth taxes' (or their equivalent) is no longer 'whether' but 'how'.

These are examples of a much greater challenge: how to adapt socially and culturally to a context in which tectonic innovation is not an occasional, overwhelming event but business as usual; in which it becomes a matter of democratic urgency to ensure that all citizens are equipped to deal with the pace of change – not simply by state measures such as the distribution of laptops (welcome as that is), but by the much more difficult recognition that there can be no meaningful equality of opportunity or social fairness without a transformation in the way in which we prepare, and continue preparing, every citizen for life in a storm of change. This is a new form of civic obligation: the collective duty to ensure an acceptable level of technological resilience and literacy for all.

Identity, ignorance and innovation: what unites these three themes is the challenge they present – to endure a period of fragmentation, turbulence and bewildering change with the social, cultural and cognitive tools necessary to forge a new commonality and a new sense of shared human decency. What comes next? That is entirely in our hands.

PART ONE

IDENTITY

CHAPTER 1
THE RISE OF IDENTITY POLITICS

A change is gonna come

Sam Cooke, 1964

On a bright summer's morning in July 2020, the people of Bristol, still growing used to the initial relaxation of coronavirus lockdown restrictions, and (as it turned out) a premature taste of returning normality, awoke to a surprise. For more than a month, a bare stone plinth in the city centre had acted as a daily reminder of the dramatic protest on 7 June – one of countless responses around the world to the killing of George Floyd – in the course of which a statue of the 17th-Century slave trader, Edward Colston, had been torn down and flung into Bristol Harbour.

But the plinth was bare no longer. Where the effigy of Colston once stood there was now a sculpture of Jen Reid – a prominent demonstrator on the day the original statue was brought down – with her fist raised triumphantly in the air. The acclaimed sculptor Marc Quinn had collaborated in secret with Reid to create this replacement, entitled 'A Surge of Power (Jen Reid)', below which a cardboard placard had been placed, bearing the words 'black lives still matter'. The entire operation, involving ten people arriving in two lorries at 5am, had been carried out without the knowledge of the municipal authorities.

Resplendent in the morning light, Quinn's statue in black resin and steel was a dazzling riposte to those who claimed that the protests of the previous month had been a destructive outburst of mob rule with no constructive or serious agenda. An image of a hateful, exploitative past had been replaced – after a short interlude – with an image of civic agency and hope. More than that: the statue epitomised a shift in the political conversation, and the realm of the possible. Only a few years before, such an audacious act of citizen rebellion and creativity would have been unthinkable. Now, it made all the sense in the world, a study in visual grace that had arisen from a moment of impatient rage. After a few days, Quinn agreed to remove the new statue at his own expense. But the point had been made.[1]

When a potent word or phrase punctures its way into mainstream political discourse – 'post-truth', 'privilege', 'fake news', 'left behind' – there are often heated primacy arguments about its precise origins. Yet, unusually, it is more or less universally acknowledged that the notion of 'identity politics' as a significant political concept was introduced by the Combahee River Collective in 1977.

This group of black feminists took its name from the South Carolina river where, in 1863, the great abolitionist and 'conductor' on the Underground Railroad, Harriet Tubman, led a legendary raid that liberated 700 people from slavery.[2] Active in north-east America during the late Seventies, the collective – which included Audre Lorde, Cheryl Clarke, Barbara Smith, Chirlane McCray and Demita Frazier – is remembered for its intellectual retreats, at which the basis of a new politics was hammered out. Its 1977 statement of principles included this all-important passage: 'This focusing upon our own oppression is embodied in the concept of identity politics. We believe that the most profound and potentially most radical politics come directly out of our own identity, as opposed to working to end somebody else's oppression. In the case of Black women this is a particularly repugnant, dangerous, threatening, and therefore revolutionary concept because it is obvious from looking at all the political movements that have preceded us that anyone is more worthy of liberation than ourselves.'[3]

What did this mean? In its powerful and uncompromising language, the collective had defined a form of political struggle that found its focus and took its inspiration from the location of the self in group membership, and specifically in the position of that group in the power structure of society. As David Lammy, the senior Labour politician and campaigner, has put it, identity politics is 'a broad term that signifies political movements in which oppressed groups mobilise and adopt political positions with the aim of correcting a perceived shared injustice. The premise that underpins identity politics is that there is some deep similarity, or essential continuity, between the experiences of different individuals within one oppressed group.'[4]

This is a useful working definition, informed by Lammy's many years of activism for racial and social justice – notably, after the 2011 riots in England, the 2017 Grenfell Tower tragedy and the Windrush scandal of 2018, in which dozens of people were wrongly detained or deported or both. It also helps to explain the common thread running through a series of movements that have transformed the political landscape in recent years: the global #MeToo campaign against sexual harassment; the activism of Black Lives Matter, especially since the death of George Floyd; the trans rights movement; and the mobilisation of 'gender-critical' feminists, who believe that the fact of biological sex is imperilled in contemporary culture, law and regulation.

The notion of 'identity', of course, had enjoyed cultural prominence long before the Combahee River Collective welded it to a political project four decades ago. In particular, the German-American psychologist Erik H. Erikson (1902–94) had popularised the proposition that confusion and neurosis about one's role in groups and the social order were of the essence in explaining personal developmental difficulty: the so-called 'identity crisis'. In a series of exploratory essays in the Sixties, Erikson had himself begun to explore the potential implications of his work for broader understanding of youth, 'woman's position in the modern world' and 'race and the wider identity'.[5] In Erikson's analysis: 'The individual belonging to an oppressed and exploited minority, which is aware of the dominant cultural ideals but prevented from emulating them, is apt to fuse the negative images held up to him by the dominant majority with the negative identity cultivated in his own group'.[6] There is much in Erikson's work that informs contemporary debate on identity politics. But he was less interested in group membership – 'communal identities' in his terminology – and its political meaning than in individual struggle and psychological turmoil.

The understanding of the self through the prism of communal identity is not a modern phenomenon, but as old as our species. Humankind is not only super-social – defining itself through group relations – but naturally tribal. Neuroscience has shown that our empathy is stimulated by those who are fellow members of our group, whether that group has profound origins, as in the case of religious affiliation, or has just been decided quite arbitrarily by (for example) *the flip of a coin*. Functional magnetic resonance imaging (fMRI) suggests that our neural response to an image of somebody from the same community – *of whatever sort* – being caused pain is stronger than a similar picture of a person from another group.[7] The default position in history has been to put tribe before individual, and to explain personhood as a subset of group identity. As the late Jonathan Sacks, the former Chief Rabbi, observed, identity politics is, from this perspective, only 'the latest iteration of a story that goes back before the birth of civilisation'.[8]

In law, culture, ritual and social practice, the medieval impulse was to locate the individual with reference to a matrix of group memberships, rather than a bespoke set of personal characteristics.[9] Though Geoffrey Chaucer understood the importance of idiosyncrasy – the drama of individual flaw, foible and folly – *The Canterbury Tales*, like so many medieval texts, is first and foremost a study in groups and archetypes, their shared habits, characteristics and narratives. In the centuries that followed, individualism began the long march across the landscape that did so much to shape modernity: in religion (the Reformation), in culture and humanism (the Renaissance) and the quest for universal principles that would transcend all that was local, parochial and tribal (the Enlightenment).

Yet the group is, and has always been, an irrepressible force in human affairs – as the Romanticism of the 19th Century demonstrated in its passionate counter-Enlightenment mission. Loyalty to the particular, personal definition by membership, selfhood as a feature of communal identity: these are indelible features of the human condition, relentlessly resistant to rationalism, universalism and individualism. Hamlet the prince is torn to pieces by the contradictions of individual personhood, by the tension between the man as the 'paragon of animals' and the self-loathing 'quintessence of dust'. But – to an extent we easily forget – *Hamlet* the play is at least as absorbed by the differing ranks of its protagonists, by the competing loyalties of hierarchy and family and, ultimately, by the 'state of Denmark' itself. Even the most compellingly introspective text in the English language bristles with expressions of group identity and allegiance.

So, on entering the fraught argument about identity politics, it is very important to acknowledge that this is not really a new debate at all – or at least that there is nothing unfamiliar in forms of discourse that push group membership to the fore. What *is* new and deeply significant is the urgency that this discourse has acquired in the first quarter of the 21st Century, the centrality that it has achieved, and the form that the ensuing controversy has taken. The question is why this has happened.

For some who have sought to answer the question, the rise of identity politics is essentially a pathological phenomenon, a wrong turning by progressives that has done at least as much harm as good. According to the political scientist Francis Fukuyama, for instance, it has become, for some of its champions, 'a cheap substitute for serious thinking about how to reverse the thirty-year trend in most liberal democracies toward greater socioeconomic inequality'.[10]

In a ferocious polemic written after the election of Donald Trump, the Columbia University professor Mark Lilla, attacked identity politics as 'a pseudo-politics of self-regard and increasingly narrow and exclusionary self-definition' composed of 'hypersensitive movements that dissipate rather than focus the energies of what remains of the left'. These campaigns, Lilla continued, 'are losing because they have retreated into caves they have carved for themselves in the side of what was once a great mountain'. And this, he concluded, was a betrayal as well as an error: 'the most damning charge that can be brought against identity liberalism is that it leaves those groups it professes to care about more vulnerable than they otherwise would be'.[11]

Much of this critical analysis has focused upon the institution of the university and its 21st-Century evolution. With some justification, it has been argued that the college campus – especially in the English-speaking world – is no longer reliably a gymnasium of the mind and has become, to a greater or lesser extent, a forcing house for various social justice causes that (again, to varying degrees) threaten the core purpose of higher education as the rigorous transmission of truth, knowledge, expertise and the skills of dispassionate inquiry.

In their book *The Coddling of the American Mind* – inspired by an earlier article in *The Atlantic* – Greg Lukianoff and Jonathan Haidt address a broad range of social failures that (they argue) are conspiring against the best interests of young people from their earliest years to their time at university.[12] While not attacking identity politics per se, Lukianoff and Haidt describe an institutional landscape in which protected groups are actively encouraged to call out supposed danger, in which 'safety' is a greater priority than exposure to intellectual risk and a 'vindictive protectiveness' seeks out and punishes those who allegedly imperil students with their offensive speech or opinions.[13]

To an alarming extent, the contemporary university only encourages the aversion to risk of modern parenting, the decline of free play and the tendency of 'iGen' (the digital generation born after 1995 that started arriving on campus in 2013) to live life virtually through social media and apps rather than in the real world.[14] On campus, speech codes, 'no-platforming' and safe spaces are becoming ever more commonplace. Though this phenomenon is most marked in American universities, the question of free speech in publicly funded higher education institutions is already being investigated by the British Conservative government with a view to possible toughening of the relevant legislation.[15]

Citing the lessons of cognitive behavioural therapy, Lukianoff and Haidt argue that this new culture of 'safetyism' foolishly encourages young people to let feelings and impulses, rather than deliberative thinking, govern their impression of reality. And in such a setting, as they observe, 'the potential for offense-taking is almost unlimited' and *intent* is an irrelevance compared to *impact*.[16] Whether I meant to upset you or not is of absolutely no importance when measured against your sense of personal grievance – and any suggestion to the contrary is in itself a 'microaggression' (one of the countless verbal, behavioural or environmental indignities faced by disempowered, marginalised and minority groups). In this context, Lukianoff and Haidt identify an important division in contemporary identity politics:

> Identity can be mobilized in ways that emphasize an over-arching common humanity while making the case that some *fellow human beings* are being denied dignity and rights because they belong to a particular group, or it can be mobilized in ways that amplify our ancient tribalism and bind people together in shared hatred of a *group* that serves as the unifying common enemy.[17]

This is a distinction to which we shall return.

The shift described by Lukianoff and Haidt is real enough, and familiar to anyone who has spent time in recent years at American or British universities. One should always be alive to the power of ideas, to the unexpected, unacknowledged ways in which they travel from the scholarly grove to the chanceries of power and the streets where the crowd marches. As Keynes famously wrote: 'Madmen in authority, who hear voices in the air, are distilling their frenzy from some academic scribbler of a few years back.' Isaiah Berlin warned likewise that 'philosophical concepts nurtured in the stillness of a professor's study could destroy a civilization.'

That said, and as important as it is, the changing character of campus culture cannot possibly account in full for the rise of identity politics in the past decade; what is happening in higher education can just as easily be understood as a symptom rather than a cause, a vivid microcosm of much broader and more powerful forces.

Central among those forces is the technological revolution. In its infancy, the World Wide Web was expected to nurture cooperation, collaboration and pluralism – and, in many respects, it has done precisely that. What was not foreseen until the advent of the smartphone and the conquest of the world by social media was the extent to which it would do precisely the opposite. As much as digital technology enables us to treat the planet as a village, it also nurtures online huddling, tribalism and the retreat into echo chambers. As Barack Obama observed in his farewell address in January 2017: 'We have become so secure in our bubbles that we start accepting only information, whether it's true or not, that fits our opinions, instead of basing our opinions on the evidence that is out there.'

As any user of Twitter can attest, social media tends to amplify the shrill, drown out nuance and encourage conformation bias. It strengthens the (already powerful) gravitational pull of tribe, and reinforces the message that we are safer, better informed and more likely to prosper if we cluster online with those who share our characteristics, beliefs and experiences. Human beings already have a tendency towards so-called 'homophilous sorting' – our neural impulse to stay close to those who are like us.[18] Digital technology gives algorithmic force to that tendency, driving us towards content that will strengthen our existing tastes, assumptions and prejudices.

This is the social infrastructure of contemporary identity politics. As important as real-life rallies have been to its rise – the Women's March on Washington in January 2017, the BLM protests of May and June 2020 – its true engine is to be found in the digital world. It is Twitter hashtags, Facebook pages, WhatsApp groups and viral YouTube videos that have made possible the light-speed formation of local, national and global groupings and maintained their solidarity. Analogue-era campaigns that relied on continuous or regular physical gathering were always vulnerable to division, sabotage and the corrosions of fatigue – one has only to explore the history of black activism and the Civil Rights movement in the Sixties to grasp that this is so.[19] In contrast, digital campaigns constantly morph, adjust and adapt to changing circumstances and pressures. The genius of the #MeToo movement in 2017 was that, with a single six-character hashtag, in the weeks that followed the original *New York Times* story on Harvey Weinstein by Jodi Kantor and Megan Twohey, there arose a spontaneous worldwide solidarity among women who had been sexually harassed and abused that would have been inconceivable before the advent of the new technology.[20]

It is hard to exaggerate the significance of this shift for political practice generally, and impossible to understand the rise of identity politics without a sense of this broader landscape. As Philip N. Howard argues in his seminal book *Pax Technica*: 'The state, the political party, the civic group, the citizen: these are all old categories from a pre-digital world'. We need, Howard suggests, to look at the world through fresh eyes and see it 'as a system of relationships between and among people and devices'. Politics 'used to be what happened whenever one person or organisation tried to represent another person or organisation'. Now, he says, 'devices will be doing much of that representative work in the years ahead'.[21]

The point is not that politics has changed (change is a constant in the political sphere). In this case, it has *moved house*, shifting from institutions, non-governmental organisations and office-based campaigns to digital networks. The full significance of contemporary identity politics cannot be understood without reference to this transference of power from institutions to networks. The speed with which the real-life protests after George Floyd's death arose in cities around the world was surprising only if you forget the instantaneous, nimble character of social media as a force of collective mobilisation. In the past, such protests would have taken days, and possibly weeks, to organise. Now, they can be brought into being with a single Facebook post. It has never been easier to maintain contact and affiliation with an identity group or one of its representative faces. What were once called 'flash mobs' – physical gatherings generated by online alerts – are now a standard feature of political discourse and a primary vector for identity politics.

Contemporary university culture, the disaggregation of progressive politics into caucuses and single-issue causes, the technological revolution: all these help to explain what has happened. But what is surprising is that, in this case, so many of those who have tried to understand the rise of identity politics have declined to use Occam's Razor: the philosophical principle that, of any given set of explanations for an event occurring, the simplest one is most likely to be correct.

To a remarkable extent, the traction achieved by identity politics in the past decade has been explained as an unfortunate error, a foolish misstep in the history of liberal democracy that must be corrected as soon as possible. Progressives who stand in the tradition of liberalism, individual rights and responsibilities, and Enlightenment values have been much too slow to ask what is, in truth, the obvious question. What *demand* is it that these new movements clearly meet that was not being met by standard forms of liberalism and social democracy?

For conservatives, the question is either an impertinence or an irrelevance. In his book *The Madness of Crowds*, the best-selling polemicist Douglas Murray suggests that the new politics of gender, race and trans activism is, in fact, 'a new metaphysics . . . a new religion'.[22] Under this rubric, he assembles some persuasive evidence that many who espouse identity politics are unwilling to debate their core claims or subject them to rational scrutiny. Murray observes that 'a set of tripwires have been laid across the culture', often making it hard to engage in civil discussion of certain issues and subjects. As the potential impact of words is prioritised over intent, so it becomes harder to speak openly: 'To speak in public is now to have to find a way to address or at least keep in mind every possible variety of person, with every imaginable kind of claim – including every imaginable rights claim'.[23] In this respect, he has a point: it has become all but impossible for feminists to debate the implications of trans rights for same-sex areas or the definition of the word 'woman' without ferocious accusations of 'transphobia' or even threats of violence (in 2018, in Hastings a meeting of the group A Woman's Place UK was imperilled by a bomb threat[24]).

Less convincing is Murray's insistence that the grievances at the heart of identity politics are either non-existent or grossly exaggerated. On the subject of race, for example, he claims that 'most of us had hoped it had become a non-issue'.[25] A non-issue? The most charitable response to this claim is that it is a triumph of hope over experience – and statistics.

As a starting point, consider the following UK data on racial disparities:

- 51 per cent of people in youth prisons are black or minority ethnic (compared to their 13 per cent representation in the population as a whole).[26]
- Between 1990 and 2017, one-third of all those stopped by the police in England and Wales under 'stop and search' procedures were from ethnic minority backgrounds.
- Over the same period, one in five deaths after shooting by the police was accounted for by people from black and ethnic minority backgrounds.[27]
- BAME Britons were more than twice as likely to die from Covid-19 in the first wave of the pandemic than white people.[28]
- White home ownership rates are more than twice those of black Caribbean people and more than three times those of black African Britons.[29]
- White British students are more than three times as likely to achieve high grades than black Caribbean pupils.
- Between 2014 and 2016, black mothers were five times more likely to die in pregnancy than white women.[30]
- Black people are more than three times as likely to be detained under the Mental Health Act.
- In 2018, black people had the highest unemployment rate of any ethnic group at nine per cent – more than twice that in the white population.

- In 2017–18, black households were over five times as likely as their white counterparts to be officially categorised as 'statutory homeless' in England.
- Ten out of 32 colleges at Oxford University failed to give a place to any black British pupils in 2015 (some measures have since been taken, but progress is slow).
- Only 5 per cent of board directors in FTSE-250 companies who disclosed their ethnicity are BAME.[31]
- One-third of FTSE-100 companies still do not have a single ethnic minority board member.[32]

Now consider the following UK data on gender disparities and injustice:

- The number of rapes reported in England and Wales rose by nine per cent in 2018–19 year on year, but the number of convictions fell dramatically from 2,635 in 2017–18 to 1,925 in 2018–19[33] (more than 90 per cent of rape victims are women).
- In the year ending March 2019, an estimated 1.6 million women experienced domestic abuse.
- The police in England and Wales receive more than 100 calls on average per hour related to domestic abuse. But only 18 per cent of women who experience such attacks report them to the police.[34]
- In 2019, 13 per cent of women were subjected to verbal and visual harassment at work. Five per cent reported being groped or physically harassed.[35]
- One in four young women are scared that they will be sacked if they officially report workplace harassment.[36]
- The gender pay gap among full-time employees stands at 8.9 per cent – a fall of only 0.6 percentage points since 2012.

And here are some statistics to give a sense of the adversity that the LGBTQ+ community continues to face in the UK:

- Homophobic hate crimes reported in London were up in 2019 from 2,607 in 2018 to 3,111.
- Between 2015 and 2019 the number of recorded hate crimes based on sexual orientation across England and Wales increased from 5,591 to 14,491 – a rise of 160 per cent.
- Reported hate crimes against transgender people nearly quadrupled in the five years after 2014 to 2,333 in 2019.[37]
- Nearly a third of trans and non-binary people say that they attempted suicide in 2019–20.[38]

Bullet-point statistics are no substitute for the personal testimony of those whose experiences, suffering and frustrated aspirations they aggregate. But they are a useful riposte to those who insist that the grievances of identity groups are overblown. They also drain some of the mystery from the rise of identity politics. When one considers this landscape of social injustice, imperfectly portrayed in a selection of data, the better question is: why has it taken so long?

This brings us to what Martin Luther King called 'the fierce urgency of now' (a phrase also much loved by Obama). Higher education institutions and social media have, it is true, proved to be hospitable settings for the rise of identity politics. But the root causes of the recent rush towards group activism, often on a global scale, are, I think, to be found elsewhere – and I would identify two principal, closely interrelated factors that have contributed to this particular moment in political history.

First, the financial crash of 2008–9 and its aftermath have prompted a series of huge socio-economic questions, most of which remain conspicuously unanswered. The taxpayer-funded bailouts that saved global capitalism from meltdown seemed initially logical – but have not been matched by a serious self-appraisal by corporations and the financial sector beyond (often insulting) warm words and the 'greenwashing' industry of 'corporate social responsibility'. Job insecurity, wage stagnation and the trap of the gig economy have become the norm for the majority of earners – and that was before the recessionary impact of Covid-19.[39] Meanwhile, the richest one per cent now owns half the world's wealth. As Robert B. Reich, former US Labor Secretary, has put it with caustic precision, we have ended up with 'socialism for the rich and capitalism for the poor' – bailouts for banks, belt-tightening for everyone else – and profound distrust in the global economic system.[40] According to the Edelman Trust Barometer survey of 34,000 people in 28 countries published on the eve of the 2020 World Economic Forum in Davos, 56 per cent now believe that 'capitalism as it exists today does more harm than good in the world'.[41]

This marks quite a descent since the fall of the Berlin Wall in 1989 and the GATT talks that led to the formation of the World Trade Organization six years later. To the extent that the Cold War was a struggle between two systems of economic organisations, capitalism had prevailed absolutely. Three decades on, this triumph has been substantially tarnished not only by structural dysfunction but also by the growing sense that the system is rigged to favour a tiny oligarchy rather than being equitable in any meaningful sense. Those who continue to defend the status quo, on the grounds that it has reduced absolute poverty, reveal only how little they have to show for thirty years of global mastery.

The only failure greater than this crisis of capitalism is the marked inability of its antagonists to come up with a better system. Though there is a huge bibliography of titles (scholarly and popular) that attack the existing structure, their proposals, when stripped of rhetoric, rarely add up to more than higher taxation, a modest shift away from the absolute fixation with growth, and – especially popular – a universal basic income for all citizens.[42] What has not emerged (and shows no sign of emerging) is an alternative system of economic organisation that is sufficiently plausible to command more than marginal political support. Capitalism remains stuck in a dark room, trying to work out why everybody hates it and what, if anything, it can do to fix that.

This economic stalemate has been one of the foremost factors in the rise of identity politics. When political leaders such as

Bernie Sanders in the US and Jeremy Corbyn in the UK have tried to assemble electoral coalitions around old-fashioned affiliation to socio-economic class and offered equally familiar statist responses to poverty and inequality, they have failed. Meanwhile, minority groups have been disproportionately affected by the economic hardship that this serially unsuccessful cohort of politicians has tried to address.

In their book *Identity Economics*, George A. Akerlof and Rachel E. Kranton argue that classical economics is fatally blind to questions of group membership and to the limitations that such memberships can place upon an individual's fortunes. 'Because identity is fundamental to behaviour,' they write, 'such limits may be the most important determinant of economic position and well-being'.[43] The most obvious manifestation of this is occupational segregation – the subtle and not-so-subtle forces that drive the sexes towards different jobs. For all their public commitment to equal employment and diversity, 'employers will usually hire men for men's jobs and women for women's jobs'.[44]

It is striking, for instance, that only seven per cent of US nurses are men. Worse, fictitious resumés sent into employers bearing common names among whites, such as 'Greg' and 'Emily', have been shown in studies to result in 50 per cent more interview requests than those for (say) 'Jamal' or 'Lakisha'.[45] Similarly, African American applicants for bank loans are eight per cent more likely to be rejected than whites. Identity, in other words, is intimately entangled with economic prospects and vulnerabilities. With that in mind, it should be no surprise that – as progressive economists and politicians have bickered over the future of capitalism – the disempowered, marginalised and anxious should have sought solidarity and political collaboration in their respective identity groups.

The second force nurturing the present growth of group activism – and the sense of group vulnerability has been the looming success of right-wing populism and extremist nationalist ideology in the past ten years. No understanding of contemporary identity politics is possible without a clear-sighted grasp of these dangerous forces and the response they have compelled from the very groups that they seek to marginalise, vilify and (in some cases) destroy. In the UK, a third of all terror plots to kill between 2017 and 2019 were planned by the far Right – now recognised by MI5 and the Metropolitan Police as a threat comparable in scale and reach to Islamic jihad.[46] Across Europe, there has been a horrific surge in anti-Semitism, often connected to conspiracy theories as demented and bizarre as they are dangerous and malign.

In the decades after the Second World War, Nazism was a sufficiently recent memory to mark out certain ideological terrain as forbidden. When, in 1968, the Conservative politician Enoch Powell made his infamous 'rivers of blood' speech, he was not only sacked from the shadow cabinet; he also (inadvertently) defined a rhetorical border which respectable politicians would not cross. His speech, in ways Powell had not intended, established the boundaries of acceptable debate in the UK on race, immigration and multi-ethnic society.

Those boundaries endured for four decades – but they have now melted away. In the age of digitised network politics, the distinction between the fringe and the mainstream is no longer obvious: instead, there is a continuum of activism and rhetoric that stretches from the centre of politics to the most hideous recesses of the online world. As the line between what is acceptable and unacceptable has been blurred, notionally mainstream politicians may piggyback on a far-Right position – partially distancing themselves from more barbarous language (the 'Breaking Point' poster, for instance), while leaving ample space for voters to believe that they are privately sympathetic to the extremist view in question. What does it tell centrist Conservatives that their leader, Boris Johnson, has been in contact with President Trump's former chief strategist and the godfather of the alt Right, Steve Bannon? Nothing good.

The banishing of alt-Right provocateurs from the principal social media platforms and the electoral setbacks suffered by the populist Right in specific countries (notably, of course, Biden's defeat of Trump) have bred an unjustified complacency in some quarters about the future of right-wing 'identitarianism' (the white nationalist flipside of progressive identity politics). Driven into private social networks, the alt Right is as busy as it ever was – but now operates out of sight, in contrast to the moment of celebrity enjoyed after Trump's 2016 victory by a handful of online 'influencers' such as Milo Yiannopolous, Lauren Southern, Alex Jones and Stefan Molyneux.

It is a grave mistake to think that the waning public prominence of such figures necessarily signals the defeat of the alt Right and what it stands for. It is also an error to imagine that the sense of communal solidarity fostered by the pandemic will automatically endure and defeat the forces of division and polarisation that have been so prevalent in recent years. The recessionary pain unleashed by coronavirus – especially as it leads to ever more painful levels of unemployment – is precisely what nationalists have always sought out and exploited.

This is the price of populism: the insistence that there are simple answers to complex problems, and the readiness to play any game to secure and hold on to power. Senior politicians used to argue that effective border control was necessary precisely to *prevent* the rise of far-Right nationalism. In contrast, today's populist governments stir up emotions instead of restraining them.

As we have already seen, when Trump declared that there were 'very fine people' on the neo-Nazi side of the Charlottesville riots he crossed a line – and many others around the world have followed. Why, more than thirty years after the publication of Margaret Atwood's *The Handmaid's Tale*, did Hulu's television adaptation of the original novel so grip the collective imagination? Because it captured the lightning of the moment in a bottle of dystopian genius. What felt in 1985 like a cautionary tale – a warning against a patriarchal tyranny fuelled by extremist sentiment – seemed more like a deafening klaxon in 2017 and the years that followed.

It cannot be stated too often: at a moment in history when liberal democracies most need statesmanship, we have been rewarded in too many countries with a chorus of dog whistles, a disgraceful display of plausible deniability and a rush to the bottom of the barrel where the deadliest demons lurk. One has only to look with clear eyes and listen to what is actually being said: from the more extreme Brexiteers to the thugs of the English Defence League; from a US president who tweets racist rhetoric without shame and says that Nigerian immigrants should 'go back to their huts' to the nationalist rhetoric of Trump's Polish counterpart, Andrzej Duda; from the stain of anti-Semitism in Corbyn's Labour Party – a wretched legacy for his successor, Sir Keir Starmer – to the sharp rise in hate crimes in England and Wales.

It is against this threatening backdrop that identity politics has risen, refusing to accept the racist, extremist, misogynist politics that are becoming increasingly commonplace around the world. It is a natural defensive reflex against clear and present danger. What did we expect?

CHAPTER 2

LIBERALISM AT THE CROSSROADS – THE CHALLENGE OF IDENTITY POLITICS

What is it that you wanted me to reconcile myself to? I was born here more than 60 years ago. I'm not going to live another 60 years. You always told me that it's going to take time. It's taken my father's time, my mother's time, my uncle's time, my brothers' and my sisters' time, my nieces' and my nephews' time. How much time do you want for your progress?

James Baldwin interviewed in *James Baldwin: The Price of the Ticket* (1989)

The US Declaration of Independence is one of the greatest and most inspiring documents drafted in human history, an inspiration for almost two and half centuries to nation-builders, democrats and champions of liberty all over the world. That said, its most famous contention is also its most tenuous: 'We hold these truths to be self-evident . . .'

Self-evident it may have been to Thomas Jefferson, Benjamin Franklin and their fellow signatories that 'all men are created equal, that they are endowed by their Creator with certain unalienable Rights, that among these are Life, Liberty and the pursuit of Happiness.' Those phrases remain resonant and – for many – galvanising. But, stripped of their rhetorical power, they are mere assertions, based on a philosophical error: namely, that any truth is 'self-evident'. The central paradox of America is that this very declaration and the nation-building that followed were made possible by the enslavement of millions.

Perhaps the greatest intellectual bequest of the Enlightenment era – of which the declaration is one of the most significant texts – is the principle of verification. According to this intellectual framework, philosophical inquiry, rational debate, academic research and the pursuit of truth must be subjected to the most rigorous tests, analysis and scrutiny. It is axiomatic that all claims are vulnerable to challenge, negation or improvement. Doubt is what fuels the machine. That, one might say, is the whole point: the foundation upon which modern liberal, pluralist societies have been built.

By design, therefore, liberalism is open to attack. In contrast to totalitarian or theocratic ideologies, it provides a framework rather than a final analysis. Far from crushing dissent, it is structured to give dissent a voice (this was the purpose of the First Amendment of the US Constitution). It is perhaps the only system of thought ever to have positively invited heresy. As a consequence, it is the natural condition of liberalism to be 'in crisis' (as countless headline-writers and authors have asserted).

Contemporary liberalism is beset by a curious blend of fatalism and arrogance. Liberals often declare that their principles are in mortal danger – from right-wing populism, from the puritanism of the millennial Left, from Islamist terrorism. But they have not adapted well to the modern condition, to the new technological context or to the fast-changing demands of our globalised, fragmented, polarised society. Liberalism has lost its talent for healing itself.

The populist Right has proved more adept at capitalising upon the 'deep story' of disenfranchisement that was so important to the 2016 US presidential election and the Brexit referendum. No world leader was quicker than Vladimir Putin to understand the potential of digital technology to disrupt the democratic process in other countries – to destabilise rival nations for a fraction of what the Soviet Union paid for its weapons systems. In an interview with the *Financial Times* in 2019, the Russian president said that 'the liberal idea' had 'outlived its purpose', in an era when the public was ever more anxious about migration, open borders and multiculturalism. Liberals, he declared, 'cannot simply dictate anything to anyone just like they have been attempting to do over recent decades'.[1]

In the US and Britain, populist governments have shown themselves to be intermittently indifferent to the rule of law – the software of any stable liberal society. It remains extraordinary that Boris Johnson believed he could get away with suspending ('proroguing') Parliament to expedite Brexit – a decision that the UK Supreme Court ruled in September 2019 was 'unlawful, void and of no effect'.[2] That such a ruling was necessary at all showed how battered liberal assumptions had become in mainstream British politics, how shameless the readiness of ministers to defy clear legal principle. Nonetheless, Johnson went on to win a famous victory in December of the same year. Liberal outrage at his conduct had (to say the least) not translated into an appealing political counter-narrative (in Labour's case, this failure was symbolised by the determination of the movement to stick with Jeremy Corbyn: a leader who comforted the party's mass membership but was woefully inadequate as a plausible prime minister).

The election dramatised a persistent problem – namely the tendency of those who claimed that they wanted to beat the populist Right to put self-indulgence before imaginative and energetic new strategies. Progressives had failed, yet again, to develop an emotional delivery system that addressed experience, hope and memory.

In America, the Joe Biden-Kamala Harris ticket fared better against Trump. But their campaign amounted to little more than a referendum upon their adversary – who, even then, in spite of his appalling mishandling of the pandemic, secured a remarkably high level of support at the ballot box (more than 74 million votes). The Democrat victory was, by definition, a landmark, bringing to an end perhaps the worst presidency in the history of the republic. But its promise was one of pain relief rather than of visionary expectation. Whatever his own legacy proves to be, Biden did not prevail in 2020 because he had forged an inspiring new version of the American Dream.

In response to the rise of identity politics, the liberal reflex has mainly been one of performative appeasement or indignation. Challenged by those asserting the claims of group identity, many supposedly progressive individuals and businesses have frozen like rabbits in headlights – promising, in a blizzard of hashtags and vague commitments to 'diversity' or 'inclusion', to do their bit for social justice. An analysis by the Tortoise Responsibility 100 Index in July 2020 of the FTSE-100's response to the killing of George Floyd showed, for example, that 19 of the 100 companies had tweeted in solidarity with Black Lives Matter, 14 CEOs had issued statements and only 12 of the 100 companies had recently proposed targeted action against racism.[3]

Worse still is the suggestion that identity politics is somehow an impertinence or an irritating distraction from the liberal project. In his book *The Once and Future Liberal* (cited in the last chapter), Mark Lilla rails against what he regards as 'narcissism with attitude' and those who are 'under the spell of movement politics'. This form of political activism, he insists, is an obstruction to political action, though it has bewitched a generation into believing otherwise. 'We need no more marchers,' Lilla concludes. 'We need more mayors'.[4]

Lilla is a passionate, erudite and often witty polemicist. 'The identity liberals' approach to fishing,' he says, 'is to remain on shore, yelling at the fish about the historical wrongs visited on them by the sea, and the need for aquatic life to renounce its privilege'.[5] But these qualities are not matched by humility or the slightest inkling that the rise of identity politics might, just conceivably, be more than an embarrassing wrong turning by young people and their campus teachers.

His answer to the predicament in which contemporary liberalism finds itself is a more robust sense of citizenship and progressive patriotism: 'The only way out of this conundrum is to appeal to something that as Americans we all share but which has nothing to do with our identities, without denying the existence and importance of the latter.' This is indeed the case – but his argument falls at the first fence by failing even to countenance the possibility that identity politics might have something to teach traditional liberals.

It is a principal claim of this book that the rise of identity politics is much more than an aberration, and that – far from being a disaster for progressivism – it is a necessary wake-up call, and one that offers a series of lessons for those (like myself) who still believe that liberalism is a sound foundation for political inquiry and action. Faced with the speed, viral spread and sudden clamour of the #MeToo, BLM and trans movements, the instinct of many liberals has been to adopt a defensive crouch and wait for the storm to pass. But the storm is not going to pass; or, more accurately, fresh storms are on the way. The better response is to understand where they have come from and what they have to say about the shortcomings of contemporary liberal democracy. To revert to the metaphor of software: liberalism needs a thorough reboot.

Take, for instance, the treasured concept of the 'veil of ignorance', most commonly associated with the philosopher John Rawls and his classic liberal primer, *A Theory of Justice* (1971). According to Rawls, our conception of justice depends upon our recognition of a 'purely hypothetical situation':

> Among the essential features of this situation is that no one knows his place in society, his class position or social status, nor does anyone know his fortune in the distribution of natural assets and abilities, his intelligence, strength, and the like. I shall even assume the parties do not know their conceptions of the good or their special psychological propensities. The principles of justice are chosen behind a veil of ignorance. This ensures that no one is advantaged or disadvantaged in the choice of principles by the outcome of natural chance or the contingency of social circumstances. Since all are similarly situated and no one is able to design principles to favour his particular condition, the principles of justice are the result of a fair agreement or bargain.[6]

Rawls's hypothesis – for that is what it is – has proven enormously influential as a basis for argument about liberal values and social justice. The problem with the 'veil of ignorance' is that it is so far removed from reality and its operations. Indeed, like the still-prevalent notion of 'colour-blindness', its intellectual prominence has helped to lull many white liberals into a false sense of confidence that their ideals are being enacted simply because they espouse them. The rise of identity politics in the early 21st Century shows that the 'veil of ignorance' is an ideal more often cited than applied.

In his book *Natives,* the British rapper and activist Akala describes a lived experience that is as remote as could be imagined from the Rawlsian template:

> In some cultures, they mark your entrance into adulthood with a spiritual quest, a physical challenge, a camping trip, a commune with the elders or with an exchange of long-held ancestral wisdom. In the inner cities of the UK, teenage boys racialised as black are instead introduced to the fact that the protection of the law does not apply to our bodies. There is no equality before the law. The whole of society knows this to be true, yet they pretend otherwise. When you meet your own powerlessness before the institution that claims to be protecting you, you feel both stupid and cheated.[7]

Indeed, what Akala describes is not a society structured around belief in the 'veil of ignorance' but one in which those let down by its institutions have clear sight of the grotesque truth that lurks behind the pretence of equal treatment:

> To be black, poor and politicised in Britain is to see the ugliest side of the police and indeed of Britain itself; it is to see behind the curtain and not be fooled by the circus, and to feel crazy because so many others cannot see what is so clear to you.[8]

In her memoir *BRIT-ish*, Afua Hirsch describes a similar cognitive dissonance and the frustrations of growing up in 'a nation convinced that fairness is one of its values, but that immigration is one of its problems' and experiencing 'the uniquely British combination of convenient ignorance and awkward squeamishness'.[9] On the one hand, black and ethnic minority Britons are expected to conspire in the myth that racial injustice is, at worst, a rapidly declining problem; on the other, their experience provides them with daily evidence that structural racism is a clear and present threat to their full citizenship. 'I'm truly sickened,' writes Hirsch, 'by the hypocrisy of the ongoing and undeniably racially skewed limits on opportunity, accompanied by a complacent official rhetoric about diversity that is crowned occasionally with open racism'.[10]

Terrible evidence of this has been provided in recent years by both the Grenfell tragedy and the Windrush scandal. Of the 72 people who perished in the tower-block inferno on 14 June 2017, only seven were white Britons and the Grenfell inquiry has heard that the tragedy was inextricably linked with race. The residents had repeatedly raised concerns – to no avail – about the fire safety of the building with Kensington and Chelsea Tenant Management Organisation, which was meant to supervise it on behalf of Kensington and Chelsea Borough Council. The complaints of richer residents of the borough – one of the most affluent local authority areas in the country – about noisy sports cars were dealt with by the town hall. But the mortal fears of Grenfell residents (tragically prophetic) went unheeded.[11] Understandably, the Grenfell Next of Kin group asked the official inquiry – which was suspended for four months due to the pandemic – to 'investigate the extent of institutional racism as a factor'.[12] The derelict remains of the building stand as a grim testament to the enduring social divides that still scar the capital city, and a reproach to those who claim that London treats all its citizens equally.

The Windrush scandal, which came to light in 2018, affected thousands of Britons of Caribbean descent who were wrongly investigated as part of the Conservative government's 'hostile environment' policy – supposedly intended to target illegal immigrants. The Windrush generation of newcomers, which took its name from the *Empire Windrush* ship that arrived from the Caribbean in June 1948, took up residence under the terms of the British Nationality Act of the same year, and did not require, and were not given, any documentation upon entry to the UK. After 2002, at least 164 British citizens were detained or deported without justification, and many more were left unemployed, indigent and denied access to public services – in spite of working and paying their taxes for decades.[13] Thus, the descendants of the enslaved, invited to the very country whose slave traders had stolen millions of Africans from their homeland, were subjected to the indignity of proving that they deserved to live in the UK at all – often with appalling consequences. To those who say identity politics is unnecessary or an indulgence, the Windrush scandal should act as a reminder that government, when acting in bad faith or carelessly, can still strip its citizens of the identity that they (correctly) assumed was theirs as of right.

It is from this gap between theory and practice – between rhetoric and reality – that identity politics has surged forth. Were the playing field level, as is so often and lazily asserted, then such discourse would be no more than special pleading. But it is precisely because the playing field remains so slanted that such activism remains necessary, and is growing in confidence. As David Lammy puts it: 'In my experience, advocates of identity politics focus on liberating certain oppressed groups only because they believe in equality and liberty for every human being'.[14]

This is an essential insight that too many opponents of identity politics fail to confront. What they construe as awkwardness, or ideological sectarianism, or a contrarian desire to divide progressivism into constituent parts is almost invariably driven by a different objective: namely, a desire for full citizenship and – as a precondition of that – a broader recognition that not all groups enjoy the full rights of that legal and civil status. The hashtag #MeToo speaks of a yearning to escape the captivity of silence and find solidarity with women who have experienced similar mistreatment. The slogan Black Lives Matter is not an attack on white lives but a reproach to society as a whole: it should not be necessary in a civilised community to say that the lives of any group *matter* – scarcely a high bar in the democratic reckoning. But – as the death of George Floyd and many other police killings have shown – it *is* necessary to say this.

As Ta-Nehisi Coates, national correspondent for *The Atlantic*, writes in *Between the World and Me*, framed as a letter to his adolescent son, African Americans grow up horribly habituated to the 'banality of violence' in everyday life:

> I am writing you because this was the year you saw Eric Garner choked to death for selling cigarettes; because you know now that Renisha McBride was shot for seeking help, that John Crawford was shot down for browsing in a department store. And you have seen . . . men in the same uniforms pummel Marlene Pinnock, someone's grandmother, on the side of a road. And you know now, if you did not before, that the police departments of your country have been endowed with the authority to destroy your body.[15]

It is humbling that any father should have to write such words to his child – a warning, naming previous victims, of lethal danger waiting for him on the streets of his home city. That they should have to be written about the world's most powerful democracy, in the 21st Century, is extraordinary. But they *do* have to be written. What Coates is describing to his son is precisely the systemic racism that was evident in the impassivity of former police officer Derek Chauvin's features as he choked the life out of George Floyd with a knee chokehold in 8 minutes and 46 seconds.

The response of contemporary liberal democracy to such horror has tended to be woefully inadequate, following what is, by now, a fairly standard pattern. It addresses the specific case (though not always adequately or quickly – even Chauvin and his fellow officers at the scene were not arrested immediately). It promises investigations and inquiries (in June 2020, Boris

Johnson announced a new government commission to look into racial inequalities, though the involvement of his policy chief, Munira Mirza, was an instant source of controversy because of her well-known scepticism about the concept of 'institutional racism'[16]). And then those investigations are published with varying degrees of fanfare and political enthusiasm – before taking their place in the in-tray of government. It is a regrettable fact that, all too often, such inquiries are appointed not to inspire, frame and inform action, but to keep it at bay.

Speaking on the BBC's *Today* programme in June 2020, Lammy – by then restored to Labour's front bench as shadow justice secretary – questioned the need for yet another commission: 'I made 35 specific recommendations in the Lammy review [into the treatment of BAME individuals in the criminal justice system]. Implement them. There are 110 recommendations in the Angiolini review into deaths in police custody. Implement them. There are 30 recommendations in the Home Office review into the Windrush scandal. Implement them. There are 26 in Baroness McGregor-Smith's review into workplace discrimination. Implement them.'[17]

More than 20 years have now passed since the publication of the 1999 official inquiry into the murder of black teenager, Stephen Lawrence, which famously identified 'institutional racism' in the police. Yet, as recently as February 2019, the author of the original report, Sir William Macpherson, admitted that there is 'obviously a great deal more to be done'.

Giving evidence on his own report to the House of Commons Justice Select Committee in March 2019, Lammy expressed regret that, in many respects, 'things have got worse since completion of the review'. How, he continued, could trust in the justice system be preserved 'when you are 240 per cent more likely to be convicted for a drug offence if you are black than if you are white'? Why, furthermore, had the government rejected his recommendation of targets – not quotas – for BAME representation in the judiciary?

At the heart of this is a broader question: why has the British tradition of incremental reform stalled so badly? Most

obviously because reform of this sort is often procedurally challenging. It requires not only adequate funding, but stamina over
many years. It relies upon thoughtful interaction between multiple agencies. And this is rarely easy.

But there is a second and more troubling reason. To confront
the problem of racial injustice does indeed require a command
of policy detail. But – much more straightforwardly – it calls
upon those with power to confront the ugly realities of the society over which they preside.

In truth, this ought to be no more than an empirical exercise:
at this point in history, it should be a civic imperative to look at
the way the world works, has worked for centuries, and to
respond with decency. Yet this requires a psychological realign-
ment that makes many white people deeply uncomfortable,
privately resentful of all that is implied and simultaneously fearful of culture wars with the far Right if they take action. And
this malaise has been, in some areas, a recipe for policy paralysis. The rise of identity politics is, in part, a response to that
paralysis and a collective posing of the question: if not now,
when?

Another concept with which many liberals have struggled is
the notion of 'privilege'. Its modern usage as a term to signify
unearned advantage and positioning is generally traced back to
Peggy McIntosh, a women's studies scholar at what was then
called the Wellesley College Center for Research on Women, and
her 1989 paper 'White Privilege: Unpacking the Invisible
Knapsack' (itself a shorter version of an earlier study)[18]. The
essence of McIntosh's thesis was that the most important characteristic of privilege was the disinclination to recognise it:

> I have come to see white privilege as an invisible package of
> unearned assets that I can count on cashing in each day, but
> about which I was 'meant' to remain oblivious. White privi-
> lege is like an invisible weightless knapsack of special provi-
> sions, maps, passports, codebooks, visas, clothes, tools,
> and blank checks.

47

The conundrum that McIntosh sought to resolve was this: why did women in her seminars feel intellectually marginalised by male students who were, on the face of it, agreeable and decent? As she told the *New Yorker* in 2014: 'I came to this dawning realization: niceness has nothing to do with it. These are nice men. But they're very good students of what they've been taught, which is that men make knowledge'.[19]

Having set aside the question of personal virtue and turned her focus to structural advantage, McIntosh further acknowledged that such advantage applied to racial inequality as much to the relative power of the sexes:

> Describing white privilege makes one newly accountable. As we in women's studies work to reveal male privilege and ask men to give up some of their power, so one who writes about having white privilege must ask, 'having described it, what will I do to lessen or end it?' After I realized the extent to which men work from a base of unacknowledged privilege, I understood that much of their oppressiveness was unconscious. Then I remembered the frequent charges from women of color that white women whom they encounter are oppressive. I began to understand why we are just seen as oppressive, even when we don't see ourselves that way. I began to count the ways in which I enjoy unearned skin privilege and have been conditioned into oblivion about its existence.

Again, the precondition of such an inventory necessitated at least a partial rebellion against the confining moral individualism which had been the basis of her intellectual, educational and social formation. Her 'schooling', she observed, gave her 'no training in seeing myself as an oppressor, as an unfairly advantaged person, or as a participant in a damaged culture.' And, crucially, McIntosh identified the core problem as a misconception that what really mattered was the individual, her 'moral state' and 'her individual moral will'.

McIntosh then listed a series of statements that identified the specific character of these advantages: For instance: 'I can if I wish arrange to be in the company of people of my race most of the time'; 'I can avoid spending time with people whom I was trained to mistrust and who have learned to mistrust my kind or me'; 'If I should need to move, I can be pretty sure of renting or purchasing housing in an area which I can afford and in which I would want to live'; 'When I am told about our national heritage or about "civilization", I am shown that people of my color made it what it is'; 'I can be sure that my children will be given curricular materials that testify to the existence of their race.'

These, and statements like them, were the unpacked contents of the 'invisible knapsack'. To some, Mcintosh's list looked like a showy act of penitence or a series of generalisations that erased social nuance and personal circumstance. Was a disabled poor white woman really more 'privileged' than a middle-class black man with a high-paid job? Did 'white privilege' trump all other considerations? But her purpose was precisely to force a reckoning, pre-empting the backlash that her observations would (and did) provoke: 'For me white privilege has turned out to be an elusive and fugitive subject. The pressure to avoid it is great, for in facing it I must give up the myth of meritocracy. If these things are true, this is not such a free country; one's life is not what one makes it; many doors open for certain people through no virtues of their own'.

In the three decades since McIntosh's paper, the notion of privilege has entered common parlance (notably as something that needs to be constantly 'checked')[20]. For reasons she foresaw, it has enraged both conservatives and liberal individualists, who (correctly) see her ideas as a foursquare challenge to the notion that *personal decisions* are by far the most important weave in the social fabric, and that our achievements, such as they are, are the product of meritocratic sifting. It is uncomfortable to be told that structural advantage might be at least as important as our personal qualities – in some cases, more so. If you have been educated not to think about 'whiteness' or 'maleness', then it is a fundamental challenge to your self-perception to face the possibility that they are essential to your position and status in society. But this has always been McIntosh's point: black people, women and other groups facing disadvantage have *always* understood that such structures exist, precisely because they are held back by them. Winners are less inclined to analyse the reasons for their success, especially if those reasons violate the rules of meritocracy.

The most common charge made against McIntosh (by the bestselling Canadian psychologist and polemicist Jordan Peterson amongst others) is that she takes insufficient account of the complexity of personhood, and the multiplicity of factors that form an individual's identity.[21] Douglas Murray argues that the notion of privilege is too blunt an instrument to be meaningful: 'Is a person with inherited wealth but who has a natural disability more privileged or less privileged than a person without any inherited wealth who is able-bodied? Who can work this out? Who would we trust to work it out?'[22]

In fact, McIntosh saw this objection coming and explicitly acknowledges the need for 'a more finely differentiated taxonomy' than her own first-draft list and the inadequacy of focusing solely upon whiteness and maleness: 'since race and sex are not the only advantaging systems at work, we need similarly to examine the daily experience of having age advantage, or ethnic advantage, or physical ability, or advantage related to nationality, religion, or sexual orientation'. Murray's claim that the operations of privilege are difficult to judge is at the heart of her case: that honesty and candour about unacknowledged advantage is very hard indeed.

Nor – contrary to what some who cite her work might claim – does McIntosh dispute the notion that personal conduct can and does play a legitimate part in social status: what she calls 'earned strength'. Her purpose is not to make us see ourselves as puppets on the strings of structural forces and to abandon the notion of free will, but to make us aware of those forces and, as far as possible, to *liberate* us from their twitching control.

The liberal impulse is to recoil from ideas such as 'white privilege' because they emphasise group characteristics and identity, and challenge the value of individualism and meritocracy as explanatory tools. But, as Lammy has pointed out, this is a false dichotomy. 'For those from privileged positions, the continued importance of identity categories is understandably hard to recognise,' he writes. '[T]hey have the luxury of thinking of themselves merely as people or, more accurately, as individuals'.[23] Notice that Lammy is not dismissing the notion of individualism – merely questioning its value as an all-purpose tool of analysis when certain people are held back because of their membership of one group and others prosper because of their membership of another.

The debate begun by McIntosh escalated spectacularly after the publication of Robin DiAngelo's book *White Fragility* in 2018. An instant bestseller, it topped the US charts again in the wake of George Floyd's killing and continues to stimulate a fierce argument over its central theme.[24] According to DiAngelo, a diversity consultant, social relations have been distorted by 'the power of the belief that only bad people were racist' and the extent to which 'individualism allowed white people to exempt themselves from the forces of socialization'. Like McIntosh, she suggests that 'our simplistic definition of racism – as intentional acts of racial discrimination committed by immoral individuals – engenders a confidence that we are not part of the problem and that our learning is thus complete'; and that when 'a racial group's collective prejudice is backed by the power of legal authority and institutional control, it is transformed into racism, a far-reaching system that functions independently from the intention or self-images of individual actors.' It follows from this that 'People of color may also hold prejudices and discriminate against white people, but they lack the social and institutional power that transforms their prejudice and discrimination into racism; the impact of their prejudice on white is temporary and contextual'.[25]

As for 'white fragility' itself – a term first coined by DiAngelo in 2011 – this refers to the sensitivities of white people when challenged to acknowledge their place in a fundamentally racist structure, and the effort expended to protect those sensitivities (which DiAngelo has often seen erupt in her seminars and classes).[26] 'We whites who position ourselves as liberal', she argues, 'often opt to protect what we perceive as our moral reputations, rather than recognize or change our participation in systems of inequity and domination'.[27] The morally intolerable consequence is that racism is not addressed, in order to spare the feelings and vulnerabilities of white people.[28]

The conservative polemicist Ben Shapiro denounced the book as 'insane' and 'unfalsifiable, cultish bullsh***'. John McWhorter, a contributing writer at *The Atlantic*, who is black, declared *White Fragility* to be 'a racist tract' and 'the prayer book for what can only be described as a cult', its assumptions 'deeply condescending to all proud Black people' and DiAngelo 'less a coach than a proselytizer'.[29]

We should take seriously McWhorter's challenge that this is 'a book about how to make certain educated white readers feel better about themselves'. In the entire landscape that has been lit up by the rise of identity politics, there are few spectacles less edifying than whites seeking to centre themselves by the new performance art of ideological self-mortification (which is very far removed from intelligent listening and self-education). Such hand-wringing fuels egos – quietly – but has no social worth whatsoever.

It is true, furthermore, that DiAngelo's absolutism does her no favours. By employing the 'Kafka trap' – any denial of complicity is only proof of guilt – she makes it hard for white people to respond to her book in a nuanced way. She seemingly offers only a binary choice: submit totally to her principles, or retain the stigma of the implacable racist. This is a weakness: not because she is wrong about the prevalence of structural injustice, but because her prose is less persuasive than admonitory.

Nonetheless, *White Fragility*, for all its flaws, is an important book, a powerful analysis of the asymmetric character of the racialised landscape she describes, and a manual that should not be ignored by those who are seeking a path forward for contemporary pluralism. It also assembles an impressive body of research, demonstrating that white children as young as six exhibit discriminatory behaviour.[30] Hard as it is to imagine a person who could meet DiAngelo's standards, she is right to continue the critique of individualism and meritocracy launched by McIntosh, and to assert that 'temporarily suspending individuality to focus on group identity is healthy for white people'.[31] Like McIntosh before her, she has shaken up assumptions and offered a bracing corrective to complacency.

Let me be absolutely clear: I still believe that liberalism and pluralism are the cornerstones of a decent society. In our globalised, interdependent, fractured world, they are more important than ever. Those who speak of a 'post-liberal' world are generally hazy, I find, about the particular freedoms which they themselves are willing to give up. But the rise of identity politics is a much-needed challenge to those who believe that liberal ideals are carved in stone, and that they should command automatic respect; or that anything, in an age of continuous and hectic change, could ever reasonably be considered 'self-evident'.

CHAPTER 3

WHERE IDENTITY POLITICS GOES WRONG

I don't want you to be safe ideologically. *I don't want you to be safe* emotionally. *I want you to be* strong. *That's different. I'm not going to pave the jungle for you. Put on some boots, and learn how to deal with adversity. I'm not going to take all the weights out of the gym; that's the whole point of the gym. This is the gym.*

Van Jones, CNN commentator, University
of Chicago's Institute for Politics, February 2017

My first job in journalism was at the free speech magazine, *Index on Censorship*, in 1991. I was a researcher, which meant sorting through clippings and letters about persecuted activists, writers and whistle-blowers around the world; learning how to sub-edit (on page – the organisation was not yet fully computerised); and generally being available when one of the section editors needed something done. The cramped offices were in a tall building overlooking Highbury Fields in north London, and the editor was the revered Argentine journalist and dissident, the late Andrew Graham-Yooll. The atmosphere was one of frantic amateurism and passionate commitment. I loved it.

In those days, the battle for free speech was an unambiguously progressive cause. True, there were some outstanding conservatives involved in its defence – notably the late philosopher Sir Roger Scruton, who, in his work for the Jan Hus Foundation, had taken extraordinary physical risks assisting dissidents during the Cold War in Czechoslovakia and other parts of Eastern Europe. But – broadly speaking – most of those of those working for *Index* or supportive of it were of the liberal left. The defence of free speech was (by definition, it seemed) part of the battle against tyranny, autocracy and oppression. It was the dispossessed and the disenfranchised who most needed the right to speak and write freely. The geopolitical backdrop was clear: the fall of apartheid (remember Steve Biko's 'I write what I like'); the end of the Cold War, in which dissident writers such as Vaclav Havel had played such a luminous part; and the Rushdie Affair, in which a brutal theocracy had sentenced an author to death over the contents of a *novel*. To be a strong defender of free speech was a mark of basic decency, and indicated an understanding that all social rights flow from this and other core civil liberties (to paraphrase the great developmental economist Amartya Sen: famines do not happen in democracies).

How long ago that moral clarity now seems. The primacy of free speech in political culture has been significantly eroded in the intervening decades, crowded out by a very different form of political analysis and a generational shift in priorities. According to a survey of students in the UK by the think tank Policy Exchange published in November 2019:

- 44 per cent said they agreed that the feminist Germaine Greer should be prevented from speaking at Cardiff University after she was accused of transphobia (versus 35 per cent who thought she should be allowed to speak).
- 41 per cent agreed with the decision to withdraw the controversial Canadian psychologist Jordan Peterson's fellowship at Cambridge University (versus 31 per cent who disagreed).
- The range of students consistently supportive of free speech ranged from three-fifths to a half.[1]

In the US, a poll published by the Campaign for Free Speech found that:

- 51 per cent of Americans think that the First Amendment, which provides constitutional protection for free speech, is outdated and should be rewritten, rising to 59 per cent among 18–34 year olds.
- 61 per cent of Americans think free speech should be restricted in contexts – such as in universities and on social media – where there is the potential to be hurtful or offensive.[2]

The mass of polling data available on this subject is not without nuance, and its interpretation remains, quite properly, open to fresh interpretation. But it would be idle to deny that the right to free speech has lost the position in the hierarchy of values that it once occupied.

Why is this so? In May 2019, I wrote a piece for *Tortoise* to mark the 40th anniversary of the controversy surrounding *Monty Python's Life of Brian* – considered blasphemous by those who tried to ban it – and the 30th anniversary of the Iranian *fatwa* against Salman Rushdie. When I asked Jodie Ginsberg, the then chief executive of *Index on Censorship*, why this once-cherished freedom was no longer such a priority, she observed that the high-profile controversies involving free speech now often involved alt- or far-Right activists such as Alex Jones, Milo Yiannopolous and Tommy Robinson. Frequently the target of campus protests or 'de-platformed' from social media sites, they – and others like them – had subsequently postured as the victims of 'politically correct' censorship.

The co-opting of the language of liberalism and freedom of expression by the Far Right is one of my greatest concerns at present. It is having a hugely damaging effect on freedom of expression because it sends the message that free speech is only for privileged white men, rather than a universal value that benefits all, and in particular minority and oppressed groups. It's vital that progressives and liberals reclaim this value as being core to promoting tolerance and equal rights – not antithetical to it. We need to be pushing harder for organisations like *Index* to be the voice of freedom of expression rather than allowing paid-for controversialists on the right becoming free speech's de facto spokespeople.[3]

Ginsberg's point was well made. So much media attention had been paid to the (often-orchestrated) clashes between alt-Right speaker and protestors that the basic value of free speech was at risk of being eclipsed. In this context, it is worth reflecting that, around the world, 80 journalists were killed in 2018; 348 detained; and 60 held hostage. Authoritarian and totalitarian regimes continue to imprison dissidents, ban books and police ideas as a matter of course. Yet there is no doubt that – in the West – much less energy is expended upon the defence of free speech than was the case 30 years ago.

To understand why this is so, one needs to recognise the consequences of the digital revolution and of the cultural forces that have arisen alongside it. When I was working at *Index*, the World Wide Web was only two years old: high-speed broadband, the smartphone and the cacophony of social media were just around the corner in broad historic terms, but the impact that they would have was scarcely imagined by those who assumed that, as its centrality grew, the Internet would be a unifying, civilising force.

The hurricane of speech, sound and imagery that followed was quite unlike anything that had preceded it in human history: only the proliferation of print in the 16th Century and of television in the middle of the last come close. And – like all storms – it has left, and continues to leave, wreckage in its wake. As the *Times* writer James Marriott wrote in August 2019:

No generation has been exposed to more offensive points of view and dangerous situations than the one which came of age online. In a recent viral Twitter thread, a mother complained that her teenage boys were deluged with 'racist, sexist, homophobic and antisemitic' jokes on the internet. Parents piled in with similar stories and I was reminded of the time I sat in a maths class at the age of 12 and listened to a group of boys behind me eagerly discuss the violent and graphic pornography they'd all watched together on the internet. They were hardly coddled ... I think this explains much of my generation's ambivalence towards free speech. If you've grown up online, the awfulness of human beings is pressed into your face at all times. We are all angry puritan preachers jostled by unsavoury types in a crowded market. The urge to purify can be hard to resist. To a baby boomer, 'free speech' means something noble: the right of *Times* columnists to criticise the government. To millennials, free speech looks ugly. It conjures the Reddit forum dedicated to posting pictures of dead children and sick young men congratulating mass shooters on achieving a new 'high score' on the website 8chan.[4]

Marriott is right about the specific context in which his own generation has come to weigh up the pros and cons of free speech, and the contrast with the cultural setting in which my own grew up: we got Havel, Rushdie and Mandela, whereas his got Holocaust denial, torture porn and 8chan (or 8kun as it became).[5] So those of us who still believe in free speech – now more than ever, as it happens – have to accept their responsibility to make the case.

In his pointed observation that his generation is not 'coddled', Marriott is taking issue with Greg Lukianoff and Jonathan Haidt, whose book, *The Coddling of the American Mind*, was mentioned in Chapter 1.[6] Whether or not you agree with their overall analysis – that an overprotective generation of parents has conspired in a culture of 'safetyism' that serves their children poorly in the long term – Lukianoff and Haidt assemble an impressive and depressing series of case studies that illustrate what has gone wrong on many North American campuses.

To give a few examples: in 2015, Erika Christakis, a lecturer at Yale Child Study Center, wrote an email questioning whether it was appropriate for the university's administrators to give guidance about Hallowe'en costumes. While acknowledging 'genuine concerns about cultural and personal representation', Christakis expressed her own alarm about 'the growing tendency to cultivate vulnerability in students', and asked: 'What does this debate about Halloween costumes say about our view of young adults, of their strength and judgment? Whose business is it to control the forms of costumes of young people? It's not mine, I know that.'

The email prompted an outraged petition signed by scores of Yale students and alumni: 'You ask students to "look away" if costumes are offensive, as if the degradation of our cultures and people, and the violence that grows out of it is something that we can ignore'.[7] Note the sudden escalation to the possibility of 'violence'. A debate about who should, or should not, tell adult students what to wear at Hallowe'en had now become an argument about physical endangerment.

Christakis's husband, Nicholas, was the master of Silliman, one of Yale's residential colleges, and was confronted by 150 students in the courtyard outside the couple's home.[8] In the tense dialogue that ensued, he repeatedly showed himself willing to listen to the students' concerns. They made clear that a full apology for his wife's email was the only way that he could show himself properly penitent and mindful of their grievances. He and Erika were accused of being 'racist', 'offensive', 'creating an unsafe space' and (again) enabling 'violence' (a charge which they of course denied). One student shouted at him: 'Who the fuck hired you? You should step down! It's not about creating an intellectual space! It's not! It's about creating a home here . . . You should not sleep at night! You are disgusting!'[9]

Though many of the couple's academic colleagues expressed private support, remarkably few came forward to defend them publicly. The president of the university responded to the controversy by sending out an email acknowledging the students' pain and making a commitment to 'take actions that will make us better'. At the end of the university year, the couple resigned their respective positions at the residential college. 'We remain hopeful', Nicholas wrote, 'that students at Yale can express themselves and engage complex ideas within an intellectually plural community. But we feel it is time to return full-time to our respective fields.'

The 2017 case of Bret Weinstein, a biology professor at Evergreen State College, Washington, is even more unsettling. Since the Seventies, the college had observed a traditional 'Day of Absence' every April, on which staff, academics and (latterly) students of colour had stayed away from campus: a means of making their importance felt, through their temporary absence. In 2017, however, the organisers of the ritual decided that white students and teachers should stay away instead.

Weinstein was well known as a committed progressive – a supporter of Bernie Sanders and champion of the Occupy Wall Street movement. But he did not agree with the proposed change to the Day of Absence at Evergreen. As he wrote to Rashida Love, the college's Director of First Peoples Multicultural Advising Services: 'There is a huge difference between a group or coalition deciding to voluntarily absent themselves from a shared space in order to highlight their vital and under-appreciated roles, and a group or coalition encouraging another group to go away.'

On 23 May – more than a month after the Day of Absence had passed, according to Weinstein, 'almost without incident' – a crowd of students marched to his office and denounced him as a 'piece of shit' who should 'get the fuck out'. Like Nicholas Christakis at Yale, Weinstein invited them to join him in 'dialectic, which does mean I listen to you and you listen to me'. The response was dismissive: 'We don't care what terms you want to speak on'.[10]

This was only the beginning. The protestors next turned their wrath on the college's president, George Bridges, and confronted him outside his office. Again, they were uninterested in dialogue: 'Fuck you, George, we don't want to hear a goddamn thing you have to say . . . You shut the fuck up.' At subsequent meetings, Bridges was told not to use his hands, denounced for his 'fucking nerve', and even told to 'hold it' when he said: 'I need to pee'.[11] Students chanted 'Hey hey! Ho ho! These racist faculty have got to go!'

Weinstein was told by the campus police chief that, for his own safety, he should leave the university precincts. On 2 June, a quarter of Evergreen's faculty signed a letter demanding that he be investigated. In September, Weinstein and his wife, Heather Heyling, agreed on a legal settlement with the college and resigned from their academic posts.

Perhaps the most extraordinary example of this campus phenomenon is the experience of Lindsay Shepherd, a teaching assistant at Wilfed Laurier University in Ontario, in November 2017. As part of a course on 'Canadian Communication in Context', Shepherd played her students two short clips from a TVOntario programme, in which Jordan Peterson was featured on a panel discussing Bill C-16, which added 'gender identity or expression' as a prohibited ground for discrimination to the Canadian Human Rights Act. In the clips, Peterson objected to the enforced use of transgender pronouns, and was shown in disagreement with a fellow Toronto University academic, Nicholas Matte, who said: 'I don't care about your language use. I care about the safety of people being harmed.'

To her surprise, Shepherd was summoned to a meeting with her supervising professor, Nathan Rambukkana, the head of her academic programme, Herbert Pimlott, as well as Adria Joel, manager of Gendered Violence Prevention and Support at the university. To their (subsequent) surprise, Shepherd was wise enough to record the encounter.[12]

Early in the conference, Rambukkana challenges Shepherd on Peterson's 'critiquing' of feminism and trans rights.

Shepherd: I'm familiar. I follow him. But can you shield people from those ideas? Am I supposed to comfort them and make sure that they are insulated away from this? Like, is that what the point of this is? Because to me, that is so against what a university is about. So against it. I was not taking sides. I was presenting both arguments.

Rambukkana: So the thing about this is, if you're presenting something like this, you have to think about the kind of teaching climate that you're creating. And this is actually, these arguments are counter to the Canadian Human Rights Code. Even since . . . C-16, ever since this passed, it is discriminatory to be targeting someone due to their gender identity or gender expression.

The terms of the debate are now set. Shepherd is arguing that her students are entitled to hear Peterson's views as part of their education. Rambukkana objects that what Peterson says does not belong to the realm of regular academic discussion.

Rambukkana: Do you see how this is something that is not intellectually neutral, that is kind of 'up for debate', I mean this is the Charter of Rights and Freedoms.
Shepherd: But it is up for debate.
Rambukkana: You're perfectly welcome to your own opinion, but when you're bringing it into the context of the classroom that can become problematic, and that can become something that is, that creates an unsafe learning environment for students.
Shepherd: But when they leave the university they're going to be exposed to these ideas, so I don't see how I'm doing a disservice to the class by exposing them to ideas that are really out there. And I'm sorry I'm crying, I'm stressed out because this to me is so wrong, so wrong.

Though distressed, Shepherd seeks guidance on what harm she has caused.

Shepherd: What I have a problem with is, I didn't target anybody. Who did I target?
Joel: Trans folks.

Shepherd: By telling them ideas that are really out there? Telling them that? By telling them? Really?

Rambukkana: It's not just telling them. In legitimizing this as a valid perspective—

Shepherd: In a university all perspectives are valid.

Rambukkana: That's not necessarily true, Lindsay.

Next, Pimlott weighs in with comparisons to the Nazi era and, again, emphasises the question of student safety.

Pimlott: I would find it problematic if my tutorial leaders were representing positions that didn't have any substantial academic credibility to that evidence.

Shepherd: But he's still a public figure . . . this was on a TV show. He's still a public figure.

Pimlott: He's a public figure, and a lot of people there like [the US white supremacist] Richard Spencer of, I don't like calling them alt-right, it gives them too much legitimacy, but Richard Spencer, right? The Nazis actually used, this is a historic – issues around the free speech idea in the 1920s in Weimar Germany as an issue around which . . . is what they're using now. We know that someone like Richard Spencer is using theories and ideas that don't have any academic credibility. He's a public figure. But in terms of, if we introduce someone, we give them greater credibility in a certain condition.

Shepherd points out again that she was merely showing video clips and expresses bafflement that this could be seen as malicious or felt to be harmful:

Shepherd: OK, so by proxy me showing a YouTube video I'm transphobic and I caused harm and violence? So be it. I can't do anything to control that.

Rambukkana: OK, so that's not something that you have an issue with? The fact that that happened? Are you sorry that it happened?

Shepherd: I know in my heart, and I expressed to the class, that I'm not transphobic and if any of them – again, I don't know what they said – but I don't think I gave away any kind of political position of mine. I remained very neutral, and uh—

Rambukkana: —that's kind of the problem.

In the controversy that followed the release of the tape, the university and Rambukkana apologised and an independent investigation found that the interview had involved 'significant overreach.' Lawsuits and countersuits followed. Shepherd has since turned her back on the Left and become an impassioned free speech activist.[13]

The Wilfred Laurier case is important, not because it has been exactly replicated on every campus in the Western world, but because it so vividly and unexpectedly disclosed a way of thinking that has indeed become commonplace in university life and is intimately entangled with the rise of identity politics. It has been visible in the UK higher education sector, too: in the regular 'no-platforming' of controversial speakers, including feminists such as Linda Bellos and Germain Greer, on the alleged bases that their views are 'transphobic' or otherwise objectionable. In 2019, the Conservative government published guidelines on free speech standards for publicly funded universities – in itself an undesirable intervention by the state in the activities of notionally independent institutions.[14]

The intellectual ancestry of this approach – especially prevalent in humanities and social science departments – may be traced back to Herbert Marcuse (1898–1979) and the so-called Frankfurt School of Critical Theory. In particular, Marcuse has bequeathed to today's champions of identity politics the dangerous distinction between 'repressive' and 'liberating tolerance'. His argument was that the inequalities and differentials of power in society are so great, and the masses so indoctrinated, that what we generally describe as tolerance is, in fact, deeply repressive in its outcomes. 'The function and value of tolerance,' he argued in the essay *Repressive Tolerance* (1965), 'depend on the equality prevalent in the society in which tolerance is practised.'[15]

This is, of course, fabulously convenient for those seeking an excuse for illiberalism. A 'liberating tolerance', by definition, would therefore 'mean intolerance against movements from the Right, and toleration of movements from the Left'. Tolerance may be safely withdrawn from organisations and campaigns 'which promote aggressive policies, armament, chauvinism, discrimination on the grounds of race and religion, or which oppose the extension of public services, social security, medical care, etc.'[16] How potentially useful is that vague 'etc' – a signal to Marcuse's devotees to behave intolerantly towards all and any groups that they believe hostile to their socially just objectives. Meanwhile, those who have been burdened by the fascistic teaching of the capitalist establishment will need a deliberately skewed counter-education 'slanted in the opposite direction'.

Marcuse's arguments are the political equivalent of the unnamed US army major in the Vietnam War who reportedly said: 'We had to destroy the village in order to save it'. According to his logic, the unjustly skewed political configuration of contemporary society legitimises almost any withdrawal of civil liberties in the name of a higher common good. In the context of early 21st-Century culture wars, this position has been modified to fit the needs of the moment. Free speech is a decidedly secondary consideration when compared to what is vaguely described as student 'safety' or the 'enabling' of 'violence' (again, ill-defined).

To spell it out: I think that the notion of white privilege is one that needs to be taken much more seriously than it has by some liberals and is an overdue corrective to some of the complacencies that have bedevilled modern liberalism. But that does not mean that anyone, in whatever context, and on whatever grounds, ought to be able to silence their interlocutor simply by pointing the finger at alleged 'privilege': that is not how a successful pluralist, interconnected society works, or could ever work.

It is also true that access to powerful modes of communication is unevenly distributed. But it is less true than at any time in history. In the modern information economy, the means of production are almost zero-cost – an absolute novelty in human affairs. This is not to say that every person with a Facebook or Twitter account enjoys the same power as, say, the BBC, or the Murdoch news empire. But it does mean that all forms of legacy media – or 'MSM' as they have become pejoratively known – are held to account to an extent and on a scale that would have been inconceivable only a few years ago. The marketplace of ideas may not yet be a level playing field but it is open to new entrants as never before – billions of them, limited only by the number of characters they can post in a single tweet and the number of followers or YouTube viewers they can attract.

It is understandable that identity politics should have become so engaged with this issue. An oppressed or disenfranchised group is bound to feel that its voice has been insufficiently heard and to ask questions accordingly – of publishers, media-companies, tech corporations, political parties, the professions, institutions of state and cultural organisations. All these, and other agencies, need to take these questions very seriously, and explain why the answers have been so long in coming. As I explained in the last chapter, the rise of identity politics has, in this, and in other respects, been a much-needed and entirely constructive adrenaline shot to the body politic.

The wrong turn has been to regard the Babel of the modern world as a zero-sum game. To simplify this proposition hugely: my voice will only be heard if yours is not. My feelings count more than your freedoms. Your speech is so obnoxious that it is not *like* violence but *actually* violence. You cannot speak unless I feel 'safe' in every sense of the word. If I cannot actually censor or silence you, I will seek to drive you out of the public space by 'cancelling' you. Any repercussions for your professional or personal life will be categorised as legitimate 'accountability' and just deserts for your 'problematic' statements, however long ago they were made, irrespective of context or intent. And – in case you were wondering – I reserve the right afterwards to say that 'cancel culture' does not exist.

Let us deal first with the most intellectually shoddy aspect of this, which is the equation of speech and violence. It is an equation that is increasingly made by students: 81 per cent of them according to a survey in October 2017 by McLaughlin & Associates for Yale's William F. Buckley, Jr. Program.[17] Of course, speech can and does *lead* to violence, which is why, thanks to the landmark US Supreme Court case in 1969 of *Brandenburg vs Ohio*, the protection of the First Amendment does not protect 'advocacy . . . directed to inciting or producing imminent lawless action'. In England and Wales, there are various forms of incitement to violence or harassment that are prohibited in statute, including, for instance, incitement to racial hatred under the Public Order Act 1986, to which the crime of stirring up religious hatred was added by the Racial and Religious Hatred Act 2006. Inciting hatred on grounds of sexual orientation became a criminal offence under the Criminal Justice and Immigration Act 2008.

Quite different claims are now made for so-called 'assaultive speech'.[18] Such is the power of speech that the concept has proved seductive: the profound emotions and stress that hurtful, unpleasant or otherwise obnoxious words can cause invite the conflation of speech and violence. As Lisa Feldman Barrett, a professor of psychology at Northeastern University, argued in a *New York Times* piece in July 2017:

If you spend a lot of time in a harsh environment worrying about your safety, that's the kind of stress that brings on illness and remodels your brain. That's also true of a political climate in which groups of people endlessly hurl hateful words at one another, and of rampant bullying in school or on social media. A culture of constant, casual brutality is toxic to the body, and we suffer for it. That's why it's reasonable, scientifically speaking, not to allow a provocateur and hatemonger like Milo Yiannopoulos to speak at your school. He is part of something noxious, a campaign of abuse. There is nothing to be gained from debating him, for debate is not what he is offering.[19]

Not so fast, argued Lukianoff and Haidt in an *Atlantic* piece four days later. It is a considerable leap of logic from the statement that 'speech can contribute to a harsh environment that brings about stress' to the statement 'speech is violence'. As they wrote, the second statement is not only philosophically slippery:

> [It] tells the members of a generation already beset by anxiety and depression that the world is a far more violent and threatening place than it really is. It tells them that words, ideas, and speakers can literally kill them. Even worse: At a time of rapidly rising political polarization in America, it helps a small subset of that generation justify political violence. A few days after the riot that shut down Yiannopoulos's talk at Berkeley, in which many people were punched, beaten and pepper sprayed by masked protesters, the main campus newspaper ran five op-ed essays by students and recent alumni under the series title 'Violence as self defense.' One excerpt: 'Asking people to maintain peaceful dialogue with those who legitimately do not think their lives matter is a violent act.'[20]

Thus does the distortion of logic lead to a truly harmful conclusion. If speech is violence, then violence used to halt such speech must be defensible: a blank cheque for pre-emptive acts of assault and aggression. No civilised community can possibly operate according to such rules or allow such inexact use of language.

A close cousin of this linguistic distortion is the claim that feelings should be the prime variable in the regulation of speech. The new primacy of emotion over rationality in the 21st Century in the political arena has been much discussed, especially in the context of conspiracy theory, fake news and post-truth.[21] As the classical liberal notion of free speech has lost ground, so it has become increasingly easy to object to language on the basis of its emotional impact rather than its moral intent. As we have seen, the uneven distribution of power between identity groups and the legitimate grievances of the disadvantaged mean that such impact must be heeded and those who draw attention to it treated with respect. But – again – it is a flaw of logic to argue that, because this is so, anyone who is offended has the power of veto over any form of speech that they happen to find insulting.

Ruth Simmons, Brown University's president from 2001–12, first African American president of any Ivy League university, and Brown's first female president, put it well in her inaugural convocation address: 'You know something that I hate? When people say, "That doesn't make me feel good about myself." I say, "That's not what you're here for." . . . I believe that learning at its best is the antithesis of comfort. [I]f you come to this [campus] for comfort, I would urge you to walk [through] yon iron gate . . . But if you seek betterment for yourself, for your community and posterity, stay and fight'.[22]

This is not, it must be stressed, an argument for incivility or discourtesy. It is an argument about the proper place of emotion in civilised debate and the extent to which hurt feelings can clinch or even invalidate a discussion. Nobody has an emotional veto.

Indeed, it should be obvious that no pluralist community can negotiate its differences on the basis that any such negotiation may be terminated by the claim that some of its content is offensive. As the Oxford University professor, Timothy Garton Ash, has put it: 'you are – taking this to its logical conclusion – giving everyone a right to exercise a veto simply by pronouncing the words "I am offended", rather as a single seventeenth-century Polish nobleman could block a piece of proposed legislation by pronouncing the words "*liberum veto*!" '.[23]

A modern society bound by such constraints could not long survive, let alone prosper: they would be a high road to stultification, silence and decay. A covenant whose first commandment is 'Thou shalt not say' is no covenant at all. Yet this principle is indeed creeping into political and social discourse, and not only on campuses. Nowhere has it been more vivid than in the furore over trans rights and the politics of gender.

It is a fact of modern society that gender fluidity and transgenderism are on the rise. Though the statistics are inexact, trans people are estimated to account for between 0.3 and 0.8 per cent of the UK population.[24] In the 2021 census, British citizens will be able to enter their chosen gender, in addition to a mandatory question on biological sex.[25] Trans people, it is shamefully clear, are disproportionately vulnerable to attack and vilification: data released by the Office for National Statistics in July 2020 showed that they are twice as likely to be victims of crime than non-trans people.[26] More than a quarter of trans people in the UK have attempted suicide, and 72 per cent have self-harmed at least once.[27]

One would have thought that this particular issue could be discussed compassionately and with reason. It poses questions – some of them entirely granular and practical – about social organisation, the difference between biological sex and gender, and the competing claims and vulnerabilities of trans people and biological women. Rarely has there been a clearer case in which to respect the philosophical 'principle of charity' – which demands that, in discussion, one interprets a speaker's statements in the most reasonable way possible. But that is not what has happened.

In practice, the debate over trans rights has been as fiercely contested as any in modern times. It routinely ignites social media with abuse and counter-abuse. It has generated one of the most furious divisions in contemporary identity politics: between trans activists on the one hand and 'gender-critical' feminists on the other. It has split the LGBTQ+ movement down the middle and become a ferocious bone of contention amongst progressives more generally. Anyone who has tried to organise a public event on this question can attest not only to the difficulty of persuading the two sides to face each other in the same room, but also the security risks that are posed by any such attempt. How did a discussion about the distinction between biological sex and gender degenerate into threats to rape and murder, and bomb scares?

Trans people argue that they were 'assigned' the wrong gender at birth and that the answer to the consequent 'dysphoria' they suffer is to identify otherwise – as male, female or gender-fluid – and to live accordingly. They object to the extent to which this process remains 'medicalised' by the 2004 Gender Recognition Act, according to which a new gender recognition certificate is issued by a medical and legal panel. Their demand is that this undoubtedly bureaucratic and often demeaning procedure be replaced by self-identification: in other words, if you say you are a woman or a man, you are. This approach has attracted considerable support across the political spectrum as a civilised way to acknowledge the path that trans people follow and to diminish the obstacles that stand between them and a life of dignity. But it is absurd to deny that this notion of gender – its total personalisation – presents major challenges to the way in which society is organised and the vulnerable are protected.

In most civil rights issues, there are, broadly speaking, the powerful and the disempowered. White privilege is an important concept precisely because it reminds white people of the racialised advantage that they have, and all too easily forget. The battle for gay rights has been – reduced to its essentials – a campaign to persuade straight people that full equality should be enjoyed by everyone, regardless of sexual orientation. But the debate on trans rights is different because it involves the vulnerabilities of *two* groups rather than one: the entirely reasonable demand of trans people to be treated with respect, and the no-less-reasonable expectation of biological women to retain the rights of privacy and same-sex spaces for which they have fought so hard.

As anyone familiar with this argument knows, my last sentence will be regarded by some as intrinsically 'transphobic'. The hashtag #transwomenarewomen (or #TWAW) denotes a blanket denunciation of anyone who dares to question the proposition that trans women should have access to all facilities presently used by biological women and girls: rape crisis centres, toilets, changing rooms, the activities and camps of Girl Guides, domestic abuse refuges and so on. Those who point out the ludicrous injustice of trans women who still enjoy the physiological advantages of male biology participating in women's sport are similarly labelled as 'transphobes' or 'trans exclusionary radical feminists' (TERFs). Labelling of this sort – mostly online – becomes a way of shutting down debate and concealing nuance.

Merely to pose such practical questions – it is argued by some – is to question the very 'existence' of trans people and certainly to deny their 'human rights'. No distinction is permitted between the core principle – trans people need to be respected, assisted and protected from oppression – and the practical implementation of change, which will necessarily involve complexity, subtlety and exemption. Indeed, for some trans people, the notion of 'debate' on these matters is *in itself* abhorrent and even genocidal in character.

This section of the identity politics map became the scene of especially bitter hostilities in June 2020, when the *Harry Potter* author, J.K. Rowling, posted a long essay on the question of sex and gender.[26] Rowling questioned various aspects of the trans agenda, especially the demand for self-identification. As a survivor of domestic abuse, she worried that this inescapably would put biological (or 'natal') women in harm's way:

> I want trans women to be safe. At the same time, I do not want to make natal girls and women less safe. When you throw open the doors of bathrooms and changing rooms to any man who believes or feels he's a woman – and, as I've said, gender confirmation certificates may now be granted without any need for surgery or hormones – then you open the door to any and all men who wish to come inside. That is the simple truth.

Having made such an intervention, Rowling must have expected a response, especially when, in a separate tweet, she compared the clinical and counselling services involved in transitioning to 'a new kind of conversion therapy'. Even so, the backlash that her posts provoked was astonishing in scale, scope and venom. The stars of the *Harry Potter* films, such as Daniel Radcliffe, Emma Watson and Rupert Grint, denounced her views. Two of the biggest fan sites associated with the books and movies distanced themselves from Rowling.[29] She was vilified as transphobic, bigoted and a traitor to the values of her own fiction despite her passionate declaration that 'my life has been shaped by being female. I do not believe it's hateful to say so.' The author's central and repeated claim – that biological sex is real – might not seem particularly contentious. But, in the most super-charged argument within contemporary identity politics, she had crossed a line, and was now pronounced an absolute and unpardonable heretic. She was, to use the word of the moment, 'cancelled' – that is to say, cast out, rejected, excluded from respectable discussion.

As the controversy escalated, Rowling and 150 of her fellow writers – including Margaret Atwood, Noam Chomsky, Gloria Steinem, Wynton Marsalis and Malcolm Gladwell – signed a letter to *Harper's Magazine* to address what they diagnosed as a crisis in liberal discourse:

> The forces of illiberalism are gaining strength throughout the world and have a powerful ally in Donald Trump, who represents a real threat to democracy. But resistance must not be allowed to harden into its own brand of dogma or coercion – which right-wing demagogues are already exploiting. The democratic inclusion we want can be achieved only if we speak out against the intolerant climate that has set in on all sides.[30]

The central argument of the letter was that progressives were harming the causes they championed by mimicking the intolerance of the radical Right:

> It is now all too common to hear calls for swift and severe retribution in response to perceived transgressions of speech and thought. More troubling still, institutional

leaders, in a spirit of panicked damage control, are delivering hasty and disproportionate punishments instead of considered reforms. Editors are fired for running controversial pieces; books are withdrawn for alleged inauthenticity; journalists are barred from writing on certain topics; professors are investigated for quoting works of literature in class; a researcher is fired for circulating a peer-reviewed academic study; and the heads of organizations are ousted for what are sometimes just clumsy mistakes.

In a sign of how far the battle lines of contemporary culture wars have shifted, many of the letter's detractors referred to its signatories as members of an elite who were in no position to claim that their voices had been silenced.[31] Rowling's inclusion on the list inevitably invited the supplementary charge that the entire exercise was, by definition, 'toxic' and 'transphobic'. What would once have been seen as a straightforward statement of liberal values was now seen – by some, at any rate – as the howl of an entitled older generation bewailing their impending irrelevance and the diminution of their power.

In the *Guardian*, the left-wing campaigner and musician Billy Bragg dismissed the *Harper's* letter accordingly:

Many of those who attached their names to the letter are longstanding cultural arbiters, who, in the past, would only have had to fear the disapproval of their peers. Social media has burst their bubble and they now find that anyone with a Twitter account can challenge their opinions. The letter was their demand for a safe space.[32]

Correctly, Bragg identified the democratisation of voice in the age of digital technology and network politics:

The ability of middle-aged gatekeepers to control the agenda has been usurped by a new generation of activists who can spread information through their own networks, allowing them to challenge narratives promoted by the status quo.

Then, however, he made a huge conceptual leap in his assessment of what free expression should actually mean in this new context:

> Although free speech remains the fundamental bedrock of a free society, for everyone to enjoy the benefits of freedom, liberty needs to be tempered by two further dimensions: equality and accountability. Without equality, those in power will use their freedom of expression to abuse and marginalise others. Without accountability, liberty can mutate into the most dangerous of all freedoms – impunity.

The very blandness of this passage is suggestive. Nobody decent is against 'equality' or 'accountability'. But by what means should these criteria 'temper' free speech? And according to whose evaluation? One can only assume that Bragg meant that social media now acts as a new meta-constitutional check and balance, weeding out objectionable opinion and unsound thinking by sheer force of numbers. But he did not elaborate.

As is so often the case when identity politics ignites on social media, the Rowling controversy fast launched a secondary sub-debate on whether or not 'cancel culture' actually exists.[33] What cannot be denied is that people have lost their jobs for expressing views that are demonstrably mainstream, but do not meet the restrictive standards set by specific social justice movements. In December 2019, an employment tribunal upheld the sacking by the think tank the Center for Global Development of the tax expert Maya Forstater – who was supported by Rowling – after she claimed on Twitter that 'men cannot change into women'.

Again, Judge James Tayler was happy to see free speech limited in this case:

> Even paying due regard to the qualified right to freedom of expression, people cannot expect to be protected if their

core belief involves violating others' dignity and creating an intimidating, hostile, degrading, humiliating, or offensive environment for them.[34]

Forstater's case was not isolated. In November 2019, Garden Court Chambers launched an investigation into one of its own barristers, Allison Bailey, after she hailed the launch of the LGB Alliance, of which she is a founder member, and posted on social media that 'Gender extremism is about to meet its match'.[35] Accusing her bosses of bowing to a transgender 'hate mob', Bailey raised £60,000 to fund her employment tribunal claim against her chambers and Stonewall, alleging that the LGBTQ+ charity – which opposes the LGB Alliance – had conspired in an attempt to 'intimidate and silence' her. Stonewall would not comment directly on the case but Garden Court Chambers denied acting unlawfully or colluding with Stonewall. In a further twist, her page on the crowdfunding site, CrowdJustice, was temporarily suspended in June 2020 after complaints were received about its content.[36]

In July 2020, furthermore, the Scots author, Gillian Philip, was sacked by her employer, Working Partners, after she backed Rowling on Twitter. In a statement, she said that she was 'disappointed that the hard work and professional attitude I have brought to my work for HarperCollins and for Working Partners counted for nothing in the face of an abusive mob of anonymous Twitter trolls. It is concerning that my concerns about women's legal rights and spaces have been presented as "transphobia", and that this accusation has been allowed to stand by my former employers.'[37] Working Partners claimed the decision had not been taken 'in direct response to the nature of Gillian's personally expressed views' but was a consequence of her associating a collective 'pen-name with her personal views on Twitter.'

Such cases raise legitimate questions about natural justice and the appeasement of social media mobs by fearful employers. But they are also a symptom of a broader phenomenon, and one that does no service to the strategic objectives of identity politics. The impulse to restrict, to 'cancel', to drive out objectionable opinion, is in danger of becoming the central mission of those engaged in these campaigns. And this is neither wise nor sustainable.

What is most striking about the fixation upon obnoxious and offensive speech is that – leaving aside its propriety – it so rarely has beneficial consequences. As Nadine Strossen, the former president of the American Civil Liberties Union, makes clear in her book *Hate,* the history of such restrictions has been inglorious and, to an under-reported extent, counterproductive. It is no accident, Strossen argues, that the notion of 'hate speech' laws originated in the fallen Soviet bloc, or that so many such regulations – however well-intentioned – have had the unintended consequence of censoring those who most need a voice. In December 2015, for instance, a report by the European Commission against Racism and Intolerance (ECRI) concluded that European 'hate speech' laws could be enforced 'to silence minorities and to suppress criticism, political opposition and religious beliefs'.[38] Strict hate speech laws in France and Germany have apparently done nothing to thwart the popularity of the *Front National* or *Alternative für Deutschland*, or the rise in anti-Semitism across Europe.

As early as 1992, Human Rights Watch warned that 'there is little connection in practice between draconian "hate speech" laws and the lessening of ethnic and racial violence or tension' – a conclusion that the European Parliament has since felt compelled to echo. In 2015, Agnes Callamard, Director of the Columbia University Global Freedom of Expression initiative, observed that although 'European governments have produced more laws . . . prohibit[ing] "Hate Speech" than any other region, with the possible exception of the Middle East', the societies over which they preside are still 'ravaged by intolerance and . . . increasing inequality' – citing 'rising levels of violence and hate, anti-immigrant, anti-Roma and anti-Semitic rhetoric'.[39]

In historical terms, the present progressive tilt towards restriction and 'cancellation' is an aberration from a consistent pattern in the evolution of progressive ideas. For Abolitionists, free expression was all-important. In his fight against slavery, Frederick Douglass always regarded the First Amendment as the guarantor of the rights of the oppressed and minorities (rather than, as is so often claimed today, the friend of the powerful). 'Liberty is meaningless', he said in 1860, 'where the right to utter one's thoughts and opinions has ceased to exist. That, of all rights, is the dread of tyrants. It is the right which they first of all strike down. They know its power.'

In 1905, when the black writer and activist W.E.B. Du Bois and 28 others met at Niagara Falls, Ontario – forced to do so because American hotels refused to serve blacks – they demanded not only equal access to public facilities and voting rights but also freedom of speech. In one of his later works, *In Battle for Peace* (1952), he remained of the same mind as he observed the cruel strictures of the Cold War. 'It is clear still today that freedom of speech and of thinking can be attacked in the United States without the intellectual and moral leaders of this land raising a hand or saying a word in protest or defense,' he wrote. 'Than this fateful silence there is on earth no greater menace to present civilization'.[40]

The late US Congressman, John Lewis – a figure who connects the era of Martin Luther King with the presidency of Barack Obama – was quite explicit in drawing the same connection. 'Without freedom of speech and the right to dissent,' he said, 'the Civil Rights movement would have been a bird without wings'.[41]

The same might be said of the protests that arose in and around Berkeley in the 1960s. When McCarthyism was a recent memory, and students were seeking the right to protest the Vietnam War and social injustices on campus, the right to free expression became central to their demands. In October 1964, Mario Savio, a civil rights activist of Sicilian-American descent, and 500 of his fellow students marched on Berkeley's administration building, demanding the abolition of all restraints upon freedom of speech in the University of California system. This marked the beginning of what became the Berkeley Free Speech Movement (FSM).[42]

On 2 December, in Sproul Plaza, a crowd of 6,000 students rallied to the cause – and heard Savio deliver a speech that would be long remembered as one of the most passionate defences of free expression ever made:

> There's a time when the operation of the machine becomes so odious, makes you so sick at heart, that you can't take part! You can't even passively take part! And you've got to put your bodies upon the gears and upon the wheels . . . upon the levers, upon all the apparatus, and you've got to make it stop! And you've got to indicate to the people who run it, to the people who own it, that unless you're free, the machine will be prevented from working at all![43]

Savio's bequest to the movements that followed was his understanding that free speech was the essential component of such activism, and the heart of all freedoms. In 1994, only two years before his death, he spoke in poetic language of this enduring belief:

> Diogenes said: 'The most beautiful thing in the world is the freedom of speech.' And those words are in me, they're sort of burned into my soul, because for me free speech was not a tactic, not something to win for political [advantage] . . . To me, freedom of speech is something that represents the very dignity of what a human being is . . . That's what marks us off from the stones and the stars. You can speak freely. It is almost impossible for me to describe. It is the thing that marks us as just below the angels.[44]

Given Savio's legacy and the importance of the movement he led, it is ironic that Berkeley should have been the venue for one of the most notable anti-free-speech showdowns of the identity politics era: the clashes surrounding the proposed appearance by right-wing provocateur, Milo Yiannopolous, on 1 March 2017, cancelled by campus police after the protests descended into violent confrontation and property damage.[45] The anti-Milo activists carried placards bearing slogans such as 'No safe space for racists' and 'This is war'.

Arguably, this is precisely what the arch-trickster of the Right had been after all along. President Trump himself could scarcely contain his glee, tweeting the following day: 'If U.C. Berkeley does not allow free speech and practices violence on innocent people with a different point of view – NO FEDERAL FUNDS?' To be fair, the university authorities condemned the violence that had forced the cancellation of the event and defended Yiannopolous's right to speak – while distancing themselves from his values. All the same, the contrast between the Savio era and the spectacle on television screens of masked protesters letting off firecrackers to close down an event was not lost on those who remembered the illustrious liberal past of the campus.

The impulse to silence, restrict and scold is the greatest weakness of contemporary identity politics. The refrain that 'the debate is over' – whatever the debate in question is – is both nonsensical and irrelevant: first, because debate is never over in a pluralist society; and second, because most of the debates which animate those who are immersed in politics have yet to trouble those who are busy making ends meet or otherwise fail to follow every detail of contemporary ideological discourse. As a rule of thumb, when a debate is declared 'over' in the rarefied world of campaigns and activism it is probably just starting in real life.

In his prophetic account of these attacks on free expression, *Kindly Inquisitors*, the journalist and fellow of the Brookings Institution, Jonathan Rauch, makes one of the best cases yet mustered for free speech as a force for social progress. In his afterword to the expanded edition in 2013, Rauch cites the case of Frank Kameny, who was driven from the US Army Map Service in 1957 because of his homosexuality and, with great courage, persevered as a campaigner for gay rights until his death in 2011. It was central to Kameny's approach that homophobic ideas needed to be smoked out and confronted. As Rauch, who is gay, observes:

Suppression of anti-gay speech and thought, had it been conceivable at the time, would have slowed the country's moral development, not speeded it. It would have given the illusion that the job was done when, in fact, it was only beginning. It would have condescended to a people fighting for respect ... You cannot be gay in America today and doubt that moral learning is real and that the open society fosters it ... The answer to bias and prejudice is pluralism, not purism. The answer, that is, is not to try and legislate bias and prejudice out of existence or to drive them underground, but to pit biases and prejudices against each other and make them fight in the open.[46]

Mill made a similar point in *On Liberty* (1859): 'Wrong opinions and practices gradually yield to fact and argument: but facts and arguments, to produce any effect on the mind, must be brought before it.' In this respect, censorship – of whatever sort – can foster a risky complacency: social media companies are richly entitled to ban whomever they please from their platforms. Twitter is not publicly owned, nor a part of the public sector. It can impose whatever community standards it likes.[47] But it is a mistake to imagine that the purge of the alt Right from this and other platforms – or the use of demonetisation to force extremists from YouTube – will kill off the poisonous ideas that such ideologues peddle. Indeed, the retreat of the far Right to private social networks has arguably made it harder to track its strength.[48] Either way, there is an absolute difference between the *banning* of a belief and its *defeat*. As Rauch continues:

The main way we eliminate hate is not to legislate or inveigh against it, but to replace it – with knowledge, empirical and ethical ... minorities are the point of the spear defending liberal science. We are the first to be targeted with vile words and ideas, but we are also the leading beneficiaries of a system which puts up with them. The open society is sometimes a cross we bear, but it is also a sword we wield, and we are defenceless without it.[49]

The further question posed by Rauch is no less pointed: 'And what about the day when right-wingers get the upper hand? Will *they* be "fair"? . . . no one stays on top for long.' Indeed they don't. And there is no shortage of evidence in the world today that the power to censor or limit speech is still more often used to defeat progressive causes than to advance them. Left-of-centre intellectuals have fled Jair Bolsonaro's Brazil to avoid persecution. Consider, too, the record of Viktor Orban's government in Hungary, which has shut down an entire university, removed subsidy from higher education departments that displease the ruling Fidesz party and subjected state and private media to extraordinary control.[50]

Censorship of one sort normalises censorship of all sorts; today's speech code of which you approve paves the way for tomorrow's crackdown that you dread. As the left-wing journalist Glenn Greenwald has argued:

This is how hate speech laws are used in virtually every country in which they exist: not only to punish the types of right-wing bigotry that many advocates believe will be suppressed, but also a wide range of views that many on the left believe should be permissible, if not outright accepted. *Of course* that's true: Ultimately, what constitutes 'hate speech' will be decided by majorities, which means that it is minority views that are vulnerable to suppression . . . If you empower state authorities to decide which ideas are permitted and which are not – to assess which ideas contain enough 'hatred' to justify banning – it is not likely but *inevitable* that those laws will ultimately be used to outlaw the ideas you like.[51]

Consider, too, the American Library Association's list of books that faced bans in 2018: five of the top ten had LGBTQ+ themes.[52] The Southern Poverty Law Center has faced repeated calls to brand Black Lives Matter a 'hate group'. Trump repeatedly threatened to curtail core First Amendment rights, arguing, as he did in July 2019: 'Free speech is not when you see something good and then you purposely write bad, to me that's very dangerous speech, and you become angry at it, but it's not free speech.'

To fulfil its potential, identity politics needs to end its destructive embrace of this issue and change trajectory: the ideals of those who seek emancipation, equality and full citizenship are not advanced by the compulsion to silence anyone who dares to dissent or query their agenda. Indeed, in what Garton Ash calls the 'cosmopolis' of modern pluralism, such dissent and interrogation of all ideas is not only a constant but a necessary process. It is how change comes about.

This has been one of the consistent and most impressive themes of Barack Obama's public rhetoric, especially when addressing the young: namely, that 'being ... an activist ... involves hearing the other side and ... engaging in a dialogue because that's how change happens.' He often cites the Civil Rights Movement, pointing out that 'it happened because ... the leadership ... consistently ... sought to understand the views' of their opponents. Encouraging students to 'have an argument with' those with whom they disagree, Obama zeroed in on the folly of being guided solely by feelings: '[y]ou shouldn't silence anyone by saying ... "I'm too sensitive to hear what you have to say." '[53]

All orderly societies, it is true, constrain certain categories of language: slander, libel, incitement to violence, content that endangers national security, and so on. No group outside the public sector – digital or otherwise – is obliged to provide a platform to anyone. There will be times when common courtesy obliges us not to speak as freely as we might otherwise. We can, and do, say that a politician has said something so vile that he or she should resign. And not all self-restraint is an act of weakness: voluntary silence can be as powerful as reckless clamour.

The key is to ask where our collective *predisposition* lies. Is our *default position* that all speech is allowable unless there is an overwhelming reason to restrict it? And – most important of all – who gets to make those decisions? The warning 'be careful what you wish for' has become a cliché. But it is sharply applicable in this case. It is a grave error to assume that the censors will always be on the side of the common good as you happen to see it. History teaches that such powers are often seized and turned to socially regressive ends. Identity politics is at an important and exciting moment of its development. But if its champions persist in their obsession with the control of speech, they will be jeopardising everything that they already have achieved and could go on to accomplish.

CHAPTER 4

IDENTITY POLITICS IS HERE TO STAY – AND THAT'S A GOOD THING

The dogmas of the quiet past are inadequate to the stormy present . . . As our case is new, so we must think anew, and act anew. We must disenthrall ourselves.

Abraham Lincoln, Annual Message
to Congress, 1 December 1862

The rise of identity politics is not a mortal threat to, or a mob-led distraction from, successful pluralism. Quite the opposite, in fact: it is a signal that, if correctly understood and heeded with respect, can enrich and strengthen liberal democracy in the 21st Century. Like any fledgling movement, it is not without flaws or conceptual errors. But the core lesson of identity politics – that the merits of individualism and meritocracy are hard to impress upon groups still suffering from historic injustice, daily indignity and, in some cases, threat to life and limb – must be acknowledged. As the American writer William Deresiewicz puts it (in his analysis of contemporary higher education), 'being treated fairly is itself a form of privilege'.[1]

The global response to the killing of George Floyd was a serious warning to those complacent enough to believe that the institutions of liberal democracy heal themselves automatically and incrementally. But it was also a challenge: a demand for greater imagination, a readiness to listen, and – above all – a sense of mission. For how can progressives of any sort be remotely content, when such an affront to every civilised value is still possible, captured on cell phones, on the streets of a major city in the most powerful country in the free world? Like the #MeToo movement, this heinous act calls upon all those in a position to do better, to respond with humility and urgency. Shame and gestures are no longer enough. It is a time for action.

How to go about this? Here are six ideas – proposed principles for a future route map in the next decade and beyond. They are not definitive or intended to be so. But they are a start:

1. THERE ARE NO LANES

Time to address the elephant in the room: what on earth makes me think I can write about identity politics *at all*? Why don't I just 'stay in my lane'?[2]

If this strikes you as an odd question, I suggest you better acquaint yourself with some of the literature on the subject, or take a stroll through the relevant digital lanes of YouTube or Twitter. Much of the debate about identity politics is actually a *procedural* row – an extended point of order – consisting of a secondary argument about who is entitled to discuss it in the first place.

So, unfortunately, it is necessary for me to pre-empt this argument. I am a 53-year-old straight white man – 'cisgender', as trans activists would put it (which is to say I continue to identify with the gender 'assigned' to me by a 'health professional' in Lewisham Hospital in January 1968). I was educated at a private school and Oxford University, where I went on to hold a college Fellowship. I have edited a famous weekly magazine, regarded by many (inaccurately, in my view) as the in-house journal of the Conservative Party, and written columns for mainstream national newspapers for much of my adult life. I have sat on government commissions, chaired a think tank, own my own home in London . . . you get the idea. By most reckonings, I am a one-man privilege carnival, and an avatar for patriarchy and power.

So what am I *doing*, rushing into this particular minefield of sensitivities and grievances? Didn't I get the memo? Most writers in my particular demographic have either taken strongly against identity politics, or, more often – and in the interests of a quiet life – crept away from this particular field of inquiry.

The first response is, as I hope I have made clear, quite wrong; and the second is craven. If you believe, as I do, in the marketplace of ideas and the never-ending flux of pluralism, then you should be prepared for ideas that challenge the very foundations of what you believe. Indeed, that is the whole point, the very essence, of living in a heterogeneous, democratic society. It is fundamental to all inquiry – academic, scientific, journalistic – to be braced for, and excited by, the new. It is also a duty of any commentator worthy of the description to stay tuned, and to engage with social and intellectual innovation. If you think the argument – just about any argument – is over, you really *should* call it a day and shuffle off the stage with the golden carriage clock (or Apple watch) marking long service to the commentariat.

This point needs to be made, because the argument about who is entitled to speak about what now bedevils so much contemporary conversation about identity, gender, race, sexuality and social justice. Before the debate even starts, there is a sort of primary contest in which the entitlement of each and every person to join in the conversation is carefully audited – usually, though not exclusively, online.

This is useful and justified if the intention is to ensure a diversity of voices: which is why (to take one example) most progressively inclined men now refuse to appear on 'manels' (men-only speaker panels), a format now happily in sharp decline. It is also, in many cases, a question of common sense. A good 90 per cent of decent commentary consists of listening and researching. Citizenship is meaningless without the *readiness to listen*. For those who enjoy privilege in all its forms, this readiness is especially important: they have a special obligation to listen, without interruption, to the stories and lived experiences of those who are less advantaged, to those whose lives are different to their own.

Let it be emphasised: this a matter of basic respect, not an act of civic charity. There are few things more revolting than white liberal people congratulating themselves for attending an event that has enhanced their 'awareness' or broadened their horizons. The essence of listening is to realise that it's *not about you* (which is why I regret the structural necessity of this section).

One of the most welcome effects of the surge in identity politics has been to encourage a little more humility and restraint. It has prompted much re-evaluation, reconsideration and reflection – the opposite of the cognitive complacency that is the rust of a functioning, healthy democracy. It has inspired some of those with power to 'pass the mic' a little more often to those who lack it. It has encouraged the gatekeepers of media platforms, political representation and employment opportunity to ask hard questions about the fairness of their procedures and actions – questions that are only beginning to be answered.

So it is *as a citizen* that I address the question of identity in this section – respectfully, but without apology. Nobody is obliged to read what I write, or listen to what I say, or to provide me with a platform. Equally – as long as I observe the law governing speech – I can say and write what I like. How I exercise that right is a matter of judgment. But a non-negotiable right it remains all the same (as is the right of anyone else to respond in kind).

This is not a fashionable assertion to make at present. But so what? As I wrote in the last chapter, the right to free expression needs to be embraced afresh, as a first principle, but also because its survival and prosperity are – contrary to what is often asserted today – so important to the progressive objectives of those who espouse identity politics.

Without curiosity, there is no democracy.[3] It is a core characteristic of citizenship – of belief in the public space and in social responsibility – to take an interest in that which does not directly affect oneself. Without the readiness to speak and to listen to those who are aggrieved, or thwarted, or impassioned about emancipation, there is no progress. Nor, one might add, is there any art. As the novelist and essayist Zadie Smith has written:

. . . what insults my soul is the idea – popular in the culture just now, and presented in widely variant degrees of complexity – that we can and should write only about people who are fundamentally 'like' us: racially, sexually, genetically, nationally, politically, personally. That only an intimate authorial autobiographical connection with a character can be the rightful basis of a fiction. I do not believe that. I could not have written a single one of my books if I did.[4]

No society that demanded such restrictions could function long. Indeed, who would want it to? Pluralism is not only, as the political philosopher John Gray has written, 'an historical fate'. It is also a desirable one.[5] To listen to contemporary nativists who long for a return to imagined 'mono-culturalism' – or, at the extremes, new 'ethno-states' – is dreary work. Garton Ash's 'cosmopolis' has arisen because it is fundamental to the human condition to move, to trade, to commingle and interact. Multiplicity is the essence of modern life. It is a noisy bazaar of interdependence, exchange and synthesis. In such a place, how could there possibly be 'lanes'?

2. COMPREHENSIVE HISTORY

It is too easily forgotten that history is, or should be, a *discipline*, not a narrative designed to bring comfort to this or that group. Of course, as post-modernists insist, stories and power relations invariably squirrel their way into all texts. There is no such thing as a historical account that is entirely free of bias or artful omission. But that should not dissuade us from seeking to produce such an account: to hone, improve and enhance the historical ledger, and to bring an ever-broader range of sources, voices and perspectives to bear on the analysis.

This question has been central to contemporary identity politics. As the respective memoirs of Afua Hirsch and Akala, and David Olusoga's brilliant book *Black and British*, make quite clear, there is a gravitational pull in our culture and institutions away from an honest reckoning with the role slavery played in Britain's past, the suffering caused by colonialism and its continued legacy in our social dynamics.[6] A joint report by the Runnymede Trust and the TIDE Project (University of Liverpool) in July 2019 found that, in spite of the theoretical commitment of the National Curriculum to teaching 'how Britain has influenced and been influenced by the wider world'; 'the expansion and dissolution of empires'; and 'the process of change, the diversity of societies and relationships between different groups', this commitment is only patchily upheld in the nation's classrooms.[7] Pupils' access to this aspect of the curriculum depended overwhelmingly on the modules and texts set and available in their schools. Though some resources such as the website 'Our Migration Story' are available as a guide for those pursuing such courses, more than 70 per cent of teachers surveyed said that they would like properly organised training in the teaching of Empire.[8]

The suspicion of such initiatives as a supposedly left-wing assault upon the teaching of history are wildly overblown. True, there is a separate, largely performative campaign to vilify specific historical figures, especially Winston Churchill: not, please note, to take due account of their errors, the harm they caused and the beliefs they espoused that would now be considered profoundly bigoted, but to carry out the historiographical equivalent of 'cancellation'.

An egregious example of this was the experience in October 2018 of Scott Kelly, a retired American astronaut, who quoted Churchill in a tweet prompted by the controversial confirmation of Brett Kavanaugh as a US Supreme Court Justice. 'One of the greatest leaders of modern times, Sir Winston Churchill said, "in victory, magnanimity",' Kelly wrote. 'I guess those days are over.' Kelly can scarcely have guessed what would happen next. Like an asteroid storm smashing into a capsule, seething trolls attacked him on social media for citing a leader who was, allegedly, 'just as good as Hitler', 'responsible for the Bengal Famine of 1943', a 'bigot' and 'a mass murderer and a racist'.[9]

Stunned by the sheer ferocity of the response, Kelly capitulated, expressing deepest contrition: 'Did not mean to offend by quoting Churchill. My apologies. I will go and educate myself further on his atrocities, racist views which I do not support.'

Reflexive caricature does no more service to history than omission of huge tranches of a nation's past. As it happens, the question of Churchill's culpability in the Bengal Famine is not as straightforward as is often alleged: the principal causes of that disaster were cyclones and regional mismanagement. Indeed, on 7 October 1943, Churchill declared in Cabinet that one of Sir Archibald Wavell's priorities as viceroy of India must be to ensure that 'famine and food difficulties were dealt with' – a demand he continued to make persistently in his personal contacts with Wavell. This is not to acquit him of all blame but to insist upon a precise reading of the sources. The perennial reassessment of such figures as Churchill is the essence of history. Their capricious obliteration by social media warriors is not.

How much more valuable are the erudite criticisms of, for instance, the 175 historians, including 13 fellows of the British Academy, two past presidents of the Royal Historical Society and the director of the Stephen Lawrence Research Centre, who wrote to the Home Office in July 2020 to complain about the historical element of the UK citizenship test. As they observed:

The official handbook published by the Home Office is fundamentally misleading and in places demonstrably false . . . People in the colonies and people of colour in the UK are nowhere actors in this official history. The handbook promotes the misleading view that the empire came to an end simply because the British decided it was the right thing to do. Similarly, the abolition of slavery is treated as a British achievement, in which enslaved people themselves played no part. The book is equally silent about colonial protests, uprisings and independence movements.[10]

The handbook falsely claims, for example, that 'While slavery was illegal within Britain itself, by the 18th century it was a fully established overseas industry' – a misrepresentation of contemporary British jurisprudence. The handbook also states that 'by the second part of the 20th century, there was, for the most part, an orderly transition from empire to Commonwealth, with countries being granted their independence' – a gross oversimplification of a turbulent and sometimes violent process of change.

As Olusoga noted at the time, there was a direct connection between the BLM protests of the summer and this initiative – a common understanding among the signatories and their supporters that the response to George Floyd's killing needed to metamorphose from a moment of shock into a movement driving change:

> This is another manifestation and a version of our history that whitewashes the difficult parts and if this is the history we're telling to new fellow citizens then I somewhat despair. With the Black Lives Matter movement what we've seen is organisations and institutions all over the world listen in ways that they haven't been able to do previously. So I'm hopeful that the Home Office will reappraise this handbook and its version of British history and offer new British citizens a fuller and more frank understanding of our past.

The question of statues and their place in the public space is one that has been front and centre in identity politics discourse, especially since the Charlottesville riots, which were initially sparked by neo-Nazi and Ku Klux Klansmen defending an effigy of the Confederate general, Robert E. Lee. In Chapter 1, I mentioned the toppling of Edward Colston's statue in Bristol during the BLM protests after George Floyd's death. In June 2020, the governing body of Oriel College, Oxford, voted in favour of the removal of a statue of Cecil Rhodes, the archimperialist, mining magnate and white supremacist, who was one of its most munificent benefactors (the matter was deputed to a commission, set to report in 2021).

My own views on statue-toppling have evolved. In 2016, when the 'Rhodes Must Fall' campaign was first surging in Oxford, I was persuaded by the argument made by the Cambridge classics professor, Mary Beard, and her advice to her fellow Britons 'to look history in the eye and reflect on our awkward relationship to it, and what we are actually beneficiaries of, not simply to Photoshop the nasty bits out'.[11] Our built environment is composed of geological strata, and we need to confront each layer of that collective history with candour and courage.

The problem is that such a position is only half an argument. What happens when you do confront such figures as Rhodes – or Colston for that matter – and ask whether they truly deserve continued prominence in the public space? In a *Guardian* article, Olusoga again made the point pithily:

Today is the first full day since 1895 on which the effigy of a mass murderer does not cast its shadow over Bristol's city centre. Those who lament the dawning of this day, and who are appalled by what happened on Sunday, need to ask themselves some difficult questions. Do they honestly believe that Bristol was a better place yesterday because the figure of a slave trader stood at its centre? Are they genuinely unable – even now – to understand why those descended from Colston's victims have always regarded his statue as an outrage and for decades pleaded for its removal?[12]

The statue of Rhodes on the façade of Oriel College is not presented as an architectural fossil or a terrible warning. Its continued prominence undoubtedly communicates a measure of reverence, commemoration and even celebration. And – though the balance of judgment may be more nuanced in other cases – such prominence is not defensible in a 21st-Century, multi-ethnic, international university town. The Rhodes statue belongs in a museum, where its significance and provenance can be studied impartially, comprehensively and with academic rigour. It will still be available as an artefact for scholarly analysis. But its social function will be changed dramatically – and correctly.

The same is true of the many statues of Confederate generals across the American South – a great many of which were erected not to honour the fallen of the Civil War but to enshrine the values and racist laws of the Jim Crow era – the age of segregation and voter suppression that was ended (and then incompletely) only by the Civil Rights movement in the Sixties. We should not yield to the wrecking instinct of the vandal, or the worst forms of icono-clastic fever that have long been a feature of religious puritanism. But we can modify the public spaces in which we live, work and study, by common agreement, sensibly and systematically. We should not erase Rhodes or General Lee from the history books. But we do not have to walk in their shadow.

History is not putty. We should not mould it to our strategic needs, or to bring us comfort. But we are obliged to tell the whole truth about our collective past, to rescue the powerless from what E.P. Thompson called 'the enormous condescension of posterity' and to speak with honesty about the crimes and errors that scarred our national past. We must do so without fear or favour.

3. AFFIRMATIVE ACTION – WHERE IT IS NEEDED

The term 'affirmative action' entered the political mainstream in 1965, when President Lyndon B. Johnson signed an Executive Order (amended to include women in 1967) mandating federal contractors or subcontractors with 50 or more employees or more than $50,000 in contracts to 'take affirmative action to ensure that applicants are employed, and employees are treated during employment, without regard to their race, color, religion, sex or national origin.' The strategy was expanded in 1969 by President Richard Nixon and his secretary of labor, George Schultz. It has been a matter of controversy ever since – not least because the US courts have taken such an interventionist approach to its enactment.

In the UK, the question has been less systematically addressed and described, with less fanfare, as 'positive action'. The most significant legislation by far in this field is the Equality Act 2010, s.158, which allows an employer to take action for disadvantages that it reasonably believes are faced by people who share a particular protected characteristic – age, disability, gender reassignment, marriage and civil partnership, pregnancy and maternity, race, religion or belief, sex or sexual orientation. In limited circumstances, s.159 allows positive action in relation to recruitment or promotion.

In neither jurisdiction are 'quotas' lawful, in contrast to legitimate targets. So, a company board might have the declared aspiration of recruiting (say) 20 per cent of its members from ethnic minorities. But it could not lawfully entrench a fixed quota in its appointment procedures. This, it is often argued by opponents of positive action, is a distinction without a difference.

Especially in America, the question of 'affirmative action' has proved hugely controversial.[13] In practice, there is no sturdy evidence whatsoever that white men have been – as is so often complained by politicians of the Right – appreciably disadvantaged by these policies. As Melvin I. Urofsky shows in his book *The Affirmative Action Puzzle*, 'race-conscious admissions policies have a major impact on the minorities, whereas eliminating them would have only a marginal benefit for the white majority'.[14]

Another line of attack has been the objection that such strategies axiomatically demean those whom they assist, stigmatising them (it is argued) as the beneficiaries of majority charity. To this, Barack Obama had a powerful response, citing his admission to Harvard Law School and then selection as an editor of the *Harvard Law Review*. He had no idea, he said, whether he was, in either case, the beneficiary of a preferential programme. But, 'if I was, then I certainly am not ashamed of the fact, for I would argue that affirmative action is important precisely because those who benefit typically rise to the challenge when given an opportunity'.[15]

Obama's argument is supported by studies of businesses that have taken action to improve diversity amongst their employees, and found that the consequences are not only socially just but economically beneficial. In 2012, Credit Suisse found that 'companies with a higher proportion of women in decision-making roles continue to generate higher returns on equity, while running more conservative balance sheets', that 'where women account for the majority in the top management, the businesses show superior sales growth, high cash flow returns on investments and lower leverage', and that large-cap companies with at least one woman on the board outperformed their counterparts with no women on the board by 26 per cent in the previous six years.[16] According to a *Harvard Business Review* study published in 2019, '[h]aving women on the board results in better acquisition and investment decisions and in less aggressive risk-taking, yielding benefits for shareholders'.[17]

More research is needed on the correlation between board diversity and commercial success. Meanwhile, Goldman Sachs, the biggest underwriter of initial public offerings in the US, led the way in 2019 by announcing that it would no longer take any company public in America or Europe unless it had at least one person who was not a white male on its board – scarcely a high bar, you might think, but perhaps an augury of greater things to come.

In the 2020s, the real problem posed by positive action programmes is the embarrassing fact that they are still *necessary*. If meritocracy works so well, why, in 2018, were the CEOs of FTSE-100 companies more likely to be called Steve than to be women? And why were only eight per cent of executive directors female?[18] Why, between 2017 and 2019, did 12 of Oxford University's colleges admit five or fewer black undergraduates, and why were there five or fewer black undergraduates on 13 of Oxford's most popular courses?[19] Why, in 2019, were fewer than a third of judges in England and Wales women, and only seven per cent from ethnic minority backgrounds (versus 65 per cent of senior judges who were privately educated)?[20] Why, between 2007 and 2017, did black male graduates face a pay penalty of 17 per cent compared to white men – equivalent to £7,000 for a full-time worker?[21]

As President Bill Clinton remarked in July 1995 of comparable inequities in American society: '[Affirmative action] should be changed now to take care of those things that are wrong, and it should be retired when its job is done. I am resolved that this day will come, but the evidence suggests, indeed screams, that this day has not come. The job of ending discrimination in this country is not over'.[22]

In the UK, it arguable that we need more such schemes, and to be much more open about the need for them. David Lammy's observation in July 2018 that the UK needed 'a heavy dose of affirmative action' had the merit both of moral clarity and a sense of urgency – both of which are often lacking from this debate.[23] As so often, it is assumed that the British practice of steady incrementalism will fix the problem. But it is perfectly apparent that this is not happening. Generations of Britons have now grown used to being told that they live in a meritocracy, when it is quite clear that this is not the case and that only the talents of particular demographics are being fully mined.

We already *have* affirmative action: but it is mostly the unspoken variety that continues, through cultural signals, understandings and unconscious bias, to benefit white men, especially those who have gone to private schools and been educated at a small group of universities. What leaves a sour taste is the hypocrisy of the status quo: that so many people talk enthusiastically about 'diversity' and 'inclusion' but are unwilling to put in the work that turns benign language into operational reality.

Not all this work need be legislative, regulatory or otherwise coercive. Witness, for example, the success of WhiteHat, the tech start-up co-founded in 2017 by Euan Blair and Sophie Adelman, which offers apprenticeships for school-leavers at prestigious companies such as Google, Facebook and Clifford Chance as an alternative to the traditional pathway of higher education towards employment at such firms. In 2019, WhiteHat already had more than 750 apprentices, of whom 65 per cent were from BAME backgrounds, almost half had claimed free school meals, and seven per cent had been in care or came from refugee backgrounds; it is now expanding from London into Manchester and Leeds.

Though not technically a 'positive action' scheme, WhiteHat certainly directs under-represented talent towards the best employers. This sort of 'pipeline' strategy, if replicated to achieve a critical mass of educational capacity, could have a significant effect upon access to the job market and the confidence of prospective applicants from a broad range of backgrounds. There are many other groups and organisations in the UK that perform this work: the mentoring charity, ReachOut; Voyage Youth, which aims to steer young people from ethnic minorities towards fulfilling employment and decrease the numbers falling foul of the criminal justice system; and Just Like Us, which helps young LGBTQ+ people in the move from classroom to workplace.

The pressure of transparency and investment decisions can also play a part in turning employment diversity from slogan to reality. In this regard, the science of behavioural economics – or 'Nudge' thinking – has useful lessons.[24] Cultural norms are not set in stone and can be moulded by aggregate forces that urge decision-makers towards benign outcomes. Certainly, the (slow but perceptible) improvement in the recruitment of women to company boards would not have occurred without the bright light shone upon businesses by researchers, index-compilers, investors and the mainstream media. The challenge is always to get beyond the appalling jargon of 'corporate social responsibility' and associated 'mission statements' to the grit of reality. Are companies really making an effort to hire more people of colour, promote more women, take serious account of applicants' backgrounds when they seek the best person for the job? Why has the Conservative Party, which at the time of writing only has 87 women MPs (compared to 277 men), not accepted the political necessity of all-women shortlists?

The myth that society is a level playing field – or anything like it – is one of the most insulting features of liberal democratic discourse. Nor is it enough to repeat the catechism of 'equality opportunity', 'social mobility' and (the newest platitude on the block) 'levelling up'. These remain ideals rather than defining characteristics of the system as it presently operates. Opportunity is more broadly distributed than used to be the case. But not enough to justify the levels of self-congratulation that are sometimes to be heard in liberal London, or the collective complacency that this reflects.

The diversity of contemporary society is not yet reflected in opportunity, position, status or power: not remotely so. Until the gap narrows substantially, we will have no reason to congratulate ourselves. This is why, as I made clear in Chapter 2, I am not instinctively hostile to Robin DiAngelo's notion of 'white fragility'. I think she is right that the self-image of white middle-class people is often a more powerful force than the honest pursuit of social justice: we are more concerned with coddling ourselves – with insisting that we could not possibly be complicit in racist structures – than with accepting the facts of the matter. Racism, sexism and other forms of oppression are still very much a part of our social system; all the more harmful, one might argue, because they are now buried beneath the glutinous rhetoric of supposed social responsibility.

This is why we should not rule out stronger medicine than that recommended by the 'Nudge' school. Voluntary reform is always preferable in a free society, especially where the relationship between different identity groups is concerned. Amicable consensus is always better than grudging compliance. All the same: the power of law and of government decision-taking is there for a reason. Probably the most successful form of affirmative action in the US has been the linkage of federal contracts to an obligation upon bidding firms to increase their representation of minority workers. Between 1974 and 1980, for example, the rate of minority employment in businesses that contracted with the federal government rose by 20 per cent, while the rate of employment of women increased by 15.2 per cent (in firms that did not do business with government, the respective increases were only 12 and 2.2 per cent).

There is no reason why the UK government and the devolved governments of Scotland, Wales and Northern Ireland (mindful of the community-specific constraints already imposed by the Good Friday Peace Agreement) could not drive through similar reforms. There are few upsides to Brexit, but one of them is the freedom to regulate the labour market free of European jurisdiction or directives. Which is to say: we could strengthen the existing provisions of the 1998 Human Rights Act and the legislation passed to comply with the European Equal Treatment Directive of 1976.

To be clear: in spite of the delusions of the nativists and the populist Right, 21st-Century society is going to become more rather than less diverse. The #MeToo movement was not a blip but a warning that old patriarchal structures are going to fall; the only question is at what pace. The politics of gender transition may be fractious, but the very strength of the debate is a clear signal that all institutions and organisations will have to recognise this shift in personal identity (and the questions it poses). Generation Z (or iGen) will not tolerate the quiet bigotries of the past and has already shown itself to be both politically engaged and all too aware of its tough inheritance. For liberal democracy to retain the trust of the majority in future it must be more than a rigged system for white middle-class men – a system that compounds its failings by, all too often, refusing to acknowledge them. Competitiveness gets a bad name when it is not fair – not, in fact, truly competitive at all.

This means retaining the *option* of quotas, both voluntary and legally imposed. If the institutions of state will not change, they will have to be mandated to do so. If companies will not modernise themselves, they will need a firmer hand to make them acknowledge the world in which they operate. That hand may be the hand of the market, the investor, the consumer or – as a final resort – the state. If the rise of identity politics has a core message, it is that the game is up.

Disadvantaged groups are not going to be appeased or pacified any longer by cheques in the post, vague pledges of good intent and policy IOUs. They will not accept a social landscape that supposedly belongs to all but, in practice, is still dominated by a single demographic, clinging on to its domain for dear life. The question is how those with the power to enact change choose to go about it – and whether they grasp the significance and profundity of what has already happened, and what is coming their way, soon.

4. JUSTICE AND REDRESS

In October 2018, the *New York Times* compiled a, chart: '#MeToo Brought Down 201 Powerful Men. Nearly Half of Their Replacements Are Women'.[25] This was a measure of how far the movement had come in a year, and how much it had achieved.

Yet much still hung in the balance. The fate of the disgraced movie mogul, Harvey Weinstein, was not yet clear; and it was widely feared, especially after the confirmation of Brett Kavanaugh as a US Supreme Court Justice in the same month, that he would somehow walk free. Both cases involved serious allegations of sexual assault against women. Though there was no other connection, the Senate's decision to confirm Kavanaugh (who strongly denied the claims) was widely interpreted as an omen that Weinstein might escape justice.

That Weinstein did not do so was of immense symbolic importance. In March 2020, he was sentenced by Judge James Burke at the New York Supreme Court to 20 years' imprisonment for a first-degree criminal sex act and a further three years for third-degree rape of a woman.[26] No such penalty can ever erase the pain and trauma that Weinstein, and many men like him, have caused and continue to inflict upon women. But his conviction and sentencing were significant, nonetheless. They offered a glimmer of hope that the institutions of criminal justice – as well as the sunlight of social media and activism – might provide some redress to the survivors of sexual harassment.

I revert to my point in Chapter 2 that liberal democracy is at a crossroads. Attacked by the populist and authoritarian Right around the world, it has also squandered the support of the many identity groups that feel neglected by and invisible to a system still predominantly run by white men – but insistent that it is fully aware of the need for 'diversity' and 'inclusion'. This hypocrisy is the greatest weakness and fault line in contemporary liberalism.

It is reasonable to object that Twitter can be a kangaroo court, an engine for instant demonisation. The corollary, however, is to ensure that companies' internal human resource procedures provide meaningful protection to employees who report bullying or sexual harassment. What was clear, time and again, as the #MeToo disclosures tumbled forth in 2017–18, was that most women had previously felt unable to speak out and that – far from being safeguarded by their employers – assumed that the word of powerful men would always be believed before their own. It was for this reason that, in October 2017, two UK journalists, Rosamund Urwin and Emily Reynolds, set up the Second Source (the name inspired by Simone de Beauvoir's *The Second Sex*), a scheme to offer confidential mentoring to women journalists, help them understand and assert their rights and work with companies to tackle harassment.[27] In July 2019, the UK government launched a consultation on workplace harassment to explore the need for further regulation and legislation – a welcome measure which, it is to be hoped, does not get lost in the melee of Brexit and national recovery from Covid-19.

How will the criminal justice system respond to this challenge? There is some evidence that the culture of #MeToo has made women feel more empowered to come forward. In England and Wales, for example, the number of rapes reported to police (which was already on an upwards trajectory) surged by almost 13,000 to 54,045 in 2017–18 compared with 41,186 the previous year. The annual figure rose yet again to 58,657 the following year. In sharp contrast, however, the number of convictions for rape over the same period fell from 2,635 in 2017–18 to 1,925 in 2018–19.[28]

This suggests strongly – though more research on the detail is necessary – that the system is not fit for purpose, and that a thorough examination of the manner in which reports of rape are handled, from police station to courtroom, is needed. It is a matter of profound concern – and shame – that, as Dame Vera Baird QC, the victims' commissioner for England and Wales, said in July 2020 (echoing the wording of activists), 'in effect, what we are witnessing is the decriminalisation of rape'.[29] The beginnings of a response were visible in August 2020, as it emerged that the prime minister's crime and justice taskforce is planning to set targets for the police and Crown Prosecution Service to bring more rape cases to trial.[30]

What contemporary identity politics has done, without question, is to bring fresh urgency to such questions, and to ensure that they remain front and centre in political discourse. It has also expanded the range of the possible, in ways that would have been inconceivable only a decade ago.

A prime example of this expansion is the debate on reparations in the United States. For generations, the idea that the descendants of the enslaved were entitled to restitution was regarded as a fringe proposal and one that would, in time, fade away completely. In fact, precisely the opposite has happened. In the 2020 presidential race, three contenders for the Democratic nomination – Elizabeth Warren, Kamala Harris and Julian Castro – made the case for reparations as a matter worthy of serious debate by the American people.

As the *Atlantic* writer, Ta-Nehisi Coates, put it in a hugely influential essay published in 2016:

> What I'm talking about is more than recompense for past injustices – more than a handout, a payoff, hush money, or a reluctant bribe. What I'm talking about is a national reckoning that would lead to spiritual renewal. Reparations would mean the end of scarfing hot dogs on the Fourth of July while denying the facts of our heritage. Reparations would mean the end of yelling 'patriotism' while waving a Confederate flag. Reparations would mean a revolution of the American consciousness, a reconciling of our self-image as the great democratizer with the facts of our history.[31]

As Coates makes clear, this is not simply an argument about a past atrocity. It is about the enduring legacy of that atrocity, more than a century and a half after the ratification of the 13th Amendment to the US Constitution formally abolished slavery. African Americans have been systematically excluded from the national wealth that was built on their ancestors' slave labour (for every ten cents of assets owned by an average black family, an average white household owns a dollar). In particular, black people have been excluded from home ownership by mortgage scams, zoning rules and predatory contracts.

How such reparations might be paid for, by whom and to whom, remains a matter of intense debate: some favour a windfall wealth tax, others specific housing and job schemes for less affluent African Americans. We are a long way from anything approaching a consensus. But the issue is now folded into the warp and weft of US politics (and was raised once more in the arguments over structural racism following the death of George Floyd). It may not happen. But – for the first time – it could. Indeed, as Afua Hirsch wrote in July 2020, this a debate that also needs to be conducted in the UK:

> In the Caribbean, Britain received, in the words of Nobel prize-winning economist Arthur Lewis, 200 years of free labour – from over 15 million black people, and those who were indentured from India. The proceeds from this enslavement, and the heavily exploitative years of 'apprenticed' labour that followed it, provided the profits with which Britain modernised its economy. The systemic poverty that remains in the Caribbean can be directly traced to the era of enslavement and colonialism, at the end of which Britain walked away leaving 60% of the region's black inhabitants functionally illiterate.[32]

The quest for redress and justice is always arduous. But it is important to acknowledge that this quest has been given fresh force, focus and immediacy by the rise of identity politics. The application of this pressure will – or should – continue to be central to its objectives. Those who have marched, and campaigned, and written in the name of such causes deserve credit, gratitude and support for – in the words of Mario Savio – putting their 'bodies upon the gears'.

5. PERFORMANCE AND PRACTICALITY

'Politics is a strong and slow boring of hard boards. It takes both passion and perspective. Certainly all historical experience confirms the truth – that man would not have attained the possible unless time and again he had reached out for the impossible'.[33]

Thus, did Max Weber, in his essay 'Politics as a Vocation', encapsulate the enduring challenge that faces those who would enact progress. They must locate injustice and make it impossible to ignore – with the persuasive power of the crowd, of political spectacle, of media channels that are not controlled (or wholly controlled) by the powerful. The extension of the parliamentary franchise in Britain was, as much as anything, a response to popular clamour. The advances made by 20th-Century feminism were the achievement of what Helen Lewis describes as 'difficult women' in her book of the same name.[34] The Soviet bloc regimes did not tumble because their leaders were bored, or ideologically converted.

But that is not all that Weber identified about the nature of progress. Its achievement also requires 'perspective' – and a recognition that the 'slow boring of hard boards' is necessary. As John Gray puts it in his analysis of liberalism and its discontents, whatever the revolutionary spirit craves, there is rarely an alternative to 'the long haul of politics'.

In the past, such an observation might have been a statement of the obvious. But, in our era, it is profoundly countercultural. The digital revolution and consumerisation of practically everything have nurtured unprecedented levels of impatience, a desire for instant gratification, a disdain for reflection – an emotional condition upon which the populist Right has preyed, with its fraudulent promises of simple solutions to complex problems.

Impatience is necessary to ignite the spirit of political change and to hold fire to the feet of those responsible for it. If an inquiry makes 35 recommendations, there need to be politicians and campaigns sleeplessly ensuring that they are implemented. But impatience, in and of itself, is not enough.

To this extent, Mark Lilla is correct in his criticism that identity politics is nothing without representation and electoral power: 'in a democracy the only way to meaningfully defend [minorities] – and not just make empty gestures of recognition and "celebration" – is to win elections and exercise power in the long run, at every level of government. And the only way to accomplish that is to have a message that appeals to as many people as possible and pulls them together.'[35]

To date, identity politics has been predominantly performative. It favours rallies, hashtags, social media campaigns, assertions, placards and collective indignation to the less adrenaline-soaked business of seeking office, legislating and filling the potholes of social justice. This is perfectly understandable. If you feel excluded from the full rights of citizenship, why should your instinct be to seek change by traditional means or to trust the very institutions that have let you down? The street and social media are naturally more appealing as venues for activism.

Traditional liberalism, as I have argued, has been slow to understand the deeper significance of identity politics – or, perhaps more accurately, unwilling to do so. Precisely because the new social movements have arisen from the failures of individualism and meritocracy to fulfil their promise, it is more comfortable to dismiss their activities as generational faddishness, an online cult and an irritant rather than a serious challenge. But this is delusion. What we have witnessed in the past ten years is a fundamental shift in the way that politics works – mobilised, undoubtedly, by technological change – that is not going to fade away in the face of the establishment's reprimands.

In his 2018 Netflix stand-up special *The Bird Revelation*, the comedian Dave Chappelle speaks of his 'responsibility to speak recklessly' – a professional duty which leads to some enlightening conclusions. Amongst them is his insistence, inspired in part by his study in South Africa of its post-Apartheid Truth and Reconciliation process, that all social justice movements need 'imperfect allies'. Chappelle's point – made in the context of a riff on the #MeToo campaign – is that all movements begin as expressions of purity and then (if they are to succeed) become coalitions of common interest, often finding shared interests and support in the most unexpected places. Radical green activists have often found that their interests – especially in local campaigns – intersect closely with those of traditional, Barbour-wearing conservationists. The protests around the world after the death of George Floyd were multi-ethnic to an extent never previously seen in anti-racism marches. Not every male supporter of the #MeToo movement fully understands the extent or depth of the problem – but the best of them are willing to learn. Real change begins in purity and gathers pace in coalition-building: in the search for imperfect allies.

It should be obvious that the impasse between conventional liberals and those who champion identity politics is a matter of enormous gratification to the populist Right. As long as progressives are divided – squabbling on social media about cancel culture and campus speech codes – the task of those who seek election by identifying enemies, denouncing elites, experts and institutions, and promising unattainable bonanzas will be that much easier.

On what basis, then, might such an alliance be forged?

6. IDENTITY-CONSCIOUS PROGRESSIVISM

As Stacey Abrams, the former Democratic contender for the governorship of Georgia, has put it: 'The marginalized did not create identity politics: their identities have been forced on them by dominant groups, and politics is the most effective method of revolt'.[36]

This observation, made in a *Foreign Affairs* article in 2019 responding to Francis Fukuyama's critique of identity politics, should be our starting point. No alliance between traditional liberals and the new social justice movements will be possible without a recognition that these campaigns are not an impertinence, or mere political fashion, or (worst of all) the hobby of hopelessly fragile 'snowflakes'. Such objections are both misplaced and insulting: the causes at the heart of identity politics are centuries-old but have taken new forms in recent decades (not least because incremental reform has failed). The caricature of young people as ultra-sensitive confuses adversity with fragility: today's twenty-somethings face lives that, in a great many respects, will be tougher than the experience of their parents. Their anger – over climate change, job insecurity, the shortage of affordable property, the challenge of social care and the decrepitude of the institutions they will inherit – should not be mistaken for a collective tantrum that will pass with maturity. This generational shift is real, the most important since the punk movement of the late 1970s, and its consequences are only beginning to disclose themselves.

This is not to say that those who espouse identity politics are infallible. The puritanism that some manifest – a common wrong turn taken by most impassioned movements – is counterproductive and drives away many who are interested in coalition-building. In particular, there is great strategic danger in the fixation with purity of speech and the consequent urge to 'cancel', 'de-platform' or otherwise silence those who cross an often arbitrarily drawn line. This impulse is fine if your collective ambition is to retreat into an ideological stockade and avoid the abrasions of messy, day-to-day politics with people who will often disagree with you. But – if that is your inclination – ask how much progress has been achieved in history by instinctive censors, and how much by those who embraced free expression and immersed themselves in the endless battle between speech and counter-speech.

Liberals need to acknowledge that individualism, meritocracy and universalism are ideals rather than (to date) descriptive terms. But, even as they accept the *reality* of this shortfall, they can also insist, robustly, upon the *reality* of pluralist society, in which values will always be colliding and negotiation between them is the most important feature of peaceful coexistence. As Isaiah Berlin, the father of modern value-pluralism, argued: differences of values are 'an intrinsic, irremovable element in human life'; 'the notion of total human fulfilment is a [. . .] chimera'; and such 'collisions of values are of the essence of what they are and what we are'.[37]

This means that agendas will clash, inventories of demands will be difficult to reconcile and a right that one group considers inviolable will infringe upon the hard-won freedoms of another. Liberal democracies still have plenty of heavy lifting to do on what religious liberty entails in a modern, diverse society. It must, of course, include an inviolable freedom of worship, and a right to protection by the state if that freedom is menaced in any way. But that freedom does not – for instance – automatically confer upon religious parents the right to withdraw their children from classes that teach the legal and civic fact that families now come in many different forms, and that parents can be straight or gay.[38] This involves difficult and sensitive conversations. All the more reason not to shy away from them. The silence of those whose only concern is not to offend anyone, ever, achieves precisely nothing in a complex democracy.

The same applies, as we saw in the last chapter, to the horribly divisive debate about trans rights. No decent pluralist society can be indifferent to or fail to act upon the suffering of trans people – the loneliness, bullying and harassment which is part of their everyday experience. This is a crisis of collective responsibility which has yet to be systematically addressed. But the seriousness of this social failure does not – cannot – mean that the rights and anxieties of biological women should simply be ignored. When, in 2018, a group of feminists distributed stickers with the slogan 'Women don't have penises' – not a view shared by trans activists, but still comfortably within the boundaries of the law – they were investigated by Merseyside Police and condemned by Joe Anderson, elected mayor of Liverpool.[39]

There needs to be a new progressivism which respects group identity and – in the best traditions of value-pluralism – seeks to negotiate the differences that arise from the (endless) collisions of rights that take place in a diverse society. The error of many who espouse identity politics is to insist that, as far as they are concerned, the 'debate is over'. The ideological car is parked.

But – in a busy democracy – no car is parked. The better metaphor is a dodgem rink, in which movement is constant and the challenge is to avoid collision. Since collision is inevitable, the duty of the rink managers is to ensure that nobody sustains injury. In modern society, the task of liberalism – more than ever – is to provide spaces where negotiations can take place.

Legislation has a part to play, but only a part. The Equality Act of 2010 has established a framework that raises as many questions as it answers. It provides basic legal crash barriers but is very far from a detailed manual to modern-day living (indeed, how could it be?). The hard graft will take place in other venues – digital and (preferably) real-life – under the rubric of common citizenship rather than as a zero-sum contest for rights.

This, of course, is the difficult bit, and the challenge to which there is no glib solution. As Lilla puts it: 'The only way out of this conundrum is to appeal to something that as Americans we all share but which has nothing to do with our identities, without denying the existence and importance of the latter'.[40] He is right that the best way of stirring a society into collective action is 'by consciously appealing to what we share' – demanding, for instance, that disadvantaged groups be given equal access to the American Dream, or the fruits of the British way of life. The trouble is that this is precisely what they have been asking for – for centuries, in some cases. Nobody doubts what Lilla calls the 'need to cultivate political fellow feeling'.[41] The issue is how to do so when that sense of cross-sectional community is in such poor repair and fragmentation is the norm rather than the exception.

At local level, there is much to be said for so-called 'encounter culture' – initiatives that actively seek to promote amicable dialogue between groups and, as Lammy puts it, allow 'previously isolated individuals to meet'.[42] There is, as he continues, a case for a national civic service for young people – or even a national climate service, which would oblige all school-leavers or graduates to engage in a year's paid work planting trees and undertaking related work to address climate emergency. Why not extend the principle of Voluntary Service Overseas to a parallel national service, which sends young people to work on social enterprise and charitable schemes within the UK but in neighbourhoods unlike the ones in which they were raised?

We need not be afraid of a 21st-Century patriotism, sharply distinguished from nationalism, on the basis famously set out by George Orwell: 'By "patriotism" I mean devotion to a particular place and a particular way of life, which one believes to be the best in the world but has no wish to force on other people. Patriotism is of its nature defensive, both militarily and culturally. Nationalism, on the other hand, is inseparable from the desire for power. The abiding purpose of every nationalist is to secure more power and more prestige, *not* for himself but for the nation or other unit in which he has chosen to sink his own individuality'.[43]

A generous, open version of patriotism such as this would be a cultural force to reckon with. It still exists in the cauldron of British emotion, distinct from the aggressive nationalism that powered Brexit and is still visible in the uglier strains of the immigration debate. But it would be folly to assume that, by some benign outpouring of collective altruism, such a spirit is going to rise, almost mystically, to rescue us from our present fragmentations and divisions. To hope for such a moment is lazy nostalgia posturing as fine feeling.

Any alliance between liberals and those who espouse identity politics must be fiercely contemporary. It must see the world as it is, not just as it could be. It must assume that network politics is now the norm and that most of its battles will be fought online. It must take as read the fact that public trust in most institutions – the NHS being a conspicuous exception – has plummeted and that one of the many formidable tasks facing those who seek progress is to restore confidence in the organisations, agencies and public bodies that, in the end, will enact it. One element in this might be grass-roots consultative assemblies of the sort championed by James S. Fishkin, and new intermediate bodies that stand between direct democracy (referendums) and the representative varieties: so-called 'liquid democracy'.[44] But this can only be part of a much greater enterprise – a root-and-branch renewal of the tarnished institutional structures in most liberal democracies and the social contract that underpins them. In the UK, for example, the 'to-do' list is daunting: an overhaul of outdated parliamentary procedure, the creation of a new second chamber of the legislature, the delegation of real power to metro mayors, meaningful regulation of the part played by social media in elections, perhaps even a fully codified constitution. No small task, to say the least.

Those who wish to see a new progressive alliance grow must assume, too, that most people regard the economic system as rigged against them – a suspicion that has been deepened by the recessionary impact of coronavirus. It will be in this formidably difficult context that any liberal force will have to address the core problems of the coming decades: climate emergency, automation and artificial intelligence, a transformed labour market in which there is little economic security, the social implications of increased life expectancy, the reality (in spite of nativist pipe dreams) of ever-increasing population mobility, the prospect of the next pandemic.

Lukianoff and Haidt, as we have seen, call for a 'common-humanity identity politics'.[45] In her *Foreign Affairs* piece, Abrams writes of the need for 'an expanded, identity-conscious politics' and this strikes me as a promising formulation. As she writes, there is no intrinsic reason why campaigns pursued by specific groups should not be of great benefit to others.

Embracing the distinct histories and identities of groups in a democracy enhances the complexity and capacity of the whole. For example, by claiming the unique attributes of womanhood – and, for women of color, the experience of inhabiting the intersection of marginalized gender and race – feminists have demonstrated how those characteristics could be leveraged to enhance the whole. Take, for example, the Family and Medical Leave Act, which feminists originally pushed for in order to guarantee women's right to give birth and still keep their jobs, but which men have also come to rely on to take time off from work to care for children or aging parents.

That is so. It is also an important example of the extent to which identity groups often perceive and mobilise against injustice before the liberal establishment has wrapped its collective head around the urgency of the matter. And this is of particular contemporary importance.

It is a grave error to imagine that the poor performance of particular governments or the moments of solidarity that nations experienced during the pandemic will automatically translate into a new progressivism, and it is certainly premature to assume that Biden's victory signifies something deeper than the defeat of a truly terrible president. In fact, the post-coronavirus landscape will be fertile ground for the populist Right, which nurtures and feeds off economic insecurity, social fragmentation, resentment of elites and experts, and suspicion of minorities. It is hostile to and impatient with liberal institutions; and its foundation is a patriarchal, nativist, vengeful form of identity politics very different from the varieties we have been discussing.

If liberals take the easy path of demoralised introspection in the hard years ahead, and the advocates of identity politics insist upon the purity of separateness, the nationalist Right will find ways of forcing its way between them. Donald Trump and Brexit represented the start of something, not the end. Those who are troubled by this have two options: to stand righteously in their silos, convinced of their rectitude, but powerless; or to put historic duty before ideological vanity, reach out to imperfect allies and generate a light that can change the world.

PART TWO

IGNORANCE

CHAPTER 5

BRILLIANT IGNORANCE

I want to live my life taking the risk – all the time – that I don't know anything like enough yet, that I haven't under-stood enough, that I can't know enough, that I'm always hungrily operating on the margins of a potentially great harvest of future knowledge and wisdom.
Christopher Hitchens, Prestonwood Baptist Church in Plano, Texas, 18 November 2010

One of the great privileges of writing about politics and culture for a living is that you get asked to speak at schools and universities. It's a con, really. These talks are framed as if you are doing the pupils and their teachers a favour by turning up to talk on a rainy afternoon in Bath or Lambeth or Glasgow. Often, one of the class is deputed to say something polite in thanks at the end, which is always very much appreciated.

But, if you're doing your job, it should be *you* that is asking the questions, and learning as you go. Young people, because they haven't yet been made boring by adult life, usually have interesting and imaginative things to say about their own worlds and about the world we all share. I suspect this has always been so, but it is especially true right now. As I said in Part One, we are in the midst of a serious generational shift that is much more significant that the routine changes in fashion, musical taste and youth idiom that takes place perhaps once a decade. This feels much more definitive – unlike anything since the late Seventies.

So it pays to listen. I am always happy to answer questions, but often find that students have their own still-forming answers to the dilemmas they face, and certainly their own preoccupations about the dysfunctional landscape on which they will soon be making their mark. As the dramatist David Hare says in his book on researching his plays, *Asking Around*: 'There is nothing better for a writer than to go out and be rebuked by reality.'[1]

If I had to distil what I have picked up from these (unashamedly anecdotal) exchanges, I would venture the following observations about those in their late teens and early twenties:

1. They are politically and socially engaged, alarmed by what they see as the intermittent chaos of modern life, its manifest social injustices, climate emergency, the insecure job market into which they will be venturing and a political system that is rigged, broken or both.
2. They have a common intuition that the task of repair will be left to their generation – the present cohort of decision-makers being woefully unfit for purpose.
3. They are not snowflakes: quite the opposite. Points (1) and (2) have seen to that.
4. They are more fixated by qualifications and grades than any generation in living memory.
5. They are terrified of failure, exhausted and overworked.
6. Their curriculum and course work leave them almost no time for cultural and literary exploration.
7. As a consequence, their hinterland of knowledge – beyond what they need to know to pass exams – is often relatively small.

They are, to generalise hugely, brilliant but ignorant: a generation raised to acquire 'skills' but only to enable them to jump through hoops; cut off from the fruits of civilisations by shortage of time and because they are steered away from anything that might distract them from tests and examinations; fearful of failure to an extent that stifles intellectual curiosity; conscious of political and social imperatives, but denied the breadth of experience and knowledge that is essential to active citizenship.

And let me leave not a scintilla of doubt: ***this is an indictment of my generation, not theirs***. It is my generation (and, to some extent, the one that preceded it) that has turned education into cognitive battery farming; that has reduced the cultivation of learning to a matrix of tick-box tests; that has drained the life, emotion and passion out of the most important gift – other than familial love – that any society can give its young. If, in the words of the former Yale professor, William Deresiewicz, we live in an age of 'excellent sheep', then it is the fault of the shepherds that this is so.[2]

To take one metric, but a significant one: they read significantly less than their predecessors. As Jean M. Twenge has shown in her study of iGen, a majority of teens in the late 1970s read a book or magazine nearly every day but, by 2015, only 16 per cent did so. By 2015, one in three high school seniors said that they had not read any books for pleasure in the past year, three times as many as in 1976.[3] Of the 200 San Diego State freshmen and sophomores Twenge surveyed in 2015, most said that they never read newspapers, and confined themselves to celebrity or fashion magazines. She quotes one respondent: '[I read] only if a school assignment requires it because I'd rather not spend my free time reading extensively.'

In the UK, a survey by the National Literacy Trust published in February 2020 found that – in the previous year – only 26 per cent of under-18s spent some time each day reading. This was the lowest figure recorded since the trust first started tracking children's reading habits in 2005. Overall, 53 per cent of children claimed that they enjoyed reading 'very much' or 'quite a lot' – though this was the lowest level since 2013. A third of children said they were unable to find things to read that interested them. There was also a clear gender divide in the survey: less than half (47 per cent) of boys were keen readers, compared with 60 per cent of girls.[4]

To which one possible response is: so what? Why attach so much importance to reading as an indicator of personal, moral or civic well-being? Certainly, the presentation of reading as a necessary cerebral chore, or a solemn form of secular piety, or (worst of all) a means of acquiring social status – all this has long been, and will continue to be, a disaster for those who believe (as I do) that reading is an emancipatory force, essential to the development of free thinking, the acquisition of knowledge and the cultivation of the truly critical mind. It grieves me that reading has come to be seen by so many members of this generation as a sub-category of the miserable curriculum through which they are herded, rather than a distinctly individual pleasure, a stimulus to free social discussion and a generally liberating experience.

On this, I am with Harold Bloom: 'It matters, if individuals are to retain any capacity to form their own judgments and opinions, that they continue to read for themselves'.[5] For *themselves*, please note: not to please their teachers or to reassure their parents, but to develop their own sensibilities, store of ideas and sense of possibility. There are few words in the English language less thrilling to a child's ears than 'set text'. As Neil Gaiman, the author and graphic novelist, has put it: 'Well-meaning adults can easily destroy a child's love of reading: stop them reading what they enjoy, or give them worthy-but-dull books that you like, the twenty-first-century equivalents of Victorian "improving" literature. You'll wind up with a generation convinced that reading is uncool and, worse, unpleasant.'

Books, Gaiman argues, are engines of empathy. They are also, in the best possible sense, engines of discomfort and self-examination: 'Fiction can show you a different world. It can take you somewhere you've never been. Once you've visited other worlds, like those who ate fairy fruit, you can never be entirely content with the world that you grew up in. And discontent is a good thing: people can modify and improve their worlds, leave them better, leave them different, if they're discontented'.[6]

To reiterate: this is not about pressure, but the opposite. It is about giving young minds access to great and popular literature (and great popular literature), freedom from guilt about reading, the freedom to discard books they are not enjoying or to postpone finishing them. Indeed, as Italo Calvino reminds us in his essay on reading the classics, there is a special relish to be discovered in enjoying a great text in adulthood:

> ... to read a great book for the first time in one's maturity is an extraordinary pleasure, different from (though one cannot say greater or lesser than) the pleasure of having read it in one's youth. Youth brings to reading, as to any other experience, a particular flavor and a particular sense of importance, whereas in maturity one appreciates (or ought to appreciate) many more details and levels and meanings.[7]

And far from being restrictive, Calvino's definition of what we should read is generous and open-spirited:

> There is nothing for it but for all of us to invent our own ideal libraries of classics. I would say that such a library ought to be composed half of books we have read and that have really counted for us, and half of books we propose to read and presume will come to count – leaving a section of empty shelves for surprises and occasional discoveries.

Between basic literacy and rich erudition stretches a long continuum, upon which most young people used to situate themselves according to their needs, inclinations and abilities. That continuum still exists. But it is no longer an important part of how they are taught or raised. 'Literature' has come to mean 'set texts', and (more important) what exam candidates are meant to think about them. History is composed of 'modules', most of them formatted and boxed into a form that is dispiritingly indistinguishable from rote learning. The notion that the exam course is just a start – an incentive to look elsewhere, anywhere – is now regarded as laughably outdated. The course, the curriculum, the official framework, is *everything*.

I am in no doubt at all that my own education – I am old enough to have sat O levels, the predecessor to GCSEs – was much less taxing than what today's pupils have to go through.

We worked reasonably hard, but there was always plenty of time for other pursuits organised or enabled by our school – theatre visits, sessions listening to cassettes of Radio 4 programmes, introductions to great works of classical music, flickering performances of foreign movies in the school hall. None of this had anything much to do with our CVs, and nothing whatsoever to do with our exam prospects. We were urged to read as widely as we could. It was at school that I was introduced to three works of history – Norman Cohn's *The Pursuit of the Millennium*, W.G. Hoskins' *The Making of the English Landscape* and Keith Thomas's *Religion and the Decline and Magic* – that persuaded me (much more than the essays we wrote in preparation for A level) that I wanted to read history at university. The workload was considerably less burdensome than it is today. So there was time to breathe intellectually and to look further afield. I count myself extremely lucky.

Especially so, in fact, when I talk to school pupils and undergraduates who, with the occasional exception, have never enjoyed this latitude. They are wedded to their approved reading lists, and to the interpretations that are urged upon them. They want to know what they have to do to get the grades they need to progress to the next stage: not in the healthy sense of seeking opportunity and intellectual evolution, but according to a logic that has much more in common to the pitiless logic of the computer game. To get to the next level, you have to survive the part of the game you are playing right now: that is all that counts. All else is distraction and dilettantism. There is no room for it in their Darwinian world.

Their focus is often extraordinary to behold. The constructive gloss would be to say that they are a generation that has purpose, direction and motivation. But at its heart there is often a visible bafflement, too; an intuition that there must be more to life than exams, grades, extra tuition and what amounts to educational survivalism. In their twenties, they often discover what they've been missing. That there is enjoyment, as well as advantage, to be derived from literature, essays, history, drama, poetry and music. It is depressing to note that – in my experience – this often comes as something of a revelation ('Why did nobody tell me about Andrea Dworkin/Emily Dickinson/Angela Davis/Graham Greene/Hunter S. Thompson/Charlie Parker?' – why indeed?).

This is why I regard the decline in reading as of special significance. It is a clue to something deeper, something that has gone badly wrong. Predictably, it tends to be blamed on digital devices and the dramatic increase in 'screen time' facilitated by smartphones and tablets. There is indeed a connection between digital technology and the decline of traditionally acquired knowledge, as we shall see, but it is not straightforward. It suits parents and teachers to argue that reading books has simply been supplanted by scrolling posts, but the reality is more subtle than that, and is, in some respects, more alarming. It is not so much that young people who would otherwise be reading *Anna Karenina* or *Beloved* are glued to Instagram or Facebook (although they may be). As Gretchen McCulloch shows in her book *Because Internet*, the digital life has given birth to completely new modes of speech and language.[8] And – alongside this – Gen Z's whole notion of, and relationship with, time itself has changed, too. Their sense that they are positioned in an awesomely long continuum of human existence – past, present and future – has been marred by the deranged pressures of the digital microsecond.

Meanwhile, young people are subject to an extraordinary range of demands, many of them academic. The abuse of prescription stimulants, such as Ritalin as 'study aids', has soared amongst *undergraduates*. In 2008, a study of 1,800 American undergraduates found that 34 per cent reported abuse of the medication, mostly as a way of coping with academic stress.[9] In a survey published in 2019 by Ohio State University of eight campuses, 18 per cent of students said they had used stimulants inappropriately – in 85 per cent of those cases, as a supposed study aid.[10] University of Michigan research has shown the abuse has already become more prevalent among high school students.[11] According to YouGov research in 2019, one in seven teenagers who had taken GCSE exams in the previous two years admitted to taking a 'study drug without a prescription' (eight in ten students from this level to postgraduate reported feeling stressed).[12]

The potentially lethal corollary to stimulant abuse during the week is for young people to switch to Xanax, or similar sedatives, at the weekend – a decidedly ill-advised way of calming their shredded nerves after the academic rigours of the week. According to Public Health England, the number of children being treated for addiction to tranquillisers doubled between 2016–17 and 2017–18 to 300, the clinical end of a continuum of abuse that affects thousands more teenagers.[13] Previous generations may have experimented with psychedelic drugs or cocaine as an act of petty rebellion. The wretched paradox of today's teen medication abusers is that so many of them are desperately trying to conform, work harder and please their parents and teachers – by any means necessary. Seeking admission to the very best universities, they end up (in the worst cases) in rehab.

Alongside prescription drug abuse, we are witnessing a truly appalling rise in mental health difficulties among young people. According to figures released by NHS Digital in February 2020, there were 10,168 hospitalisations in 2018–19 involving patients under the age of 30 as a result of self-harm, up from 4,749 cases in 2008–09. The number of cases involving those aged between nine and twelve – 506 – represented a quadrupling over the previous decade.[14] In 2018–19, there were 19,040 hospital admissions for eating disorders, up from 16,558 the year before and 13,885 in 2016–17. The most common age for those admitted was between 13 and 15.

In 2018, the suicide rate in Britain for young people aged 10 to 14 reached a 19-year high – an all-time peak for young females.[15] In the US, a study released by the Centers for Disease Control and Prevention in October 2019 showed that the number of suicides among people aged 10 to 24 suddenly increased 56 per cent between 2007 and 2017 – from 6.8 deaths per 100,000 people to 10.6.[16] In her book on iGen, Twenge describes in detail, with reams of data, what she calls 'An Epidemic of Anguish: Major Depressive Disorder, Self-Harm, and Suicide'.[17] The main causes, she believes, are the spike in screen time and exposure to social media pressures, the decline in person-to-person interaction and 'less print media use'.

In spite of the (welcome) new candour about mental health in public debate, and the efforts of celebrities and members of the royal family to encourage those who are suffering to speak up, the services available to all age groups are still seriously inadequate and the waiting lists for those without the means to seek private care can be dangerously long. Those politicians who speak of 'parity of esteem' between physical and mental health in public provision insult the intelligence of the public. No such parity exists, or is in prospect.

For now, we are left to fret over the problem itself and to ask how it is that we have so badly let a generation down. I do not believe that the epidemic in teen mental health problems can solely be ascribed to school and university pressure. Correlation is not causation, as any data scientist can attest. Nonetheless, it is clear enough that something has gone terribly wrong in the education system, and that one of the symptoms of that failure is a context that – at the very least – contributes to the epidemic stress and misery amongst young people, and, as we shall see, systematically robs them of a true education.

CHAPTER 6

UNINTENDED CONSEQUENCES – HOW EXAMS LOST THE PLOT

And you may ask yourself, well,
How did I get here?
'Once in a Lifetime', Talking Heads, David Byrne/Brian Eno

It is too often assumed that bad outcomes necessarily flow from bad intentions. Yet – especially in matters of government policy and public service reform – it is much more often the case that decent motives yield results that are far from the minds of the framers; or that bureaucracy and inertia snuff out the original spark of inspiration; or that the unforeseeable overwhelms the forecasts, charts and plans of clever people.[1]

In spite of what its detractors insisted at the time, the impulse in the last quarter of the 20th Century to reform, rescue and reinvigorate the UK education system reflected decent, public-spirited ambitions that were rapidly to cross party lines. As controversial as it was in its evolution, Sir Kenneth Baker's Education Reform Act of 1988 represented the culmination of decades of concern that the schools system was failing pupils, that the absence of an agreed basic curriculum amounted to a social injustice and that the teaching unions and local education authorities were blocking improvements at every turn.[2] In his memoirs, the former education secretary set out the case for transformative changes he enacted:

> I realized that the scale of the problem could only be tackled by a coherent national programme, and time was not on our side ... I had two watchwords: standards and choice. Those twin themes, exemplified by the introduction of a national curriculum with testing, and city technology schools and grant-maintained schools [free of town hall control] were the ways I intended to achieve my overriding aim. This was to improve the quality of education for *all* our children in whatever part of the country they lived.[3]

Against the wishes of Margaret Thatcher, who favoured a limited core curriculum, Baker insisted on a 10-subject superstructure, and a national testing regime for pupils at different stages of their education – the results of which would be published, school by school, in new league tables. The powers of local education authorities were dramatically reduced, and schools encouraged to leave town hall control altogether if parents so wished. In a single act of legislation – one of the most important since the war – Baker had, in effect, nationalised the hitherto-localised education system, told the teaching profession what to teach and subjected every pupil in the land to standardised testing.[4]

What was striking was not the hostility that the Baker reforms encountered – huge, and long-lasting – but the bipartisan consensus that they eventually commanded. Tony Blair's New Labour initially declared itself committed (meaninglessly) to 'standards, not structures' and focused (more usefully) upon providing schools with the resources to reduce class sizes. But, in practice, the trajectory of Labour education policy in its 13 years of office (1997 to 2010) was consistent with the Baker reforms, and a continuation of them, rather than a restoration of the status quo ante. The national curriculum and testing system were left in place. Even grant-maintained schools

– a particular grievance of the teacher unions and local education authorities – were essentially reinvented as 'academies'. David Cameron's Coalition with the Liberal Democrats, and the Conservative governments of Theresa May and Boris Johnson, have not undermined any of the fundamental principles of the 1988 Act. As an enduring act of public service reform, it is trumped in the post-war period only by the National Health Service Act of 1948.

This very brief history matters because the classroom culture experienced by today's pupils is the consequence, more than three decades on, of this single far-reaching statute. It created, in effect, a marketplace in education, enabling the best state schools to compete, in full transparency, with the private sector. It transformed the teacher–pupil relationship, subjecting it to the constraints of a national curriculum that would evolve and develop, but continued to be a looming presence in every school day. Most dramatically, it made 'pencil-and-paper' tests the bedrock of educational experience, the defining moments of pupils' experience from Reception to Year 13 (what used to be called the Upper Sixth Form).

The great irony of this legislative monument – so radical and institutionally subversive in its origins – is that it produced a system that is now ossifying in its turn. The necessary corrections of the Eighties have become over-corrections in our own time. The standardisation of schooling has become a rust on initiative, creativity and intellectual risk-tasking. The fixation with tests has narrowed the horizons of pupils and turned a defensible assessment system into an all-consuming obsession that drains the life out of education. Starting with a legitimate attempt to bring rigour to the classroom, we have ended up with a structure that rewards terrified rote learning and crushes imagination.

In his acclaimed critique of education reforms in the UK and elsewhere that have reduced classrooms to exam factories, the late Sir Ken Robinson described the priorities underlying the system:

In terms of *teaching*, the standards movement favours direct instruction of factual information and skills and whole-class teaching rather than group activities. It is skeptical about creativity, personal expression, and nonverbal, non-mathematical modes of work and of learning by discovery and imaginative play, even in preschool . . . When it comes to *assessment*, the standards movement emphasises formal, written examinations and extensive use of multiple-choice tests so that students' answers can be easily codified and processed. It is skeptical too of coursework, portfolios, open-book tests, teacher evaluation, peer assessment, and other approaches that are not so easily quantifiable. This is partly why students spend so much time sitting at desks, working on their own.[5]

Has it been worth it? Apparently not. Robinson continued:

Countries like the US and England have sacrificed much in a desperate drive to raise standards in literacy and numeracy. Yet test scores in the targeted disciplines have hardly improved. In 2012, 17 percent of high school graduates in the US were unable to read or write fluently and had basic problems with spelling, grammar, and punctuation. 'Although a few scores on the National Assessment of Educational Progress (NAEP) have slowly inched upward,' says Paul R. Lehman, a past president of the National Association for Music Education in 2012, 'many have remained essentially unchanged in recent years, and in March 2013, Arne Duncan warned Congress that more than 80 percent of the nation's schools would likely be labeled as failing in 2014 under NCLB [the 2001 No Child Left Behind Act] . . . The problems are not only in 'basic skills'. American students struggle even with elementary cultural knowledge.[6]

The problem with all such metrics-based approaches is that they are easy to understand, and easy to embed into decision-making processes. In practice, this can be a matter of life and death for schools: in 2008, Ed Balls, secretary of state for Children, Schools and Families in Gordon Brown's government – and scarcely a politician of the Right – suggested that secondary schools in which fewer than 30 per cent of pupils achieved five or more GCSEs at A*–C, including English and Maths, should face closure.

This was a warning shot against institutional failure. But it was also part of a top-down culture which nurtured a very particular kind of mediocrity. As the Confederation of British Industry observed in 2012, the 'conveyor belt' exam system 'foster[ed] a cult of the average' and incentivised teachers to focus on the overriding goal of ensuring that pupils attained C grades at GCSE. The most able teenagers were not stretched and those who needed assistance tended, inevitably, to get sidelined in the race for middle-order grades.

At the same time – consistent with this – teachers found themselves increasingly absorbed by bureaucracy, consuming time that they ought to have been devoting to lesson-planning and to extra tuition with pupils who required help. In their study of the contemporary teaching profession, Rebecca Allen and Sam Sims show that '[b]ox ticking demands – real or imagined – from school [inspectors], ceaseless curriculum reform, disruptive top-down reorganisations, and an adult culture that requires teachers to document their every move have caused a huge increase in administrative workload and a drop in morale'.[7]

Even as successive governments have hardened their commitment to standardised testing and – more to the point – the near-equivalence of 'education' with 'testing', so the evidence has piled up that the structure is not working as they so insistently claim. In his inaugural lecture in June 2013 as professor of Education and director of the Centre for Evaluation and Monitoring at Durham University, Robert Coe assessed the performance of the education system since 1994, collating a range of international data that enabled him to compare pupil performance in English, maths and science. His conclusion was stark: 'Standards have not risen; teaching has not improved.'[8]

In this respect, an unsatisfactory pedagogic philosophy survives partly because it matches the political culture of our times. A nationalised, standardised system may not make sense close up, but is easily described in media bulletins. As Allen and Sims put it:

> Ministers are largely judged by their announcements: the white papers, parliamentary statements and press releases by which they communicate their reform plans. The general public, of course, consume these announcements in short-ened clips on the evening news, or while flicking through the newspaper over breakfast. This creates a bias towards policies which are easy to describe in pithy, concrete language.[9]

The most egregious consequence of this is 'teaching to the test': the practice where, because of all the competitive, profes-sional and institutional pressures to which schools, teachers and pupils are subject, the overriding preoccupation of educa-tion becomes preparation for exams. End-of-year assessments and public exams have long been a part of school life, of course; and there is nothing *intrinsically* wrong with them, or with sensible preparation, revision and constructive encour-agement, followed by one-on-one review of marks gained and lessons learned.

But this is entirely different from educational settings in which all roads lead to standardised tests, everything else is treated as a distraction and teaching itself becomes nothing more than a response to marking schemes. (I found it uniquely depressing to discover, anecdotally, that today's pupils are taught a strict way of writing *paragraphs* – as if that most malleable and creatively plastic unit of discourse could be reduced to one-size-fits-all format.)

This danger has long been apparent to the most acute policy analysts. In July 2006, when he was shadow education secretary, David Willetts observed that teachers now found themselves 'under enormous pressure not to teach their subject, but to teach to the test . . . Much of what is valuable in education cannot be measured in tests and league tables, just as the value of life is not only about prices and markets.' Willetts continued, 'It takes a real spirit of enterprise and self-confidence for a teacher to break free of the exam module and convey the excitement of what really brought them to the subject.' Indeed: and it takes courage for an opposition party to pursue the logic of such a breach with established practice when they achieve power (the Conservatives conspicuously failed to take Willetts's advice when they gained office in 2010 – or thereafter).

In 2008, the cross-party Commons Select Committee on Children, Schools and Families also concluded that educational priorities were being subordinated to metric obsessions and their consequences:

> We believe that the system is now out of balance in the sense that the drive to meet government-set targets has too often become the goal rather than the means to the end of providing the best possible education for all children. This is demonstrated in phenomena such as teaching to the test, narrowing the curriculum and focussing disproportionate resources on borderline pupils. We urge the Government to reconsider its approach in order to create incentives to schools to teach the whole curriculum and acknowledge children's achievements in the full range of the curriculum.[10]

According to statistics compiled in 2015 from the Programme for International Student Assessment (Pisa) rankings and the Survey of Adult Skills (PIAAC), both of which are administered by the Organisation for Economic Cooperation and Development, the UK is one of the worst offenders in the developed world in this respect. The emphasis upon short-term information acquisition, rote learning and strict adherence to answer formats means that what is learned for exam day quickly fades from memory. In a travesty of educational principle, the very pressure to succeed in tests that are notionally proof of academic accomplishment is hostile to enduring knowledge and a cause of long-term ignorance.[11]

In a remarkable intervention in October 2017, the head of Ofsted, Amanda Spelman, said that the relentless focus upon public exams and national curriculum tests was denying young people the chance to acquire 'rich and full knowledge'. While she accepted that 'testing in school clearly has value', she urged teachers to spend less time marching pupils through a boot camp of past papers. 'The regular taking of test papers does little to increase a child's ability to comprehend,' Spelman said. 'A much better use of time is to teach and help children to read and read more . . . good examination results in and of themselves don't always mean that the pupil received rich and full knowledge from the curriculum . . . In the worst cases, teaching to the test, rather than teaching the full curriculum, leaves a pupil with a hollowed-out and flimsy understanding'.[12]

Spelman was right, but – as she doubtless knew – her remarks were countercultural to the point of subversion. As much as many (probably most) teachers would love to be liberated from the stultifying constraints of tests, or at least from an education system that values exam grades above all else, there is absolutely no sign of this system changing. The consequence is not only that teenagers are steered strongly towards an approved way of answering a narrow range of likely topics, and anything else that is likely to match the very specific expectations of the markers. They are also in danger of being penalised if they show originality, or intellectual audacity, or imaginative vigour.

To illustrate the point, consider the following absurdity, described in the researching of this book by Dr Ben Snook, head of History at Godolphin and Latymer School in Hammersmith, West London:

There was a question, a few years ago, on an A Level History paper about the impact of the so-called 'Great Recession' of the 1870s. A student of mine wrote what I thought was a brilliant essay, in which she argued that the

'Great Recession' was actually a myth – rather than there having been a genuine economic downturn in the UK at the time, in reality other economies – Germany and the USA, primarily – accelerated in growth, and this gave the impression that the British economy was slowing down. In reality, the UK's economy was diversifying, and moving on to a new stage of economic development. But that wasn't realised at the time. Hence the concept of the Great Depression. The essay scored very low indeed. The reasoning, once we challenged it, was that there was *no scope within the mark scheme written by the board for a student to challenge the central concept of the question* [my italics]. The Board had decided that there *was* a Great Depression; any attempt to challenge that . . . was irrelevant, because it moved too far beyond the published, established parameters within which the question had to be answered.

Snook's point is that this case was only a symptom of a deeply entrenched and (ultimately) anti-educational phenomenon.

This is an extreme example, but it applies, now, across the board, and not just in History either. We find ourselves, now, in a situation where second-guessing the mark scheme, applying the precise demands published by the boards, and doing so in a structured, precise, and really quite neurotic way, is a necessity. We've even started getting our students to underline key words in their essays to make sure that the examiners spot them. Since we've been doing that, our grades have gone up.[13]

Pause and consider, for a moment, the dreary idiocy of a system where teenagers preparing, in most cases, for university, are being advised by their teachers (at one of the best independent schools in London) to underline key words in their examination answers in order to catch the eye of the markers. And then consider the fact that the strategy worked.

Does this not strike you as an astonishing structural betrayal of a generation?

Another example: the competition, where it is permitted, between the six exam boards – AQA, OCR, Edexcel, CCEA (Northern Ireland), WJEC (Wales), and SQA (Scotland) – enables schools to game the system as consumers, taking their custom to the service provider that they think gives their pupils the best chance.

On what basis might they make such decisions? By studying past papers and course plans, and looking for the easier options. They might, for instance, light upon OCR's Latin GCSE requirements for Prose Literature, subject to which candidates are asked to 'translate' canonical texts (such as Tacitus's *The Poisoning of Claudius*) together in class and are then tested on their understanding of the texts in the exam. But the clincher is that teachers obviously lead the classroom translation, which pupils memorise by rote. They are then asked elementary comprehension questions (example: 'Which two groups of people sent these men to the training?' Answer: 'Their parents and their relatives'). In practice, the exercise amounts to a challenge to short-term memory and then an analytic test that is barely worthy of the name, and certainly not designed to stretch the minds of 16-year-olds.

Another lowering of the hurdle is the growing prevalence of multiple-choice questions. Take AQA's GCSE Biology Paper 1F, originally sat on 15 May 2018 – nearly *half* of which is composed of such questions (29 out of 64). Many of the other questions are extremely simple, requiring candidates only to draw lines on images to demonstrate a very basic level of knowledge. They are given one hour and 45 minutes to complete a paper that, with the best will in the world, could test nothing more than an ability to recall crammed information under a measure of time pressure.

A similar pattern may be observed in Edexcel's French GCSE Paper 3: Reading and Understanding in French, also from 15 May 2018. There are many multiple-choice questions, such as (in response to a short passage of writing):

4 (i) Mersault is invited to Raymond's . . .
A house
B friend's house
C office
D boss's home

And then:

4 (ii) Mersault says he . . .
A is able to go
B doesn't want to go
C has other plans
D wants to bring a friend

Look, too, at the emphasis upon short answers: precisely the sort of test methodology that lends itself to rote learning rather than true understanding. In Paper 1 of AQA's Higher Level Chemistry GCSE from May 2018, only 17 of the 100 marks available are awarded on the basis of questions worth five or more marks. The remaining 83 per cent are allocated to questions that require only short answers – exercises in short-term memory retention, in other words.

Of course, in the quest for advantage that constitutes the exam-factory system, all this is positively appealing to schools – one less thing to worry about, one more reason to feel confident of decent grades. Teachers selecting exam boards will be mindful of such attractions: forms of question that do not demand extensive responses and mesh nicely with rote learning and teaching-to-the-test. This is the marketplace within the marketplace.

It is idle to deny that this represents a significant shift in the form and content of public examinations taken by 16-year-olds. Here for instance, are some of the questions faced by O Level Biology candidates in 1974:

2 (a) What is *humus* and why is it an important constituent of the soil? By what means could a farmer increase the humus content of his soil?

(b) Describe in outline how atmospheric nitrogen could eventually, and by different ways, become part of the cytoplasm in the cells of a named herbivore. (Details of digestion and enzyme processes are not required.)

3 (a) (i) What is osmosis and how it is involved in opening and closing stomata?

(ii) How and why are stomata important in the gaseous exchange of a leaf?

(b) Describe an experiment, with a control, to demonstrate that carbon dioxide is necessary for photosynthesis in a leaf.

Now consider a selection of the questions faced by candidates for O Level History on 22 November 1982 – again, testing their capacity to write longer answers and marshal what information they have committed to memory in interesting and intelligent ways:

2. Explain the problems that William III faced in (a) Scotland and (b) Ireland, and describe the actions he took in trying to solve them.

4. Write an account of Britain's overseas trade from 1689 to 1750.

5. Account for the failure of the Jacobite movement.

Finally, a look at French O Level papers from 1984 reveals a translation question that is longer and arguably more complicated than current A level requirements. Candidates are required to write compositions that are clearly expected to be written with creativity and a broad vocabulary. Here, for instance, is the prompt for one such question:

Very late at night, you are walking home with a friend after a party. In one dark street you almost bump into a ladder (*une échelle*) and looking up you can see a figure apparently entering the house through an open upstairs window. You regard this as suspicious. Tell the story of this whole incident, the part you played and the outcome, innocent or not.

This prompt is, in itself, longer than most of the answers that are expected of candidates today. It also seeks to inspire imagination and invites irony and mischief in a way that is simply alien to the present generation of examiners.

The lazy, reflex response to the difference between past practice and contemporary methods would be to say that pupils are less able today than they were in the Seventies and Eighties, and that the system has been – to use the dreadful phrase – 'dumbed down' accordingly. A less Blimpish and more thoughtful analysis would be as follows: that the examiners, teachers and pupils of the Seventies and Eighties were operating in a *completely different context*.

Yes, teenagers wanted to accumulate a decent set of grades, to enable them to take the A levels of their choice, and to strengthen their case for subsequent university admission. But there were no league tables; there was no national curriculum; the school inspectorate had yet to be reborn as Ofsted; the arms race of inter- and intra-school grade competition simply did not exist in the way that it does today.

The papers were more challenging, but the stakes were appreciably lower. Disappointing grades were precisely that – disappointing. They did not threaten a pupil's entire future or, in aggregate, the very survival of a school. No struggling child faced the humiliating prospect of being removed from a class because she might bring down the average performance of her cohort, and thus imperil her school's ranking for the year. The exam system was simultaneously tougher – and more humane. It was a testing regime, not a grand Darwinian machine designed to churn out success, penalise failure and industrialise a grotesque parody of intellectual natural selection. It was a rite of passage, not a traumatic cause of mental illness and substance abuse. It was an important part of – but emphatically not the whole of – a child's education.

In a century of pulverising change, it is morally imperative to go back to first principles and ask whether the system we have is remotely fit for purpose. To an increasing extent, psychologists are questioning its wisdom. According to Dr Naomi Fisher, the clinical psychologist and author:

> I think we have a system where right from the beginning, we're encouraged to think of education as a competitive thing. And we're comparing children against each other, right from the start. There's quite a lot of evidence that this isn't a good thing in terms of learning . . . some of the strategies which people use for school aren't actually conducive to learning and competition is one of them. All the time we're looking at – is this child in the right level, are they behind, are they ahead? Are they gifted and talented, have they got special educational needs? Right from the moment the child goes in [to full-time education] – very young, really two or three. We're starting to look at where are they compared to everybody else.

The danger is that, on the 13 to 15-year-long route march from arrival in full-time schooling, pupils are branded successes or failures – and conscious of it – at an appallingly early age.

> The earlier that we start comparing children to other children, the earlier we start saying, 'They shouldn't be at this point', the more they're aware of that. When you're aware of that kind of thing early on, it has an effect on you. We know that children aged four or five already know whether they're clever, or not . . . And there's also research that shows that how children think about themselves actually has more effects in the long term and how they actually are performing at that age . . . We create a competitive system early on. Adults like to pretend to themselves that the children don't notice this . . . but actually the research shows that they do know.[14]

Such findings in psychology are supported by research in the ever-expanding field of brain science. As the French neuroscientist Stanislas Dehaene has argued, the emphasis upon grades in day-to-day education may not just be excessive but totally ill-conceived as a foundation of modern education:

> Grades are not only imprecise, but often delayed by several weeks, at which point most students have long forgotten which aspects of their inner reasoning misled them. They can also be profoundly unfair, as the level of exams usually increases from week to week. To use video games as an analogy, when you discover a new game you have no clue how to progress, but you start with very easy levels and are free to retry the same level as many times as you need. With 'bad' students' report cards, they aren't motivated by being able to take the same test again and again until they master it; they're given a new exercise each week, almost always beyond their abilities.

This can have subject-specific, neuroscientific consequences:

> In maths, some children suffer from genuine form of maths-induced depression because they know that whatever they do they will always be punished with failure. Maths anxiety is a well-recognised, measured, and qualified syndrome. Children who suffer from it show activation in the pain and fear circuits, including the amygdala, which is located deep in the brain and is involved in negative emotions. These students aren't necessarily less intelligent, but the emotional tsunami they face destroys their abilities for calculation, short-term memory and especially learning.

In other words, the prospect of poor grades in maths tests can induce fight-or-flight responses in children, wrecking their chances of achieving numeracy. In our remorseless focus upon grades, we are actually teaching pupils *not to learn*:

> In mice, fear conditioning literally solidifies neuronal plasticity: after the animal has been traumatised, the circuit finds itself in a similar state as toward the end of the

sensitive period, when synapses have become immobile and frozen . . . American psychologist Carol Dweck has largely studied the negative effects of this mental disposition . . . – what she calls a 'fixed mindset'. She contrasts this with the fundamentally correct idea that all children are capable of progress, which she calls a 'growth mindset'.[15]

It is interesting to note that even a world-famous, expensive public school such as Eton is exploring the extent to which even internal examinations – if excessive, or excessively prioritised – can subject pupils to undue pressure. Research published in 2018 by John Greenwood, a teacher of Russian at the college, suggests that the culture of tests divided into 'success' and 'failure' and the consequent ranking of students can demotivate 'a significant number of learners . . . in many cases, there is evidence of demotivation, a reduction in self-esteem and there is a good deal of research that indicates the negative consequences of this'. Greenwood reports the view of his colleagues that, in some cases, 'we are senselessly lowering self-esteem in boys'.[16]

So much more is known today about the neuroscience of learning than was known in the Eighties. Dehaene's research illustrates how counterproductive the present system of theatrical, terror-drenched end-of-year tests really is. He favours a much more incremental approach to testing, which he describes as 'retrieval practice' – a regular form of progress-checking that encourages long-term learning, strengthens memory without making it a receptacle for one-off regurgitation, and enables pupils to interact meaningfully with their teachers.

Neural imaging, furthermore, shows that cramming simply does not work – or not in a way that has any educational value. Force-feed the brain in a single session and brain activity actually *decreases*. A much more effective method of committing knowledge to memory is to identify a time period and divide it into chunks of 20 per cent. Hence, if you want to remember something in ten months, revisit it in an unpressured fashion every two months – a system that has been shown to reinforce learning to persuade the brain that the information deserves to be considered for long-term retention.[17]

In this respect, the difference between the sustained, systematic acquisition of knowledge and the frenzied cramming that is the lot of today's Ritalin-charged teenagers is comparable to the difference between sound nutritional habits and faddish diets that result only in short-term weight loss (and are often damaging to the dieter's physical health). The case for a root-and-branch re-evaluation of public examinations, national testing and the culture they have spawned is now overwhelming.[18]

We have become blindly dependent upon a structure of education that is now more than 30 years old. There are too many taboos, too many no-go zones in the debate on its future (such as it is). But one was inadvertently forced upon us in March 2020 when the education secretary, Gavin Williamson, announced to the House of Commons the imminent closure of all schools in response to the pandemic – and the summary cancellation of GCSEs and A levels. School closure was a sore trial for parents and pupils alike, a social experiment in home education for which nobody was prepared and for which working people had little time. Nobody was keen to repeat the experience.

Of course, the admissions process was made harder for universities and a generation of pupils found that their school careers were ending somewhat anticlimactically. The great education machine jammed horribly in August when the assessed grades were published – downgraded, in many cases, by 40 per cent from the recommendations made by schools. There were many heartbreaking stories of teenagers whose marks were lowered so significantly that they were unable to go to the universities of their choice, in spite of performing to that standard in school mock examinations.

What had happened? A central algorithm had gone to work on the recommended grades of hundreds of thousands of candidates and spat out hideously unfair consequences. It was, justifiably, a matter of national scandal and a deplorable injustice. But it was also a moment of revelation, the pulling back of the curtain in *The Wizard of Oz*. Teachers who knew their pupils had made honest assessments of the grades they should receive. The centralised system operated by the exam regulator Ofqual had rewarded them with systematically generated nonsense – and the government was forced into a humiliating U-turn, whereby candidates were, after all, awarded the grades originally recommended by their own teachers.

Even as ministers hoped for a return to normality in 2021 – hopes that were dashed by the brutal second wave of infection – a more important seed of doubt had been sown. Was this not a moment to go back to basics and question the very foundations upon which these examinations were based? Some dared to ask whether – for instance – it was really necessary to stick with the GCSE system of public examinations for all at the age of 16.[19] It even became possible for an organisation like Tortoise Media to pose the question at its annual Education Summit: 'Should we abolish exams?'

Annual practices that are etched into the national calendar – such as public examinations – soon acquire a form of immunity from deep interrogation. To ask 'Shall we have A levels this year?' is not quite the same as asking 'Should we bother with Wimbledon?' or 'Do we really need Christmas again?' But all three questions belong in the same category of collective assumption. Or at least they did, before the national coronavirus lockdowns.

These unwanted, grievous intermissions in national life forced us to examine just about everything, whether we wanted to or not. For a start, we suddenly had the time to brood, to fret over questions that would normally never arise as we pounded the treadmill of daily life. These were moments to peer over borders and see how other countries went about – for example – teaching their children.

To be fair, some have been pointing out for a while that the old model of standardised testing is no longer working, that there are other approaches on offer in other countries and that sticking with what we have is a *political choice*.[20] This is not to say that many economically powerful countries do not remain committed to a strict regime of testing, especially in Asia. In China, which topped the 2018 Pisa rankings in reading, maths and science, the entire education system is structured around a single test of life-altering seriousness: the *gaokao* or higher examination.

The test – essentially a college admissions assessment – is held over two days, takes 12 hours and covers Chinese, English, maths, science and the humanities. France and Germany also place great emphasis upon school-leaving exams, respectively the *baccalauréat* and the *Abitur*. True, the extent of national testing every few years differs from country to country. But the essential philosophy is the same: standardised testing is, in the end, what counts.

Yet it need not be so. Given the price that we have seen is paid for this kind of examination regime, is it not worth looking at the other options that are available? In the Netherlands, for instance, primary and secondary schools are highly autonomous, and, when assessments are held, the form they take is generally chosen by the school. There is a level of national and regional guidance in Spain – but schools still decide on the testing methods to be applied, and when the assessments are to be held.[21]

A more conspicuous contrast to the system presently used in the UK and many other countries is the Nordic model. Sweden has been widely praised for its emphasis upon play at kindergarten level, its practice of starting formal education at 6 or 7 rather than 4 or 5, and its radical decentralisation (the 2018 Pisa rankings recorded a recovery in the country's educational performance after a dip in previous years)[22]. But it is Finland that has provided a radical and successful alternative to the strict standardised-testing model that is now so dominant and entrenched in countries such as the UK.

The Finnish system is different in kind rather than degree. It eschews selection, streaming and formal education for children under seven. Though school-leavers sit examinations, there is very little emphasis upon standardised testing of any kind – indeed, the notion of 'teaching to the test' is one that makes little sense to most Finns. The burden of homework is light, extra tuition is unusual and the stress experienced by pupils is accordingly much lower. Yet what would be seen as unpardonable laxity elsewhere has delivered impressive results: Finland was ahead of the UK in the 2018 Pisa ratings for reading, maths and science.[23]

In 2016, a study by the Central Connecticut State University reported that Finland was the most literate country in the world, with the UK trailing in 17th place.[24] In this context, it is worth noting how, precisely, Finnish government guidance *defines* literacy: 'the basis for emerging literacy is that children have heard and listened, that they have been heard, that they have spoken and been spoken to, people have discussed things with them, and that they have asked questions and received answers.'[25] This is about as far from rote learning as it is possible to get.

The Finnish model is very far from perfect. Its Pisa rankings have fluctuated, sending fickle education policymakers off to Estonia as the next potential home of the ideal schooling system.[26] The truth, of course, is that no such system exists, and that each country has its own traditions, economic characteristics and demographic patterns that must be borne in mind when trying to import the pedagogic practices adopted elsewhere.

What *is* true is that other systems are available, other approaches possible. A nation does not have to hug standardised testing for fear of calamity. Indeed, it might ask with profit whether the cost of the embrace has grown too high, and that it is time to reassess not only what works now, but what is likely to work ten or fifteen years from now when the needs of pupils will be incomparably different to those of their counterparts in the 1990s.

Like all crises, the pandemic has acted as a solvent of long-cherished assumptions. And during the summer of 2020, a fair few teachers, education experts and even ministers (especially after the A level downgrading debacle) began to wonder privately (if they had not already done so), whether the whole system to which the nation's schools remain in thrall might be, to borrow Bentham's phrase, 'nonsense on stilts'. And – if that were even a possibility – why had we been so powerfully persuaded otherwise and for so long?

CHAPTER 7

POINTLESS PERFECTION: HOW THE MERITOCRACY MYTH KILLS KNOWLEDGE AND LEARNING

In the last chapter, we explored a national case study: how a radical project to raise standards in schools and to enhance educational opportunity in Britain degenerated into an institutionalised fear factory, in which knowledge and learning are eclipsed by the relentless quest for grades, teachers and pupils fixate upon the test rather than the substance of what is taught, and all are ranked in pitiless league tables. The consequence has been an all-too-visible decline in the quality of testing, and its reduction to tick-box, multiple-choice and short-answer formats. A great deal has been sacrificed on the altar of alleged 'standards', at a cost that may be reflected in an epidemic of mental illness amongst teens as much as the diminished educational rewards for those who endure this system.

It would be a mistake, though, to imagine that this phenomenon is confined to the UK, to schools alone or that the cultural forces that brought it about are distinctively British. All national education systems have their own idiosyncrasies, strengths and weaknesses, the product of the societies that spawned them

– the cultural expectations, the pedagogic traditions and the form taken by schooling in each particular country. One must always allow for the specific and the unique. Nonetheless, the UK is not the only nation to have reduced its children to battery hens in the name of excellence.

In his bestselling critique of US higher education, the former Yale professor, William Deresiewicz, sets out in withering detail the extent to which elite American universities have lost their soul as venues of learning, and become degree factories in which privileged but miserable young people are frogmarched through a system that drives them through courses they take because they have been told to; through exams by which they measure their very existence; towards careers that they feel obliged to pursue but which may not interest them:

> The system manufactures students who are smart and talented and driven, yes, but also anxious, timid, and lost, with little intellectual curiosity and a stunted sense of purpose: trapped in a bubble of privilege, heading meekly in the same direction, great at what they're doing but with no idea why they're doing it.[1]

And why are they doing it? Because they know no other way. Because that is what they have been raised to do, from the very beginning of their drilled and choreographed lives:

> The endless hoop-jumping, starting as far back as grade school, that got them into an elite college in the first place – the clubs, bands, projects, teams, APs [Advanced Placements], SATS [Scholastic Assessment Tests], evenings, weekends, summers, coaches, tutors, 'leadership', 'service' – left them no time, and no tools, to figure out what they want out of life, or even out of college. Questions of purpose and passion were not on the syllabus.[2]

Deresiewicz calls this 'credentialism': a system in which the purpose of life is reduced to the pursuit of accolades, gold stars, high grades and other keys with which to open the next door on the pathway of lifelong scrutiny, probation and public assessment.[3] Joy, free thinking, personal quests and sheer idiosyncrasy have no part to play in this, except secondarily, if they have led to another line-item on a college applicant's résumé (perhaps 'leadership' in a theatre group, or 'service' in a social enterprise). All that matters to this class of students – destined for what Deresiewicz aptly calls a 'hereditary meritocracy' – is 'acing' the test, getting the right answer, leaving absolutely nothing to chance. For these teenagers, the prospect of missing out on an Ivy League education is tantamount to catastrophe – far, far worse than a setback or a disappointment. In their one-strike-and-you're-out universe, failure to secure admission to one of America's top universities is almost literally unthinkable, a rupture of their genetic coding and a betrayal of their families. It is not simply a practical question. It is an existential threat.[4]

This, in turn, reflects a fundamental shift in our collective sense of what an education is *for*. Brochures and prospectuses emphasise pastoral care, personal development and nurturing of the self. But this is largely a sham, designed to cater for a generation of parents who regard hot yoga, kale consumption and mindfulness apps as care of the soul. In every respect that matters, educational institutions are now geared to future work and affluence, prestige and the acquisition of credentials. None of these are bad *in and of themselves*. Ambition, a successful career, financial self-reliance: these are to be prized. But they are not – or should not be – the sole concerns of a young person's education.

Lukianoff and Haidt catalogue the depressing shift in the objectives of kindergarten from social interaction and self-directed play to what they call 'childhood as test prep'[5]. In 1979, an American parent being asked whether their six-year-old child was ready to start first grade would have to fill in a checklist about their ability to take guidance when crossing the road, draw and colour in a picture, tell left from right, be separated from his parents without being upset – and so on. Today, a comparable checklist will ask if the child can identify and write numbers to 100, count by tens to 110, 'interpret and fill in data on a graph' and 'form complete sentences on paper using phonetic spelling'. Progress? A change, certainly.

Open-ended free play has been replaced by whole-class sedentary instruction – so-called 'drill and skill' methods. And before you instinctively applaud this as a victory for rigour, remember that the children in question are five. Whom is this performative discipline really designed to please? Does it actually benefit the pupils, or simply dramatise what parents and policymakers think *should* be happening in the classroom? Lukianoff and Haidt – both strong believers in rigorous education – are in no doubt that the system has gone awry:

> Beginning in preschool and continuing throughout primary school, children's days are now more rigidly structured. Opportunities for self-direction, social exploration, and scientific discovery are increasingly lost to direct instruction in the core curriculum, which is often driven by the schools' focus on preparing students to meet state testing requirements. Meanwhile, especially for wealthier kids, instead of neighbourhood children finding one another after school and engaging in free play, children have after-school activities like music lessons, team sports, tutoring, and other structured and supervised activities.[6]

Thus, a system designed to enhance 'standards' risks crushing individuality and self-confidence, while launching children on to the résumé arms race of extra-curricular activities before they have learned to play, let alone play an instrument. How has this happened? How has the sensible objective of improving education mutated into a frequently counterproductive culture of manic testing, résumé-packing, dull homogenisation and – all too often – mental illness? The answer, as ever, is a convergence of factors.

The 20th Century was, par excellence, the era in which elites in democratic societies started to pride themselves upon their meritocratic character. The prime criterion – at least in principle

– was no longer social background, but character, accomplishment, dedication. To gain admission to a university, for instance, an applicant required grades rather than connections (at least in theory – the 'legacy' system in US colleges continues even today, and nepotism has not yet been driven from the corridors of great institutions).

The problem with meritocracy is threefold. Let us say, purely for argument's sake, that the system works perfectly – that talent, promise and achievement are duly rewarded. That ability is invariably discovered, encouraged and allocated power and wealth accordingly. This would be a satisfying outcome for the successful minority. But what about everybody else? What about those of more modest talents who nonetheless aspire to a decent life, a sense of enfranchisement, a life of purpose? Even the rhetoric of meritocracy and social mobility has a corrosive effect: it makes those who have not moved up the ladder of affluence, prestige and professional status feel that they have failed and are lesser citizens for it. The decline of commonality and collective spirit that I discussed in Part One is intimately connected to this. The value of the phrase 'left-behind' – much used in the anxious debates that followed the Brexit vote and Trump's 2016 victory – is often contested.[7] But meritocracy – not only by definition, but *by design* – leaves people behind.

This is the mostly unacknowledged and certainly unresolved fault line that runs through its notional idealism. Social mobility is a fine thing, and systems that reward ability are clearly preferable to those that reward privilege. But can it reasonably be claimed that they are a sufficient basis for a just and decent society? And why are we surprised when the populist Right exploits those who feel cheated by this social model? It is all too easily forgotten that the book that popularised the idea – Michael Young's *The Rise of the Meritocracy* (1958) – was a work of dystopian satire, describing a revolution against an imagined meritocratic regime in 2033.[8]

The second defect of what we call 'meritocracy' is that its prime consequence has been to reconfigure rather than abolish the caste system. In his masterly book *The Meritocracy Trap*,

Daniel Markovits, a professor at Yale Law School, shows in rich detail the extent to which a system that was designed to thwart the concentration and passing on of hereditary privilege has ended up compounding the problem (albeit in new forms).

The top one per cent's share of national income has more than doubled since its low point in the middle of the 20th Century. In 2017, the average pay of a FTSE-100 chief executive was £5.7 million, almost 300 times the median British worker's income. The old upper-class elite of cliques, clubs and connection has been replaced by the fee-paying elite of private education – open to all who can pay.

Since 1993, life expectancy in Blackpool for male residents has risen by only 2.7 years, compared to 10.4 years in Kensington and Chelsea. Geographical inequality is reflected even in enterprise: London has 112 start-ups per ten thousand inhabitants, compared to Sunderland, which has only 32. One closed elite has been supplanted by another, as Markovits notes:

> . . . meritocracy [in the UK] built a new caste order in place of the one that it dismantled, replete with its own forms of hierarchy and exclusion . . . This new "'meritocratic' business-oriented and corporate elite' built upon elaborate education and 'drawn from a narrow range of occupations" has "eclipse[d] . . . the aristocratic upper class." It represents something genuinely distinctive and not just a repackaging of the familiar. And it arises because meritocracy has achieved rather than betrayed its ideals, which (even as they genuinely liberate society from aristocracy) sustain massive and terribly damaging inequalities of both outcomes and opportunities.[9]

In the US, 40 per cent of the students at the most selective universities came from families with incomes of over $100,000 – up from 32 per cent just five years before.[10]

The third problem – most specifically relevant to the discussion of our broken education system – is that meritocracy has encouraged what might be called the cult of metrics. Its origins can be traced at least as far back as the Victorian era, when the notion that everything worth knowing was measurable began to gain traction.

Matthew Arnold (1822–88), best known as poet, critic and author of *Culture and Anarchy*, was also a schools inspector for 35 years – and a rebel against this metric fixation. As early as the 1860s, he identified the risk of teaching to the test:

> . . . it tends to make the instruction mechanical and to set a bar to duly extending it [the instruction] . . . performing a minimum expressly laid down beforehand – must inevitably concentrate the teacher's attention on the means for producing this minimum . . . the danger is the mistake of treating these two [the minimum and the good instruction of the school] as if they were identical.

In his tract, *The Twice-Revised Code*, Arnold feared that the higher social cause of education was to be sacrificed to the 'friends of economy at any price' and that children would be subjected to a system of mechanised, restrictive rote learning: 'much in it, which its administrators point to as valuable *results*, is in truth mere machinery'. [11]

That was so, and there was much more to come. In the work and studies of Frederick Winslow Taylor (1856–1915), the engineer and industrial theorist, was founded the modern school of 'scientific management'. Under what came to be known as 'Taylorism' – in his own words – 'the managers assume . . . the burden of gathering together all of the traditional knowledge which in the past has been possessed by the workmen and then of classifying, tabulating, and reducing this knowledge to rules, laws, formulae . . . Thus all of the planning which under the old system was done by the workmen, must of necessity under the new system be done by management in accordance with the law of science'. [12]

In principle, much of this was sensible and useful. The measurement of performance, collection of data and analysis of what is compiled are pillars of any rational society in which transparency, accountability and fairness are valued. When a producer interest (the group responsible for the product or service) has captured a process at the expense of consumers – cheating the customer, enforcing restrictive practices, hiding shoddy work – there is nothing like the sunlight of information to disinfect the system. For a society that was governed, as 20th-Century America was, by mass industrialisation (Fordism), the race for scientific advantage (especially after the shock of the USSR's Sputnik triumph in 1957) and the desire for economic greatness, the field of data and metrics was culturally comfortable.

Yet – like any system that strays into the fervent terrain of cult – the use of metrics has now become, in many cases, almost pathological. Numbers are a part of most arguments (this book makes use of plenty of them). But there is a line between illustration of a proposition and the reflexive reduction of that proposition to a statistic, or series of statistics. All too often now, data is used to give unearned authority to assertions; it is confused with knowledge, and poured over questions as if all intellectual issues can be solved by a sufficiency of quantitative information. Nuance and fine judgment are lost in spreadsheets. And that which cannot be straightforwardly measured is regarded as irrelevant. If you want to see neurosis in action, tell a corporate executive that you are on your way to deliver a presentation – but without a slide show of graphs.[13]

What Kenneth Cukier and Viktor Mayer-Schonberger have called the 'Dictatorship of Data' found its most famous expression in the management of the Pentagon during the Vietnam War by US defense secretary, Robert McNamara – utilising the methods he had employed as an assistant professor at Harvard Business School, and a rising star (briefly president) of the Ford Motor Company. Trying to understand the conflict in South-East Asia, 'McNamara sought Truth, and that Truth could be found in data. Among the numbers that came back to him was the "body count" [reported enemy fatalities]. The body count was the data point that defined an era'.

As fast became apparent – and was demonstrated comprehensively in Douglas Kinnard's book *The War Managers* (1977)

– McNamara's addiction to data skewed his entire understanding of the cultural, nationalistic and emotional commitment of the Viet Cong to the fight, and was based upon metrics that were at best flawed, and often completely misleading.[14]

As Cukier and Mayer-Schonberger conclude, this disastrous chapter in US geostrategic history illustrates a much broader point:

> We are more susceptible than we may think to the 'dictatorship of data' – that is, to letting the data govern us in ways that may do as much harm as good. The threat is that we will let ourselves be mindlessly bound by the output of our analyses even when we have reasonable grounds for suspecting that something is amiss . . . Education seems on the skids? Push standardized tests to measure performance and penalize teachers or schools. Want to prevent terrorism? Create layers of watch lists and no-fly lists in order to police the skies. Want to lose weight? Buy an app to count every calorie but eschew actual exercise.[15]

As trust in institutions has declined, so we have hugged metrics closer. When those who lead us let us down, numbers have the comforting aura of objectivity and they appear to banish subjectivity. And since the 1980s, when the consumerisation of public services became prevalent on both sides of the Atlantic – with the so-called 'New Public Management' school – data has become ever more important not only in the allocation of taxpayers' money but also to the ethos of public sector institutions.

In education, as we have seen, this has translated into an obsession with standardised testing, league tables and grades as (by far) the most important facet of school life. Education has become a commodity rather than an experience. The system can be gamed. Teachers teach to the test, instead of teaching. And (worst of all) the tests themselves have increasingly been turned into tick-box, multiple-choice, short-answer assessments that reward the sugar-spike of cramming rather than healthy nutrition of learning. As we have seen, what started as a well-intentioned project to improve education has, in many ways, debased it – and, worst of all, betrayed young people by forcing them into the grade factory, where what they really learn is that school is a place of endurance, relentless scrutiny (not the same as teaching) and (on occasion) near-psychotic pressure.

This scarcely deserves to be called pedagogy. Instead, it demonstrates the validity of 'Campbell's Law' – the principle attributed to the American social psychologist, Donald T. Campbell (1916–96), whereby '[t]he more any quantitative social indicator is used for social decision-making, the more subject it will be to corruption pressures and the more apt it will be to distort and corrupt the social processes it is intended to monitor'.[16]

Moreover: the system is not even working *on its own terms.* Let us accept, for a moment, the premise – explicit or implicit – that the true purpose of 21st-Century education is to prepare pupils and students for the workplace; that education and training are, in fact, synonymous. The online College Scorecard, launched by the Obama administration in September 2015 – as Professor Jerry Z. Muller puts it in his analysis of modern metrics culture – 'treats college education in purely economic terms: its sole concern is return on investment, understood as the relationship between the monetary costs of college and the increase in earnings that a degree will ultimately provide'.[17]

Even before the recessionary thunderbolt of Covid-19, youth unemployment around the world was at record levels: about 13 per cent of all 15 to 24-year-olds, or 73 million people, were out of work, the largest number on record. As the late Ken Robinson and others have noted, the skyrocketing number of graduates has also distorted the job market, as a first degree has ceased to be anything close to a guarantee of employment upon graduation. In Europe and America in the Fifties and Sixties, around one in twenty people went to university. Between 1970 and 2000, that proportion increased by almost 300 per cent. As access has increased so too has the personal cost to students of their higher education.

It is unambiguously welcome that more young people now go to university, or – more accurately – are able to do so. But the purpose of higher education has become much less clear in the process: far too many 18 to 19-year-olds now commit themselves to a costly three or four years at university because they have been told that a degree is now a precondition of decent employment of any kind. That is a wild misinterpretation of what university life should be about. And – in many cases – it is not even true. According to figures published by the Higher Education Statistics Agency (Hesa) in June 2020, nearly one in ten alumni of some British universities were unemployed 15 months after graduating – that is, without any gainful employment.[18] Analysis of the 2015 Labour Force Survey by the TUC showed that black and ethnic minority graduates are more than twice as likely to be unemployed as equivalently qualified whites.[19]

Meanwhile, a report released by the New York Federal Reserve Bank in November 2019 found that graduates aged 22 to 27 were more likely to be unemployed or underemployed (that is, working in jobs below normal expectations for their levels of experience or academic attainment) than the overall figure for the labour force – the first time this had happened for almost 30 years.[20] Does this mean that an undergraduate education is now a waste of time and money? Of course not. What is true is that degrees are now being mis-sold as pensions and other financial services have been – misrepresented as a sure-bet ticket to a certain level of prosperity and certainty.

In practice, the entire education system has been debauched on a false promise. As Deresiewicz puts it: 'it is a particularly middle-class form of ... illusion: the idea that life can be rendered predictable, reduced to an orderly succession of achievements that will guarantee security and comfort'.[21]

This section is entitled 'Ignorance' for a reason. I do not believe for a second that today's young people are less cognitively able or personally curious than their predecessors. What is the case, and has been increasingly so in recent decades, is that their collective level of *knowledge* is declining. In 2018, a YouGov survey of young Americans found that 87 per cent of high school students failed a rudimentary five-question test about US history. Only 35 per cent of them knew which presidents' faces were carved into Mount Rushmore; a mere 11 per cent could name the rights protected by the First Amendment.[22]

More worrying still, a poll in the same year conducted by the Conference on Jewish Material Claims Against Germany found that two-thirds of American millennials – those born between 1981 and 1996 – did not know what Auschwitz was, and 22 per cent of them said they had not even heard of the Holocaust, or were not sure whether they had.[23] A subsequent survey by the Conference, published in January 2020, showed that 69 per cent of French millennials and members of Gen Z (those born between 1996 and 2010) did not know that six million Jews were killed during the Holocaust. Almost half (44 per cent) believed that two million Jews or fewer perished – and 28 per cent believed that one million or fewer were murdered.[24]

As scandalous as this level of ignorance is – poor levels of knowledge of the greatest atrocity in human history, even in France which is generally thought to have a high-quality education service – the real scandal is the system that allowed this to be so. Young people are increasingly ill-prepared to deal with the online barrage of Holocaust denial and revisionism.[25] But what else did we expect from a classroom culture dominated by teaching to the test, forcing children through the hoops of short-answer, short-term-memory exams, and (crucially) turning education into a chore of iterative assessment rather than a decade and a half of personal development?

Standardised testing – to the extent that it has become the norm in the English-speaking world – swallows up time and energy. It entrenches poor priorities. What space is there for history, civics, artistic appreciation and creativity that is not just another means of stuffing your curriculum vitae? There are plenty of worthy educational goals – encouraging civil conduct, inspiring interest in the world and fostering free thinking – that are not measurable and cannot be reduced to statistics or formatted for inclusion in a league table. Where do they fit into the 21st-Century syllabus? Are they truly valued, or valued at all?

As Shout Out UK, the energetic youth media and political literacy platform, argued in 2017:

> The average GCSE student can tell you that the chemical symbol for Sodium is Na, that the Triple Entente was formed of the United Kingdom, France and Russia and that speed is calculated by dividing distance by time. But they cannot tell you who the leader of the opposition is, or even the core differences between the UK's two major political parties. School teaches you to pass an exam; an exam which will almost always prove to be entirely useless in later life. It does not teach you how to understand the fundamental workings of society and as a result, when we reach 18 and are given an incredible responsibility, we simply do not know what to do.[26]

In my experience, this partly reflects a growing sense among young people that Westminster politics is simply an irrelevance and scarcely worth the effort of intellectual investment. But the point is still well made. If you cram teenagers' minds with items of information to be retained in their short-term memory and send them swimming around the grim goldfish bowl of testing, you cannot be surprised if they do not emerge from the process as citizens-in-waiting, let alone free-thinking individuals with a hinterland of shared knowledge.

Qualitative research supports this analysis. In 2017, Dr Iro Konstantinou, an expert on class, race and identity, published the following findings from an ethnographic study carried out at a private school in London:

> The attitude of young people towards politics is not due to apathy or disengagement but a result of the wrong education they receive through the curriculum, as well as of a disillusionment with mainstream party politics ... They think that the curriculum teaches to the test and not to provide practical real-life knowledge so *'if you want to know what is going on, you have to look for the information yourself'*.

And the truth is that most of them will not. They don't feel there is enough time for them to do that and they think it is the responsibility of the school to encourage it.[27]

Whether you are sympathetic to the students' predicament or not, their testimony is further evidence that the notion of knowledge – not facts, rote learning, or even skills that are negotiable in the labour market – is at a low ebb. The idea that a fully formed person, regardless of their professional destiny, should be taught to read, think freely and engage in conversation – well, this now seems almost laughably quaint.

It was not always so. As the Stanford lecturer Denise Clark Pope recalls in her study of American schooling:

> In tenth grade, I fell in love with Walt Whitman. I went home and declared my adoration for the man and his work, adding that I had most certainly found my calling in life. Never before had I met someone whose words were so invigorating and whose poetry inspired me to try to write my own . . . Though I experienced my strongest feelings in English class, marveling at the artistry of Shakespeare, Faulkner, Emerson, and Dickinson, I also remember enjoying subjects in my science and history courses. I spent hours with friends pondering existential issues that emerged from our studies, such as the limits of free will and the origin of life.[28]

Behaviour typical of a future academic? No doubt. But what saddened Pope when she became a high school English teacher was not that her students failed to experience the same teenage passion – but that she detected not a spark of the same enthusiasm, or 'a desire to read and write as a way of understanding humanity and of exploring the world.' Her subsequent (and acclaimed) study of Faircrest High School, in a wealthy California suburb, lifted the lid on the cultural transformation since her own schooldays. As one highly regarded student, Kevin, tells her:

People don't go to school to learn. They go to get good grades which brings them to college, which brings them the high-paying job, which brings them to happiness, so they think. But basically, grades is where it's at. They're the focus of every student in every high school in every place in America and otherwise. Period . . . I wish I could say I'm an individual, and I am not going to sacrifice my individuality for a grade, you know . . . just write for writing's sake.[29]

Eve, another ambitious student, explains why she is committed to such an extraordinary work rate, including six or seven hours a day during vacations:

To get into an Ivy [League School]. That's all I can think about . . . to get in and become a successful $500,000-a-year doctor or engineer or whatever it is I want to be . . . It's very narrow-minded for me . . . I have to get accepted; then I can have a life, once I'm in . . . Lots of us are getting sick, and I am addicted to coffee; actually, I prefer to say voluntarily dependent on caffeine. See, some people see health and happiness as more important than grades and college; I don't . . . I am just a machine with no life at this place . . . This school turns students into robots. I have been thinking about it a lot. I am a robot just going page by page, doing the work, doing the routine.'[30]

The students whose lives Pope describes are people-pleasers, told by their parents that 'pressure turns coal into diamonds', calculate their GPA (grade point average) several times a day, prepared, in some cases, to cheat, used to staying up for days at a time to 'ace' grades, even to hide their extra-curricular activities from their competitors to preserve the résumé advantage. Some get ill from overwork and stress, or are prone to sudden, uncharacteristic outbursts of rage. They can be made sick by the prospect of a test, paralysed by fear of failure. The content of their education, as Pope observes, is an irrelevance in this grotesque battle for perfection: 'They studied the material, read the textbooks, and completed the assignments, for the most part, because they had to, not because they wanted to or because the subjects genuinely interested them'.[31]

The students whom Pope studied were high-achievers. But the system that they worked within failed – and continues to fail – all pupils in different ways, in different countries: the common factor being the reduction of schooling to a test regime, and the relentless quest for success in a rat race tyrannised by metrics. The pleasure that Pope took from Whitman as a pupil is now a distant memory – and would be interpreted by most involved in this culture of grade capture as a whimsical distraction from the main event.

The cost of this shift in priorities was already extremely high when Pope described it two decades ago. How much greater it is now, for a generation raised as digital natives. We are sending young people out into a world scarred as never before by misinformation, conspiracy theories, social media feeds patrolled by predatory bots and a polarised political discourse that stokes up anger instead of encouraging civil debate. At exactly the moment that they most need a sturdy defence system, we are despatching them into this landscape unimmunised. And that landscape, as we shall see, is like no other that has preceded it.

CHAPTER 8
THE DIGITAL INSTANT

Where is the knowledge we have lost in information?
T.S. Eliot

The year 2018 may one day be remembered as the moment that human beings fell behind goldfish in at least one crucial evolutionary respect. The fish that swim around elaborately decorated tanks have an attention span of around nine seconds. In 2018, the average human attention span was found to have fallen from 12 seconds in 2000 to a mere eight seconds – a shorter period than that achieved by goldfish. This is not a glorious milestone in the history of human cognition – or human anything, for that matter.

The change can be mostly ascribed to the transformative impact that digital media have had upon what it means to be a person. Though the World Wide Web has been around since 1989, and the Internet for much longer, the all-important staging posts were as follows: the creation of Facebook in 2004 and Twitter in 2006; the launch of the Apple iPhone by Steve Jobs in 2007; the proliferation of broadband tech in the same year; the release of the WhatsApp cross-platform messaging service in 2009; and the launch of Instagram the following year. Other platforms – such as the hugely popular Chinese social networking service, TikTok – have continued to emerge and establish a significant market position with dazzling speed.

Movies, television and music have migrated to streaming services so quickly that it is easy to forget that Blu-ray discs were only launched in 2002 and that the iPod seemed unfathomably advanced on its release in 2001. The world of Netflix, Amazon

Prime, Spotify and Apple Music is unrecognisably different to the digital landscape of less than 20 years ago. It is true that every century has its technological revolution, one that defines and shapes its behavioural patterns, psychology, politics and social structures. But this revolution shows every sign of being permanent: it is relentless in its forward movement and uncompromising in the changes that it compels. Even now, the possibilities of artificial intelligence are becoming clearer by the day – and they are thrilling and unsettling in equal measure. There has been nothing like this in human experience, and it is reasonable to assume that it is only in its infancy.

The sheer pace and scope of this technological storm – relentless, unceasing, indifferent – has inspired an inevitable strain of Luddism, anxiety and moral panic.[1] Much of this counter-attack is aimed at the young, for the simple reason that they spend so much time online – according to some studies, about *nine hours a day*.[2] Jean Twenge suggests a figure closer to six, though she excludes from that figure Internet activity at school.[3] In his study of the psychological impact of the new technology, Larry Rosen reports that 62 per cent of iGen teenagers check their messages every 15 minutes or less, and that 32 per cent are similarly gripped by Facebook.[4] What is not in doubt is that today's digital natives, born into a world in which the border between real and virtual life is completely porous, are accordingly creatures of dual nationality.

And this has prompted many of their elders to interpret their immersion in online media in *moral* terms – reflective of a generational lack of rigour, or intellectual laziness, or collective introspection. The most lurid example of this is the title of Mark Bauerlein's *The Dumbest Generation* – an early study, published in 2008, of the impact of digitalisation upon young minds that includes interesting observations and research but is diminished by its presumption of collective guilt:

The youth of America occupy a point in history like every other generation did and will, and their time will end. But the effects of their habits will outlast them, and if things do not change they will be remembered as the fortunate ones who were unworthy of the privileges they inherited. They may even be recalled as the generation that lost that great American heritage, forever.[5]

I think this analysis is itself lazy – an easy way of avoiding deep consideration of what this technology means, could mean and should mean in the 21st Century. A sharp contrast is provided by Gretchen McCulloch's recent book on the way in which the Internet has changed the language that we use – a study that, resisting the temptation to wallow in gloom, concludes that 'there is space for innovation, space for many Englishes and many other languages besides, space for linguistic playfulness and creativity'.[6]

You may not like the spectacle of your children staring at their phones all day, but you should at least allow that their behaviour is rational. They are, to an extent you may not care to admit, only mirroring your own addiction to your digital devices. Absolutely every stream of information and communication that they need (as well as those they choose for fun, entertainment, dating) pours forth from that little luminous screen. Yes, they are almost certainly engaged in online conversations with their friends. But they are also receiving updates on homework assignments, posts about their extracurricular activities, GPS data on where to go for their next training session or tuition lesson, updates from doctors, dentists and therapists, data on deliveries they (or you) may be expecting, news from the campus library about a book they need for an assignment – and so on, and so on. To teens raised in this technological environment, the idea of 'digital detox' makes as much sense as saying: 'Let's all live as Amish for a week. It'll be good for us.'

There is no point in creating a single, all-purpose, interactive portal through which *all* academic, social, news, club, campaigning and commercial information flows, and then behaving with prim outrage when young people consult it as regularly as they do. I once visited a prominent London private school where the teachers held forth about the damage that phones were doing to classroom order. After the session, several of the pupils pointed out to me that it was also a disciplinary offence not to keep up to date with official school emails which were, apparently, sent throughout the day. 'Which instruction do we follow?' they asked, quite reasonably. Blaming young people for whatever it is you don't like about the Internet is as silly as blaming immigrants for the aspects of globalisation to which you object.

The more constructive approach to this revolution in cognition and epistemology – that is, thinking and knowledge – is to ask what impact it is having upon us all, and upon teens in particular. I think that we have yet to grasp fully how deep this change really is. It has altered even our perception of *time*, by bombarding us with more information, emotional stimuli and momentary triggers than any medium in history. But the impact of this change is uneven across the generations.

Those of us who watched the Internet grow up, and are old enough to remember the screeching pulse of dial-up connection – and the bursting of the dotcom bubble in 2001–2 – have an entirely different relationship with this technology than our children, for whom digital media is not a tool, or something distinct from their lives, but the space where much of their living takes place.

They live in a different timestream to everyone else: captured, at any one moment, in the *digital instant*: second-by-second clusters of neural prompts, incentives and impulses that require constant processing and adaptation. The experience of a person who is following Facebook messages, WhatsApp groups, a friend's YouTube channel, school emails, a note from her counsellor, a change of timing for a music lesson, her own Instagram page to check on how many 'Likes' her latest post has attracted, an increasingly heated exchange of texts between two friends, and a series of alerts from a social enterprise that she works for in her spare time – well, this is a level of brain overload that has no precedent, and no readily available guidance system.

Certainly, attention span has been a casualty of this neurological bombardment. In June 2019, a study by researchers from Oxford, King's College London, Harvard and Western Sydney

University found that smartphone technology was depleting our ability to concentrate and eroding our ability to retain information. '[T]he limitless stream of prompts and notifications from the internet', said one of the academics working on the project, 'encourages us towards constantly holding a divided attention – which then in turn may decrease our capacity for maintaining concentration on a single task.' Digital multitasking forces users to expend 'greater cognitive effort' to maintain focus to complete any of the tasks in hand.[7]

According to Professor Russ Poldrack, a neuroscientist at Stanford University, this absence of focus means that new information may be misdirected to the wrong part of the brain. In normal circumstances, it should go to the hippocampus, which is responsible for the long-term storage of knowledge. If a person is distracted by more than one task, and constantly interrupted by social media posts and alerts, the same information may go instead to the striatum, whose job it is to house new procedures and skills, rather than facts and ideas. The upshot is that retrieval of misdirected information will be appreciably harder. 'Multi-tasking adversely affects how you learn,' Poldrack says. 'Even if you learn while multi-tasking, that learning is less flexible and more specialised, so you cannot retrieve the information as easily.'

A separate survey in April 2019, collated at the Technical University of Denmark, found that the surge in digital content demanding our attention has decreased the time we are willing or able to devote to it. Scraping data from the past 40 years in movie ticket sales, Google books, Twitter from 2013 to 2016, Google Trends from 2010 to 2018, Reddit from 2010 to 2015 and Wikipedia attention time from 2012 to 2017, the researchers found significant contraction in the time that users devote to media of any sort. For instance: in 2013, a Twitter global trend had an average duration of 17.5 hours – compared to only 11.9 hours in 2016.

Topics become popular more quickly than they used to, and fade from the hivemind with increased speed. The researchers also advanced this alarming prophecy concerning the future of political and civil discourse: 'If nothing changes, topics that are discussed publicly will reduce to a minimum amount of reported information before moving to the next, almost certainly hurting the quality of information about the topic. On the other hand, things that are only noticed over a very short period might not be relevant [in] the long run'.[8]

More than 85 per cent of teachers endorse the statement that 'today's digital technologies are creating an easily distracted generation'.[9] Few psychologists would deny that there is a connection between the surge of diagnoses of Attention Deficit Hyperactivity Disorder in young people in the past 20 years and the rise of the new technology. Astonishingly, some children as young as two and three are now being given medication for ADHD – apparently because of their excessively impulsive responses to flickering television, phone and laptop screens. As the cyber-psychologist Mary Aiken puts it, 'the mere difference between the slow pleasures of real life and the high-speed thrills of digital screens could cause an urge or taste for more excitement, a kind of *sensory-arousal addiction.*' Whether infants should be prescribed such powerful drugs is a matter for psychiatrists to debate carefully. What is clear is that the hyperstimulation of digital devices is having an impact upon the brain development even of *toddlers.*[10]

Susan Greenfield, an authority on the neuroscience of consciousness, has observed that we should not be surprised by the scale of this behavioural change, given the nature of the technological transformation. 'As a neuroscientist I am very aware that the brain adapts to its environment,' she said in 2016. 'If you're placed in an environment that encourages, say, a short attention span, which doesn't encourage empathy or interpersonal communication, which is partially addictive or compulsive ... all these things will inevitably shape who you are. The digital world is an unprecedented one and it could be leaving an unprecedented mark on the brain.'[11]

The key is that the brain will adapt to the stimuli and environment with which we present it. 'Because of the plasticity of our brains ... if you change your habits, your brain is happy to go along with whatever you do,' says Joyce Schenkein, a neuropsychologist at Touro College in New York. 'Our brains adapt, but the process of adaptation is value-neutral – we might get smarter or we might get dumber, we're just adapting to the environment.'

Because we are subjected to so much information and stimulation online, what cognitive psychologists call 'the recency effect' has become more significant.[12] There is a natural cognitive bias in the structure of our memories to recall the last thing we saw or heard – a phenomenon often observed in the deliberations of jurors or in consumers watching advertising or in those who have just heard a waiter describe the menu of the day. As the brain is overloaded with information, so the recency effect grows stronger: it is positively turbocharged by online media. You might want to remember the instruction from your boss, received five minutes ago. But your idle scroll through Instagram since then makes it appreciably less likely that you will. More than 40 per cent of digital interruptions are self-inflicted, as we choose to check our emails, DMs and WhatsApp messages, searching endlessly for the dopamine hit of a micro-boost to our self-esteem. This means that – strategically speaking – our digital behaviour is often a form of self-sabotage: we are making it significantly harder for the brain to sort and retain important information as we treat it like an epistemological punchbag.

In the digital age, the recency effect is a *global machine for the generation of ignorance*. Printed texts, though much less sophisticated than online devices, have the virtue of simplicity: as you are reading a passage on Mozart, or Maya Angelou, or Moscow, there is no risk that an Instagram image of a friend on holiday with his family will punch through the page to distract you – or a TikTok clip about people falling over, or a Twitter alert about a breaking news story.

The battle for our attention is now constant, brutal and bewildering. Impact vies with importance (and usually wins). As Larry Rosen remarks: 'While a percentage of the population has been diagnosed with [Attention Deficit Hyperactivity Disorder], our dependency on technology, the 24/7 availability of the Internet, and our constant use of devices makes us *all behave as if we have ADHD*'.[13] Recency squashes relevance. Increasingly, we are what we just saw, or heard or read: we are little more than memes with a pulse.

A secondary phenomenon – relevant in this context – is so-called 'cognitive offloading'. A study published in 2016 by researchers at the University of California, Santa Cruz, and, the University of Illinois, Urbana Champaign, found the Internet was not only changing the pattern of our memories, but, to some extent, *replacing* them. Even in the short-term confines of this experiment, participants who used Google to answer an initial set of difficult trivia questions were more likely to decide to use Google when answering a *second* set of easier trivia questions than were participants who answered the initial questions from memory. In other words, once permitted to use online media in a controlled environment, we carry on doing so.

The lead researcher, Dr Benjamin Storm, summarised the change thus: 'Memory is changing. Our research shows that as we use the Internet to support and extend our memory we become more reliant on it. Whereas before we might have tried to recall something on our own, now we don't bother. As more information becomes available via smartphones and other devices, we become progressively more reliant on it in our daily lives'.[14]

An earlier study led by Betsy Sparrow at Columbia University reached consistent conclusions. Participants did not, for instance, recall information as accurately if they believed that it would still be accessible to them online; those who believed that the information had been erased performed better in memory tests. 'Since the advent of search engines, we are reorganizing the way we remember things,' said Sparrow. 'Our brains rely on the Internet for memory in much the same way they rely on the memory of a friend, family member or co-worker. We remember less through knowing information itself than by knowing where the information can be found'.[15]

Cognitive offloading, in many cases, makes sense. If information and data can be instantly recalled by a Google search or a scroll through a shared document, then why commit it to memory? It is also true that so-called 'transactive memory' – the process by which we outsource information to individuals, experts and trusted communities – has always been part of the social fabric. But this is something different. Precisely because the Internet is a limitless storage facility it has been described as a 'supernormal stimulus' for transactive memory – in the sense that it encourages us not to delegate selected memories to printed records, friends or family, but as many as possible to a single information cloud.

As so often, the question is one of trajectory – where the altered behaviour leads us. If it frees up cognitive capacity for other useful activities – analytic, recreational, creative – then so much the better. But if it weakens the muscles of memory to the point where we cannot recall basic knowledge without the crutch of a smartphone, tablet or laptop – well, that would be considerably less desirable. There is a fascinating debate, still in its first stages, about the prospective integration of human and machine, and the eventual evolution of humanity from narrowly carbon-based life forms: so-called 'transhumanism'.[16] But this is not that.

The Internet is bad at sifting different kinds of content, at ascribing value and accurate categorisation to the inconceivably huge quantities of material it has to offer. As the University of Virginia professor, Mark Edmundson, puts it: 'The result is to suspend reflection about the differences among wisdom, knowledge, and information. Everything that can be accessed online can seem equal to everything else, no datum more important or more profound than any other'.[17] Research has shown that individuals asked to search for particular information online find it more quickly than those using printed encyclopaedias. But – and here's the rub – the online searchers were less able to recall the retrieved information subsequently.[18] As one would expect, Google may often be faster than printed sources. But online trawling seems not to succeed as well at securing brain storage on a long-term basis.

In any case, delegating all or most human memory to a hand-held device is not a step to be taken lightly. Does it truly augment our capacity as human beings or weaken our brainpower? Again, its functional value should be measured against its deeper potential to oxygenate ignorance.

There is also the question – not yet comprehensively answered – of how digital media alters the way that we actually *think*. According to a 2016 study published in the proceedings of the Association for Computing Machinery (ACM) Conference on Human Factors in Computing Systems, the brain absorbs material differently if it is experienced on digital media.[19] In particular, the consumption of content online affects 'construal levels': the fundamental level of 'concreteness' versus 'abstractness' that people use in perceiving and understanding behaviour, events and other information.

For example: participants were asked to read a short story by the author David Sedaris on either a physical printout, or in PDF format on a laptop, and were then invited to sit a comprehension test. For questions involving abstractions, those who read the printout scored higher – with an average of 66 per cent correct answers compared to a score of 48 per cent by those who read on screen. In the case of concrete questions, the performances were reversed: the digital readers scored 73 per cent compared to 58 per cent by those who used the printout of the story.

Other tests supported this core finding. It may be that, as the human brain becomes more habituated to a digital-first environment, its capacity to absorb abstract ideas from online sources grows accordingly. But this initial research shows that – at the very least – onscreen reading is qualitatively different to the use of traditional print sources. The mind does not treat the iPad and the book as differently configured versions of the same mechanism. And this has potentially huge implications for the future teaching and learning of abstract, complex ideas (as opposed to the transmission of concrete details).

In trying to understand contemporary ignorance, we also need to grasp the extent to which, in the new information ecosphere, different forms of misinformation seem to stick together and co-habit. In his study of knowledge and information in the digital age, the American science writer William Poundstone discovered a sharp correlation among Britons between ignorance of basic facts and the belief that Diana, Princess of Wales, had been murdered. Those who didn't know which famous document had been signed by King John in 1215, or what happened to the stock market in 1929, or that Alice B. Toklas did not, in fact, write *The Autobiography of Alice B. Toklas*, were more likely to swallow one of the conspiracy theories concerning Diana's fatal car crash in a Parisian underpass in 1997. In the US, there is a close correlation between those who say they will vaccinate their children, those who know that humans did not co-exist with dinosaurs, those who are aware of what the Manhattan Project was and know that the war of 1812 came before the Civil War.[20]

As Poundstone observes, the fact that forms of ignorance travel in packs is no small matter:

> [The] philosophy of broad general knowledge is facing stiff headwinds. Our media zeitgeist favours a more hedgehog-like relation to facts. We are given digital tools that enable head-first dives into deep pools of interest while excluding everything else. The promise is that 'everything else' will always be in the cloud, available on demand. Lost in this seductive pitch is that being web informed is not about context as much as it is about factoids. It is the overview that permits the assessment of the particular, that offers all-important insight into what we *don't* know.[21]

I would go further. The digital instant is not only a location in space–time that limits our recall of knowledge and the range of trustworthy information to which we may refer. It is also a place dominated by emotion rather than fact. What defines the era of post-truth is not the novelty of lies – deceit is as old as communication – but the cultural context that has arisen in which feelings have primacy over accuracy. As trust in traditional institutions and gatekeepers has collapsed and algorithms have enabled digital networks to bombard us with content that matches our emotions and instincts, so we have retreated, often unwittingly, into digital cantons and stockades. When Donald Trump's aide, Kellyanne Conway, introduced the phrase 'alternative facts' to the political mainstream, she reframed the very difference between truth and lies – as if reality were something that each of us chose from the digital buffet.[22]

The Internet only looks like a super-evolved library and communications network. Granted, it shares features with both, and with many other human organisations, artefacts and institutions besides – the hospital, the school, the university, the psychologist's clinic, the department store, the games room, the dating service, the newsroom, the cinema, the theatre, the planetary map, the restaurant, the gym, the limitless archive. But it is primarily *an emotional system* that uses the most advanced technology the world has ever seen to stimulate our dopamine pathways. It rewards the novelty-hungry part of the brain that drives the limbic system, inducing momentary pleasure, rather than the higher-level prefrontal cortex that is engaged in planning complex cognitive behaviour, personality expression, decision-making and the regulation of social conduct.

Everything else the Internet does is secondary to this overriding purpose. What defines, anchors and funds online networks is their capacity to engage and stimulate brains that are more distracted than at any moment in history. What began life as an extraordinary project in collaboration and amateur cooperation has become an untamed force that is driven by clicks, sales and the most basic of human impulses.[23]

It remains a miraculous tool – whatever its detractors say, Wikipedia (for example) is surely one of the great human inventions of the past century – and, in ways great and small, a force for good. Its finest feature remains the hyper-democracy of the technology itself: the fact that the cost of the means of production are now close to zero, and that nobody needs to own a print plant or a television station to get their message across to the world. As the open-source software champion Eric S. Raymond famously predicted, the Cathedral has been replaced by the

Bazaar.[24] Hierarchical systems have been supplanted by global networks. To quote the declaration made by the technological writer Clay Shirky in 2008: Here comes everybody.[25]

Yet it was always a delusion to believe that what became known as 'Web 2.0' would be a necessarily benign, collaborative, democratising force for decency. Like all technologies, the Internet – to mix metaphors – held a mirror up to and weaponised humanity's worst instincts, as well as its best. It has enabled the corruption of political discourse by unprecedented levels of targeted misinformation and foreign interference in democratic electoral processes. It has helped global terrorism form local franchises. It has made the most vile pornography – including images of child sexual abuse – easier to proliferate and harder to regulate. It has handed unprecedented power over human data to a tiny number of gigantic tech corporations, all vying to attract and sell the most valuable commodity in the world: our attention.[26]

So great is the scale of this transformation – and the changes to come – that it is important, as far as possible, to consider the implications with the dispassionate eye of the anthropologist rather than the panicked perspective of the moralist. As we have seen, young people are now, more than ever, captive to the digital instant and to the confines of a mayfly world which changes utterly from second to second, as the stimuli to which they are subject continue their ceaseless iterations.

In an epistemological environment of this sort, what we have traditionally called 'ignorance' is not a personal failing. It is the default setting of a system that, from commercial design to neuroscientific impact, depends upon constant churn and is actively hostile to retention, consideration and critical deliberation.

Those raised in the digital era are not Flat Earthers but *Thin Earthers*: they have very limited awareness of the true nature of the ground beneath their feet, or the multiple, roiling, groaning layers of historic magma that lie below, and the tectonic, centuries-old forces that (to an extent that is hard for them to comprehend) have shaped everything around them. Their interest in the past, such as it is, tends to be extirpatory and hygienic: to denounce anything that has gone before that does not accord with the high standards of today and of the Thin Earth of flickering images that is their natural habitat.

The question is: are we happy to go along with that?

CHAPTER 9

NEWS THAT STAYS NEWS

I knew right there in prison that reading had changed forever the course of my life. As I see it today, the ability to read awoke inside me some long dormant craving to be mentally alive . . . My homemade education gave me, with every additional book that I read, a little bit more sensitivity to the deafness, dumbness, and blindness that was afflicting the black race in America.

Malcolm X

In 1994, I went to Geneva on assignment for *The Times* to interview the great literary critic and thinker George Steiner, who had just been appointed to a professorship at Oxford University. Our conversation – first over lunch and then in his tiny office – ranged from the significance of Marx, Freud and Lévi-Strauss in the criticism of poetry, to gossip about the *New Yorker* (for which he was lead book reviewer), to Lear's cry of despair over the dead Cordelia, ancient Chinese bronzes and his lifelong preoccupation with the meaning of the Holocaust that, as a Jew fleeing France in 1940, he had escaped.

In defence of high culture, Steiner made the following claim: 'I've no right to say to anyone you should read Aeschylus and not Joan Collins, no right whatever. And yet I do. No right but a despotic, unarguable, Neronian conviction.' I am fairly sure that he meant Jackie Collins, Joan's late sister, a prolific writer of mass-market novels. His use of the word 'Neronian' – meaning 'tyrannical' – was a little eccentric. Yet that line has found its way into many books and lists of quotations; a declaration of undaunted resistance at the end of a century to the deluge of the lowbrow and dumbing down that was to come in the next.

Steiner had offered a strong opinion but also – as he conceded – done so in a way that was bound to be contentious. In daring to stand up for one sort of culture rather than another, in suggesting that some texts or artefacts or pieces of music are better than others, he had self-identified as an 'elitist', and given fresh ammunition to those who had always denounced him as a snob.

In fact, he was no such thing. In later life, he readily acknowledged that, had he been starting his philosophical journey today rather than after the Second World War, he might well have been more absorbed by the rise of emerging economies (India, in particular), by the advance of technology and by the impact of globalisation.

Throughout his writing life, Steiner was an arch-democratiser – in the very particular sense that he wanted everyone to read the great works of literature, to listen to classical music, to flex their intellectual muscles to the limit (it was his ritual every morning to take a random prose passage from a book and translate it into four languages). His mission, as he saw it, was to act as a cultural postman – *il postino*, as he called himself – remorselessly urging his students and readers to immerse themselves in civilisation and its discontents. He was a champion of internationalism and interdisciplinary exchange; he deplored chauvinism and intellectual walls.

He defended difficulty and intellectual stamina, anticipating the great populist lie of our era – that complex problems have easy solutions. Never, it should be emphasised, did he proselytise the glib argument that reading is inherently therapeutic, or that high culture makes people behave well. Indeed, the greatest paradox, with which he wrestled for his entire life, was the fact that Germany – the nation of Bach, Beethoven, Holbein and Rilke – could spawn the Holocaust; that 'Goethe's garden almost borders on Buchenwald'.

When Steiner died in February 2020, I was struck by two powerful reflections. First – sadly – that his most important works, especially *Language and Silence*, *After Babel* and *Real Presences*, are no longer regarded as essential reading. And second, that they had never been more pertinent; that the 'Neronian' claims made by the compact magus I had spoken to, a quarter-century before, had a fresh and nagging relevance to our own times.

The terrain that he made his own has been the venue of ferocious conflict in recent decades. First, the notion that there was a 'canon' of Western literature and artistic works that was specially worthy of attention and reverence has been pulverised: the 'Great Books' programmes offered by so many US campuses and the notion of a 'Great Tradition' of English literature advanced by F.R. Leavis in 1948 were subject to ridicule and vilification. Where possible, it became standard practice to mock any syllabus that gave undue prominence to the works of 'dead white European males' – that is, just about any author encompassing this particular demographic, from Plato to Fitzgerald, via Dante, Shakespeare, Milton, Flaubert and Dostoyevsky.

As so often, this radical attack – fought on many fronts – had a constructive, corrective impact, opening minds and library shelves to the literature of other traditions and the voices of the disenfranchised or ignored. In the magic realism of Salman Rushdie and Gabriel Garçia Marquez, mainstream readers found themselves engrossed in writings from the Indian subcontinent and from South America. Bookish teenagers in the Eighties were less likely to be carrying a once-hallowed text from the old canon than a copy of Chinua Achebe's *Things Fall Apart*, or the latest offering from the Virago Press (the imprint for women writers founded in 1973), or a novel by the growing contingent of openly gay or queer writers such as Alan Hollinghurst, Edmund White or Kathy Acker.

Old-fashioned critical analysis, meanwhile, was pushed aside in favour of waves of literary theory surging from continental Europe – and especially from France. Students who would once have cantered around the canonical course were now expected to understand texts as expressions of power, symbolism, prejudice and ideology. As one reads today the dense prose of Michel

Foucault, Jean Baudrillard or Jacques Derrida, it is important not to forget how *energising* their writings were in the final quarter of the past century – how much emancipation and punk vitality they offered to liberal arts faculties that had grown complacent and stuck in their ways.[1] The backlash was vigorous, too – in Harold Bloom's *The Western Canon* and, especially, *The Closing of The American Mind* by Allan Bloom (no relation).[2]

In his dissection of the new forces at work on American campuses, Allan Bloom cast the debate in millenarian language:

> This is the American moment in world history, the one for which we shall forever be judged. Just as in politics the responsibility for the fate of freedom in the world has devolved upon our regime, so the fate of philosophy in the world has devolved upon our universities and the two are related as they have never been before. The gravity of our given task is great, and it is very much in doubt how the future will judge our stewardship.[3]

'American moment' or not, this was certainly a significant punctuation mark in what became known as 'culture wars': polarised, furious, irreconcilable. On the one side, the theorists, inspired in various ways by neo-Marxism and the new schools of theory, and committed to a prototypical academic version of modern identity politics; on the other, a dwindling number of traditionalists who felt that Western civilisation was under siege by ideologues, philistines and wreckers. In different forms and under different banners, the dialectic continues to this day, often, perhaps mostly, generating more heat than light.

The most regrettable side effect of this great ideological conflict is the impact it has had upon the way in which reading is perceived: as a habit, as a pursuit, as a way of life. Already in competition with television, and now what I have called the digital instant, books (or at least certain categories of book) have lost much of their aura as forces of emancipation and empowerment. First, it is routinely argued that today's pupils need to be steered towards 'skills-based' education, preferably in STEM subjects (science, technology, engineering and mathematics), but certainly away from the humanities.

The billionaire entrepreneur Marc Andreessen captured this mindset in 2012 with his claim that the average graduate with a degree in English would 'end up working in a shoe store'.[4] In a speech in January 2014, Barack Obama said: 'I promise you, folks can make a lot more, potentially, with skilled manufacturing or the trades than they might with an art history degree'.[5] The president later expressed regret for what he had intended to be an encouraging remark aimed at those interested in vocational training. But the fact that such an eloquent (and erudite) politician could say something so dismissive about the liberal arts in the first place was remarkable.

The second, and more general, objection is that reading-based education is inherently elitist, as well as useless. It is an indulgence that only the privileged can afford, an activity that will, in the end, always entrench rather than release power. Around the edges of this argument always hangs the insinuation that no literary or historical syllabus, no matter how well-intentioned or carefully constructed, can be free of the stain of oppression, or imperialism, or sexism, or bigotry, or all the above.

Consider, then, the epigraph to this chapter, and the words of Malcolm X. When asked what his alma mater was, he replied: 'Books'. In ten years of imprisonment, the petty criminal originally known as 'Red' Little read with a passion matched by few autodidacts, and transformed himself into the figure of eloquence and erudition who is remembered and celebrated all over the world to this day.

Toni Morrison framed her lifelong love of reading differently:

That Alice-in-Wonderland combination of willing acceptance coupled with intense inquiry is still the way I read literature: slowly, digging for the hidden, questioning or relishing the choices the author made, eager to envision what is there, noticing what is not . . . I don't need to 'like' the work; I want instead to 'think' it.[6]

And here is Susan Sontag in 1992, explicitly linking her vocation as a writer to her early discovery of reading:

> I began reading at a very, very early age, and I've been a reading junkie ever since – I read all the time. I probably spend more time reading than any other thing I've done in my life, including sleeping. I've spent many, many days of my life reading eight and ten hours a day . . . The day has pockets – you can always find time to read. Reading set standards. Reading opened up to me all these norms, or – to put it in a more naive and probably truthful way – ideals.[7]

Why recruit such voices to make the case for reading? Why revert to such basic arguments at all? Because, sadly, it is necessary, and because the stakes are so high. This is not an argument about *piety* (children being patted on the head for choosing a book over a video game) but *power* (the knowledge, learning and critical abilities that are necessary to be a fully enfranchised citizen).

So far have we moved from the 'Great Books' model – and, to be clear, I am not making the case for a return to such a system – that the centrality of reading to personal formation and intellectual development has become lost in a sort of shuffle of cultural embarrassment and a bogus understanding of what is truly 'modern'. It is not exactly that reading is frowned upon – that would be absurd. But its former role, visible in Western culture from the Renaissance to the 20th-Century working-class literacy famously detected by Richard Hoggart in Northern England, has faded wretchedly.[8]

As we have seen, reading for pleasure and personal development – code for reading anything other than set texts – is in decline, and, to generalise, has shifted from a default habit of the average citizen to something more arcane, hobbyistic, even quaint. Teachers and parents still urge children, dutifully, to read. But they would rather that they learned coding. Yes, it is a life-transforming experience to read David Foster Wallace's epic novel *Infinite Jest* (footnotes and all). But wouldn't that time *really* be better spent preparing for a career as an engineer?

As a former trustee of the Science Museum Group, a campaigner against pseudoscience and someone who takes a hungry lay interest in the sciences, I find this tension absolutely tragic. In 1959, the novelist and chemist C.P. Snow famously identified 'The Two Cultures' that had produced 'mutual incomprehension' between scholars in the humanities and professional scientists. He was rightly pitiless about the failure of English dons to take an interest in even the very basic concepts of chemistry, physics and biology:

> Once or twice I have been provoked and have asked the company how many of them could describe the Second Law of Thermodynamics. The response was cold: it was also negative. Yet I was asking something which is about the scientific equivalent of *Have you read a work of Shakespeare's*? I now believe that if I had asked an even simpler question – such as, What do you mean by mass, or acceleration, which is the scientific equivalent of saying, *Can you read?* – not more than one in ten of the highly educated would have felt that I was speaking the same language. So the great edifice of modern physics goes up, and the majority of the cleverest people in the western world have about as much insight into it as their neolithic ancestors would have had.[9]

Today, the scientists would have the upper hand in such a high table discussion, much more confident – and with good reason – that their research will be securely funded ten years from now and that the political mainstream supports them against their poor, misguided colleagues in the English, history and philosophy departments. Literature may be a wonderful thing, they reflect – but it is not going to attract inward investment to campus from Big Pharma.

The high price of this intellectual partition is that it reduces learning to a zero-sum game. It presents the study of the liberal arts as part of the adolescence of our species – a youthful preoccupation to be set aside in the century of the Fourth Industrial Revolution, AI, health tech, climate emergency science, data mining and the omnipotent algorithm. I am all for young people pursuing STEM subjects and strongly support the campaigns to encourage them to do so (especially girls, who have been historically under-represented in the nation's laboratories). But there is no need to denigrate the liberal arts in order to provide a sufficient supply of engineers and life scientists to the workforce. Indeed, to do so betrays a fundamental misunderstanding of what the modern workforce – and the workforce of the future – will require.

Between 2016 and 2019 the number of pupils taking English A Level declined by a fifth – which is no surprise, really, given the educational assumptions that now predominate in the mainstream. In the autumn of 2019, Nicky Morgan, the education secretary, framed the matter thus: '[In the past] if you didn't know what you wanted to do . . . the arts and humanities were what you chose because they were useful . . . We now know this couldn't be further from the truth. The subjects to keep young people's options open are STEM subjects.'[10]

This is not necessarily so. Computer science courses, routinely presented as a sure-fire path to a stable career, no less routinely have the highest unemployment rates.[11] Which, in fact, is only logical. One of the most powerful industrial and cultural forces in the world today is automation, the process by which tasks previously performed by people are taken over by machines. This has long been a feature of the factory floor, mineral extraction and construction. But the transformation of work is no longer confined to manual labour: anything that can be routinised – which is to say, many white-collar tasks involving basic legal, accounting, marketing and other clerical tasks – can be handed over to robots.

In 2017, the McKinsey Global Institute assessed that 800 million workers around the world would lose their jobs to robots by 2030 – probably a conservative estimate.[12] The scope for robotic surgery is already huge, posing challenging ethical questions about the necessity of anything more than the most basic human involvement in straightforward procedures, and strategic problems about the training of junior doctors, as more and more of the clinical tasks that they perform as part of their professional apprenticeship are taken over by machines.[13] In 2017, a legal AI program called Case Cruncher Alpha proved better at predicting the outcome of hundreds of PPI (payment protection insurance) cases than more than 100 lawyers from respected London firms (the machine's accuracy rate was 86.6 per cent compared to 66.3 per cent for the human beings).[14] There are few areas of the financial sector where machine learning is not already transforming the way in which business is conducted.[15] Meanwhile, all those middle-class children forced by their parents to learn how to code on Saturday morning should learn that AI is now capable of writing programs itself – marking, in effect, the arrival of the computer that can teach itself to perform better.[16] A typical human programmer can come up with 400 lines of code a day: the work of a second for a machine.

Not all jobs will be automated, of course, and automation will create new forms of employment for humans – supervisory, technical, conceptual – as it always has. But we ignore the scale of the change, and its implications, at our peril. Today's pupils are not being prepared for the late 20th-Century technocratic workplace. They are being prepared for a very different environment, and one in which a specific set of talents, aptitudes and even temperamental qualities will be at a premium.

In his seminal book *A Whole New Mind*, the business and technology writer Daniel H. Pink argued that the coming revolution was not only economic and social but *neurological*. It had long been orthodox to assume that the most important (and lucrative) tasks were those performed by the left hemisphere of the brain: the side that reasoned sequentially, handled analysis, and pursued logic. The right side of the brain, in contrast, did the emotional, instinctive and empathetic work – tasks that, in the crackling heat of the Information Age, seemed old-fashioned if not actually redundant. But the very success of technology has flipped this orthodoxy on its head. As Pink writes:

> The last few decades have belonged to a certain kind of person with a certain kind of mind – computer programmers who could crank code, lawyers who could craft contracts, MBAs who could crunch numbers. But the keys to the kingdom are changing hands. The future belongs to a very different kind of person with a very different kind of mind – creators and empathizers, pattern recognizers, and meaning makers. These people – artists, inventors, designers, storytellers, caregivers, consolers, big picture thinkers – will now reap society's richest rewards and share its greatest joys.[17]

This was much more than an assertion. Pink had identified a gap between the old assumptions and new commercial practices. So when Robert Lutz was hired by General Motors as vice chairman of product development in 2001, he told the *New York Times* that his strategy would be 'more right brain . . . I see us being in the art business. Art, entertainment and mobile sculpture, which, coincidentally, also happens to provide transportation'.[18] MFAs (Masters of Fine Arts) were being sought after by canny businesses with as much vigour as MBAs (Masters of Business Administration) – with the inevitable consequence that fine arts courses received more applications and could be much more selective. Even before the full disruptive impact of Steve Jobs's transformation of Apple was felt, other corporations were intuiting that differentiation lay in design, concept and story: all handled by the right side of the brain. In the US, Pink noted, graphic designers outnumbered chemical engineers by four to one; more Americans worked in arts entertainment and design than as lawyers, accountants and auditors.

Pink's work was remarkable because it preceded both the seismic changes brought about by social media, the shift to centre stage of AI, and the new centrality of digitised emotion to the practice of politics. In the decade and a half since, Silicon Valley has hired liberal arts graduates with relish. Indeed, some of its most notable products have reflected the insights of the humanities as much as the functional capacities of technology.

Stewart Butterfield, the co-founder of the workplace platform Slack, has drawn a direct correlation between its simplicity and ease of use and his training as a philosopher at the universities of Victoria and Cambridge: 'Studying philosophy taught me two things, I learned how to write really clearly. I learned how to follow an argument all the way down, which is invaluable in running meetings. And when I studied the history of science, I learned about the ways that everyone believes something is true – like the old notion of some kind of ether in the air propagating gravitational forces – until they realized that it wasn't true'.[19]

Butterfield is far from unique. Susan Wojcicki, the CEO of YouTube, read history and literature; Jack Ma, the co-founder of Alibaba Group, holds an English degree; it is often forgotten that Mark Zuckerberg was a psychology major when he founded Facebook. As the venture capitalist Scott Hartley has put it, the 'Techie' has never needed the 'Fuzzy' – the right-sider – more.[20] To differentiate their products and retain customer loyalty, such businesses need to think more than ever about user experience, design, concepts of identity and community, and interactions that are pleasurable as well as functional. It has been said that culture is now upstream from politics. It is also upstream from business.

Which means that employers require, perhaps more than ever, the talents that a liberal arts education nurtures as much as the scientific expertise that will – naturally – remain central to the global economy. This is supported by data from LinkedIn which has shown that – far from working in shoe stores, as Marc Andreessen predicted, a growing number of liberal arts graduates are being hired by tech companies, often at a higher rate than computer scientists.

Edgar Bronfman Sr., former CEO of Seagram Company, has offered this advice to prospective students:

Get a liberal arts degree. In my experience, a liberal arts degree is the most important factor in forming individuals into interesting and interested people who can determine their own paths through the future. For all of the decisions young business leaders will be asked to make based on facts and figures, needs and wants, numbers and speculation, all of those choices will require one common skill: how to evaluate raw information, be it from people or a spreadsheet, and make reasoned and critical decisions.[21]

A decent humanities course – not only at undergraduate level, but for teenagers at school – ought to be founded on a simple proposition: that reading with understanding and writing well also teach you to think more rigorously and creatively; to speak in a persuasive and intelligent fashion; and to approach problems with an eye to precedent as well as to future imperatives. The liberal arts teach us how to learn more – a skill that is required now more than ever. As a former president of Harvard, Drew Faust, has put it, a liberal education should give young people the knowledge and abilities 'that will help them get ready for their sixth job, not their first job'.[22]

What this suggests is that the cultural oscillation between science and humanities – the divide identified by C.P. Snow – is, in fact, the problem, and that the modern world requires a fresh reconciliation of the two and a recognition that the dichotomy is false. A growing recognition that this is so is reflected in the growing use of the term 'STEAM' – inserting 'arts' into the familiar STEM acronym.[23] In part, this is a consequence of the sheer scale of the issues that are now being posed by the technological revolution. It is not enough to be able to write algorithms. We have to understand and conceptualise their social, ethical and political consequences.[24] Gene editing, for example, is clearly much more than a practical challenge: it presents dilemmas of spectacular complexity about the ethical limits of technology's remodelling of nature. We are in the foothills of working out what impact social media is going to have upon institutions, political discourse and democratic structures. Such questions cannot be properly framed – let alone answered – without a rich grasp of history, philosophy, the social sciences, literature, aesthetics and linguistics. It is simply idle to pretend otherwise.

Steve Jobs understood this completely. Launching a new edition of the iPad, he said: '[I]t's in Apple's DNA that technology alone is not enough. It's technology married with liberal arts, married with the humanities, that yields us the result that makes our hearts sing'.[25] In 2011, Yale University and the National University of Singapore joined forces precisely to bridge the chasm between Snow's two cultures, between the two sides of the brain and – for that matter – West and East. Yale-NUS College teaches its students both humanities and sciences, Plato and Confucius, Homer's *Odyssey* and the Hindu *Ramayana*. Its ethos is eclectic, global, and celebratory of the porousness between disciplines.[26]

Yet – as we have seen – such enlightened projects are relatively rare in the pedagogic landscape. It is encouraging that a growing number of universities – Birmingham and University College London (for instance) in the UK and seven colleges in the Netherlands – now offer joint honours courses in liberal arts and sciences. But such institutions remain outliers; and their spirit of open-mindedness and eclecticism is – on the whole – not reflected in schools, especially in the UK. Our children continue to be herded through an education system that values test grades over wisdom and knowledge. This compounds their captivity in the digital instant – their disconnection from the flow of time (past and future), and subjection to the recency effect. Though the evidence of the employment marketplace provides a much more complex picture, they are routinely told that liberal arts subjects are a waste of time, an indulgence and a high road to career insecurity.

I return to my belief that the key to this problem lies in reading, or its decline. Not reading at 3am, dosed on Ritalin to ace a test, but reading to free the mind. Not reading to please teachers, but reading to help you question what they tell you. Reading that equips the next generation with the tools it will need for a world of fractured, multiple identities, insecure employment, turbulent social change and an endless series of negotiations with their fellow inhabitants on this terrain of turbulence. Reading that is the gateway to other forms of creativity and curiosity.

In his acclaimed 2013 TED speech, the education researcher Sugata Mitra explained why the old system of rote learning was no longer useful – and what should replace it:

> [Today] the clerks are the computers. They're there in thousands in every office. And you have people who guide those computers to do their clerical jobs. Those people don't need to be able to write beautifully by hand. They don't need to be able to multiply numbers in their head. They do need to be able to read. In fact, they need to be able to read discerningly.[27]

And those who are taught well, in this way, will acquire the skills of ideation, broad-frame pattern recognition and complex communication that still enable humans to compete with robots.

Of course, all manner of experiences, formal or otherwise, can enhance a person's horizons and deepen their knowledge (one of my own favourites is a trip to the pioneering biomedical labs at Imperial College, London, where the future of medicine unfolds before one's very eyes)[28]. I am not making a case against any of them. But reading is (or should be) the starter-pack of a civilised life, the introductory course in learning how to be a human being at full potential. My anecdotal experience matches that of Mark Edmundson who argues in his book *Why Read?* that 'beneath that veneer of cool, students are full of potent questions; they want to know how to navigate life, what to be, what to do'[29]. Edmundson also notes, correctly, that none of the pathologies that have wrecked contemporary education are the fault of the students themselves. They did not invent the 'consumer biosphere whose air [is] now their purest oxygen'.[30]

Reading would also be a much better use of pupils' and students' time than the absurd testing regime to which they are now all subject. There will always be competitive assessment in schools and universities. Arguably, a measure of early-years assessment will remain necessary to ensure that basic skills of literacy and numeracy are taught to all children (it is a grave social injustice that one in six adults in England, 7.1 million people, have very low literacy skills as defined by the UK National Literacy Trust)[31]. But the stranglehold of testing needs to be released.

Examinations should play an appreciably smaller role in education generally, with standardised grades regarded as no more than the most basic – and preliminary – measure of a student's potential. There is no excuse for the tick-box culture that dominates schools and universities today, or the short-answer, multiple-choice questions that drive nuance and true understanding out of the testing process. As a rule, if you need a spreadsheet to assess the young people that you teach, you are in the wrong profession. Metrics should play a part in university admissions policies; but only a part. An institution that proposes to educate a person for three or four years and charge them a considerable amount of money in the process, owes them more than a cursory interview or two. Those who say they do not have time to talk to applicants at any greater length have the wrong priorities. People cannot be reduced to statistics, in spite of repeated claims to the contrary. They deserve to be more than fodder for the education machine.

It is often claimed that book sales continue to be high only because the affluent are buying more of them. Even if that is so, it is an argument for making them more widely accessible (the decline in public libraries is one of the true scandals of our time, and one that could and should be reversed at comparatively small cost to the taxpayer). The most outrageous insinuation that sometimes drifts into discussions of reading – and its decline as a habit among young people – is that books are inherently middle-class artefacts, objects of privilege. That better-off pupils can afford to spend time reading *Wuthering Heights*, or *The Handmaid's Tale*, or the poetry of Caleb Femi, but that children heading for the gig economy or a technical trade should not squander their energies on such fripperies.

This is unbelievably patronising, as well as an affront to the core value of any democracy – which is a belief in the equality of worth of every person. It also reflects a form of cultural illiteracy: ignorance of the literary continuum that connects arthouse and popular culture, Netflix with Naipaul, rap with Rilke. On this matter, we *can* disagree with George Steiner's 'Neronian' insistence. We do not have to dispense with Instagram or TikTok or movie franchises. But we shouldn't be defined by them, or accept the false choice between highbrow and lowbrow. Every time a child, offered a cultural experience, says: 'That's not for me', the response should be: 'Give it a try.' Every child who is told (much worse) that a book or a work of art or a piece of music is 'not for her' should robustly insist on experiencing it. A networked world should be just that: its phantom barriers and ramparts should be torn down, like a Berlin Wall of the mind.

What we need now is a *global curriculum*: not the narrowly national version, founded in 1988, but a syllabus of much greater flexibility that encourages pupils to think, talk, write and flourish – rather than simply to parrot answers learned from papers. To be clear: it should be global in *reach* rather than institutional structure (we need more local variation, not less). It should be much less prescriptive in the content it mandates pupils to study, and more imaginatively geared to teaching them how to think, analyse and learn. It should seek to exfiltrate pupils from the trap of the digital instant, reconnect them with the mains cable of learning and open their eyes to the great prairies of knowledge that are theirs for the taking, and the understanding of the past (and not just the victor's version) that will inform the decisions they take about the future.

No two schools or campuses will ever be the same. But they should at least offer a portal to an intellectual constellation that connects Harold Bloom's beloved Western canon to the counterculture against which he railed (we should read both); to the Black Lives Matter reading lists that were drawn up in the wake of George Floyd's murder;[32] to the remarkable cohort of woman essayists – Rebecca Solnit, Phoebe Robinson, Jia Tolentino,

Leslie Jamison, Chimamanda Ngozi Adichie, Heather Havrilesky – who presently dominate the genre; Jordan Peterson's list of Great Books;[33] the best African books of the 20th Century;[34] the ten philosophy books everyone should read;[35] the best books on medicine for the lay person;[36] or quantum physics;[37] or climate emergency;[38] or global poverty;[39] or the history of art;[40] and so on.

No such list of lists could (or should) ever aspire to be complete: these inventories ought to be porous, organic, constantly updated. And they should be liberalising rather than restrictive: try this book and see where it takes you. Become a traveller and an adventurer in the world of letters and ideas. That is the whole point. We need an entirely new politics of education, much less dependent on prescription and founded on the principle of pupil empowerment: less teaching to the test, more teaching. Needless to say, this is a much harder form of pedagogy. But it will be much more rewarding for educators than the grade factory in which they are presently floor managers.

The heroes of this project – which already exists, in disaggregated form – are committed artists such as Akala, whose Hip-hop Shakespeare Company, founded in 2009, explores the parallels between Shakespearean texts and contemporary hip-hop culture.[41] Charities such as BookTrust, which reaches 3.9 million children a year, do extraordinary work getting books into the hands of the disadvantaged and encouraging reading for pleasure.[42] Resources like the Children's Poetry Archive are freely available to introduce young people to poems at their own pace and without the pressure of being taught to the test.[43] These, and other ventures like them, are the seeds from which could blossom a new definition of what books mean to the new generation, liberating them from their present, wearisome status as slab-like objects that symbolise the purgatory of relentless testing.

And there are still courageous teachers who – often against the advice of their departmental bosses and the number-crunchers in the head teacher's side-office – take the time to inspire their pupils as well as to shepherd them through the syllabus; who direct them to a website they might like, or a poetry app, or give them a battered paperback that is not on the curriculum but might change their whole way of seeing the world. I have spoken to enough teachers to know that most of them entered the profession hoping to do exactly this but find themselves completely constrained by paperwork, targets and the pressure of league tables. To snuff out such a sense of vocation – and to so little purpose – is barely short of criminal.

It cannot be emphasised strongly enough that this is *not a restorationist mission*. It is fiercely contemporary in its objectives, mindful of the pressures of modern life and Ezra Pound's maxim, included in his *ABC of Reading* (1934), that 'Literature is news that stays news.' Getting today's children to read, widely, eclectically and for constructive purpose, is a *radical* undertaking, a task of maximal disruption. At present, we force-feed pupils and undergraduates with information. But what they need is knowledge, the connective tissue between data and wisdom. They need the tools that will enable them to navigate the stormy straits that lie ahead. The discourse of social media, celebrity culture and populist politics is one of competing certainties. But, as Edmundson notes, the ability to doubt – including to doubt oneself – is essential to a fulfilling and free life: 'The true student demands more. And to find it, she is willing, against the backdrop of all this knowingness, to take a brave step. She is willing to affirm her own ignorance.'[44]

I do not want to see the next generation retreat into docile bookishness, or docility of any kind, for that matter. What I am proposing is not whimsical, nor a *cri de coeur* from the ivory tower. It is an uncompromisingly contemporary idea, one inspired by years of observing, visiting and writing about schools and campuses. We need to impress upon pupils that a hinterland is not a privilege but a civil right: that an understanding of the culture of the world, and a grasp of the past that is drenched neither in triumphalism nor collective self-flagellation, should be a common entitlement. We need young people with the knowledge and abilities to live, work and collaborate in a world of unprecedented complexity. We need citizens who have the confidence to be more than consumers and taxpayers.

The politicians who tell you that everything is getting better in education speak the same nonsense as the Soviet apparatchiks who announced record tractor production results. Those who say, regretfully, that a better way is impossible reveal only the poverty of their own expectations. Our system is no longer fit for purpose, if it ever was. Do not settle for it.

PART THREE

INNOVATION

PART THREE

CHAPTER 10

THE AGE OF METATHESIOPHOBIA: OR HOW FEAR OF CHANGE HAS CHANGED EVERYTHING

The whole universe is change and life itself is but what you deem it.

Marcus Aurelius

You better start swimming or you'll sink like a stone, 'cause the times they are a-changing.
Bob Dylan, 'The Times They Are a-Changin' (1964)

As someone once said: Stuff Happens. At least since Heraclitus of Ephesus (*c.*535–*c.*475 BC) observed that 'everything changes and nothing stands still', it has been a staple of Western philosophy that the human condition is one of unceasing flux. An essential component of personhood is to accept change as the defining feature of life and uncertainty as the fickle friend and foe that walks beside us for all of our days.

There have been many different schools of thought about the best way in which to cope with this implacable reality, such as Stoicism (acceptance combined with a personal quest for reason and virtue), Epicureanism (a life of moderately consumed pleasures, such as friendship and feelings of joy, as the best path for a decent person), and theistic religions (most of which teach that, for those that live righteously, the sufferings of the present life are only the path to bliss in the next).

So we must tread with care in declaring uniqueness for our own age in this respect. Who are we to say that digitalisation has transformed the world more than, for instance, the invention of the wheel around 5,500 years ago? Or that the increased longevity that is testing our health and social care systems marks a greater change than the medical advances, reforms of sanitation and democratisation of health care that followed the 1918 Spanish flu pandemic? Or that climate emergency has had a more serious impact upon the collective psyche than did the prospect of nuclear annihilation during the Cold War (irrespective of whether it should or not)? Or that the coming wave of automation will be more disruptive than the First Industrial Revolution?

It is easy to forget, too, how routine dramatic demographic change actually is: before the First World War, farmers and those in domestic service were still the largest groups in most countries. The blue-collar worker's rise and fall was a story mostly confined to the 20th Century.

What we *can* say is that human beings have rarely, if ever, faced such extraordinary change on so many fronts. Almost no facet of our experience is untouched by rapid mutation, or its prospect. Digital technology leads the field as the most immediately palpable force, but it is closely followed by a suite of competitors: the hard facts of climate science; the sharp decline of job security and indefensible inequities within the globalised economy; the opportunities and challenges of increased life expectancy; the collapse of trust in traditional institutions and corresponding polarisation of politics, surge in pseudoscience and proliferation of conspiracy theories; the geopolitical tensions between West and East, closely aligned with the respective innovative capacities of the US and China; the arthritic faltering of the post-war international order and the global organisations in which it is enshrined; the continued threat of fundamentalist and far-Right terror; and – alongside all this – a generational shift in ideas, values and social priorities unlike any for forty years. Covid-19 has exacerbated all these forces, and incubated fresh perils of its own. In sum, we inhabit a moment of omnidirectional bombardment.

A word on nomenclature: I use the word 'innovation' as an umbrella term to describe these trends, transformations, technological advances and disruptions. Others deploy it more narrowly – but no less revealingly. In his compelling book on the subject, Matt Ridley defines it thus: 'Innovation, like evolution, is a process of constantly discovering ways of rearranging the world into forms that are unlikely to arise by chance – and that happen to be useful . . . It means much more than invention, because the word implies developing an invention to the point where it catches on because it is sufficiently practical, affordable, reliable and ubiquitous to be worth using.'[1]

As Ridley explains, innovation is usually more gradual than we expect. The 'eureka' moment is more often than not the stuff of legend; it involves trial and error, teamwork and serendipity; it is inexorable but tends to flourish in conditions of fragmented governance. He cites the dictum of the Stanford University scientist Roy Amara, that people tend to overestimate the impact of a new technology in the short run, but to underestimate it in the long run. Autonomous cars may be a very good example of this: we are expecting them too impatiently, will be disappointed by the pace of progress for some time; but – at a later date than initially expected – they will transform the nature of transportation.[2]

Ridley also notes the human tendency to resist innovation: 'Despite the abundant evidence that it has transformed almost everybody's lives for the better in innumerable ways, the knee-jerk reaction of most people to something new is often worry, sometimes even disgust'.[3] Coffee, margarine, the playing of music on the radio, the use of anaesthesia in childbirth, refrigerators: the list of changes that have been initially opposed with great vigour is as long as it is irrational. Mobile phones were originally regarded as the electronic equivalent of an embarrassingly flash sports car, and certainly not as the first iteration of a digital device that would become an essential tool of citizenship and everyday life.

Though I use the word 'innovation' much more broadly than Ridley to apply to a broad spectrum of changes that are affecting the world today, his analysis is instructive beyond the confines of his own thesis. Why do we resist and fear change? Partly because, as we have seen, it is almost literally inescapable. No aspect of life, no pocket of daily experience is immune from its effects. It makes demands of us that we are not necessarily equipped to meet.

Why so? In addition to the sheer scale and scope of change, we have forgotten some of the adaptive talents that enable us to cope with transformation. Both as hyperactive consumers and as beneficiaries of state services, we learned a sort of collective passivity in the late 20th Century that has contributed to the present levels of panic as we head towards the second quarter of the 21st. Our reflex is to confront change as though we are not participants in it, merely victims or supplicants. We regard ourselves as stripped of agency (which may or may not be true, depending upon the context).

Immigration is, again, a good case study. So often, we still hear that the British people 'were not consulted' about immigration levels at various points in recent history. To which the only honest reply is: *yes we were*. Each time we insisted on a properly staffed NHS (especially during a winter health crisis), on social care that was halfway decent, on a service economy that functioned, on a ready supply of plumbers, builders and decorators, on digitally ordered grocery deliveries arriving on time, we expressed a micro-preference about the way in which we wanted society to be organised. Every single one of those sectors would have collapsed without migrant labour (and may yet face serious problems now that Britain has left the EU). This was never a secret, and it is pure hypocrisy to pretend otherwise.

Every time we took this economic and social landscape for granted, we implicitly endorsed the immigration policy that preceded the Brexit vote. There is still much research to be done on the disproportionate numbers of BAME people who died in the UK during the pandemic in the spring of 2020.[4] But one of the many reasons is that members of ethnic minorities – migrants, their children and grandchildren – perform so many frontline tasks, as doctors, nurses, care workers and bus drivers, that put them in positions of exceptional risk. This alone should shame those who say that the virus has strengthened the case for their pernicious nativism.

Yet, as I argued in the Introduction to this book, immigration has become a proxy issue on a grand and alarming scale. In an essay for the George W. Bush Institute in 2018, Imam Shpendim Nadzaku, resident scholar of the Islamic Association of North Texas, identified the problem with admirable precision: 'Immigration strikes at the very heart of a central *metathesiophobia*, or fear of change. This anxiety can come from a fear of the unknown or an expectation of loss – loss of identity about religion, language, and culture and the power and privileges associated with that identity . . . [But if] only we looked back in history, we could learn that immigration is human and the associated changes present challenges and opportunities. As Americans, can we imagine an altered reality, had the immigrant parents of the many great men and women of our country never come? Within a multicultural, pluralistic society people should celebrate their diversity, not feel threatened by it. ". . . one Nation, under God, with liberty and justice for all."'[5]

In general, a society that is not frozen by theocracy or totalitarianism will oscillate between hunger for change, and fear of it. The duality of the late 18th Century was captured in the tension between Thomas Paine, champion of the French Revolution and participant in the American War of Independence, and Edmund Burke, whose *Reflections on the Revolution in France* (1790) remains perhaps the best argument for conservative values in the English language ('[a] spirit of innovation is generally the result of a selfish temper, and confined views. People will not look forward to posterity, who never look backward to their ancestors').

The 20th Century was a maelstrom of change: technological, social, political and cultural. Indeed, the transformation began before 1900. In 1913, the French poet and essayist Charles Péguy observed that 'the world has changed less since the time of Jesus Christ than it has in the last thirty years'.[6] As the late art historian Robert Hughes put it:

> ... what did emerge from the growth of technical and scientific discovery, as the age of steam passed into the age of electricity, was the sense of an accelerated rate of change in all areas of human discourse, including art. From now the rules would quaver, the fixed canons of knowledge fail, under the pressure of new experience and the demand for new forms to contain it. Without this historic sense of cultural possibility, Arthur Rimbaud's injunction to be *absolument moderne* would have made no sense. With it, however, one could feel present at the end of one kind of history and the start of another, whose emblem was the Machine, many-armed and infinitely various, dancing like Shiva the creator in the midst of the longest continuous peace that European civilization would ever know.[7]

The war of 1914–18 shattered much of that confidence and unleashed a series of geopolitical shockwaves that, one might argue, can still be felt. The century was one of astonishing violence, of social upheaval, of scientific advance, of the rise and fall of Fordist factory practices and of unprecedented genocide (including an attempt to exterminate an entire people by bureaucratised, industrialised means). The 1950s and 1960s, in particular, were the playground of the cohort of changemakers in culture and social practice described by Christopher Booker in his book of the same name as the 'Neophiliacs'.[8] Thereafter, a consumerist, individualist consensus emerged in the West, launched by Reagan and Thatcher and sealed by Clinton and Blair. It was charged by a love of new technology, comfort, convenience and pleasure – what Michael Lewis called, in 1999, the 'New New Thing'.[9]

As in every age, there was strong resistance to this: a reactionary spirit that sought to thwart the march of modernisation.

This was, after all, the century of blood-and-soil fascism as well as of civil rights, of the burgeoning of fundamentalist religion around the world as well as the microchip, of G.K. Chesterton as well as the Beatles. The year in which the Berlin Wall came down was also the year in which the Iranian *fatwa* was declared against Salman Rushdie. Progress (not coterminous with change, of course) always vied with its opposite, as it always does.

So we must acknowledge that there is nothing new or unusual about resistance to change. But what we should not ignore is that *change itself has changed*. Until recently, it was possible for a US presidential candidate such as Bill Clinton to campaign on a slogan as simple as 'Change vs more of the same' (which found its British analogue in Tony Blair's 'New Labour, New Britain'). But now the framing of populist political narratives is very different.

Insurgent campaigns such as the Vote Leave movement and Donald Trump's presidential candidacy in 2016 were explicitly driven by a promise to *turn things back*. The Brexiteers pledged to 'Take *Back* Control', just as Trump swore that he would 'Make America Great *Again*' (my italics). In both cases, the populist message was that the sensation of loss and powerless-ness in the face of change felt, respectively, by British and American voters was wholly justified – and could be addressed by robust, straightforward measures that the wicked globalist elite was withholding from the public for its own nefarious reasons. Walls would be built, Brussels defied, bureaucrats tamed, experts treated with scepticism, immigration radically reduced ... all in the name of restoring equilibrium, a 'fair shake', 'common sense', the rights of the nation, the 'will of the people' and all the other snake-oil verbiage stored in the popu-list bottle.

In the final section of this book, I seek to adopt a more honest and nuanced approach to the question of change and innova-tion. I reject absolutely the simplistic script of the populist Right, which may win some campaigns but is hopeless as a play-book for government. I look at a handful of areas of policy and human experience that have been, are being and will continue to be transformed and ask how contemporary society can achieve greater resilience in the face of change and greater agency in the face of helplessness.

This is, by definition and without apology, work in progress. It is a good time to be sceptical of sloganeers and merchants of the quick fix. Business gurus such as John P. Kotter who have studied how organisations should handle change are especially withering about what he calls 'too much happy talk from senior management'.[10] Part of the trick, as Kotter writes, is to establish the 'sense of urgency . . . crucial to gaining needed cooperation' without sowing confusion and mayhem: and the fact that this *can* be achieved is shown by the levels of compliance with the national coronavirus lockdown announced by Boris Johnson on 23 March 2020. There is much to criticise in the UK's handling of the pandemic, but the effectiveness of the initial lockdown itself was remarkable – greater, indeed, than ministers expected.[11]

As Kotter, who is now an emeritus professor at Harvard Business School, puts it: 'A higher rate of urgency does not imply ever present panic, anxiety, or fear. It means a state in which complacency is virtually absent, in which people are always looking for both problems and opportunities, and in which the norm is "do it now." '[12]

I take as my starting point that the diagnosis of *metathesiophobia* mentioned above is a useful one. This particular psychiatric disorder has many symptoms, among them:

- Thought of change or of adapting to a new environment may prompt a full-blown panic attack. The phobic may experience a few or all of the following symptoms: heart palpitations, rapid or shallow breathing, shaking, trembling, sweating, nausea or gastrointestinal distress, inability to form words, dry mouth, thoughts of death, choking and extreme dread.
- Avoidance of change. The patient creates a 'comfort zone' and is unwilling to come out of it, often going to extreme lengths to remain within it – breaking connections, telling lies, making excuses.

- To avoid change, he or she may go to great lengths, break ties, tell lies or make excuses. This can affect his or her social, personal and professional life.
- The phobic may be aware that his fear of change is irrational. However, he is unable to overcome the strength of his emotions.[13]

Does this afflicted individual not remind you of many of the collective disorders of our time? The failure to communicate? The instantly triggered panic? The retreat into echo chambers? The readiness to pay a considerable price to evade or block out change? The bouts of temporary reasonableness that do not prevent the overall pattern of irrational behaviour?

At the root of the pathology – individual or collective – is basic neuroscience. The brain prefers predictable negative consequences over uncertain outcomes. It also prefers things which it believes to be tried, tested and older. So a group of test participants who are shown a picture and are told it was painted in 1901 will tend to react to it more favourably than if they are told it was painted in 2001. We fear tribal ridicule and public failure. Our default position is to hug that which is familiar.[14]

The Harvard social psychologist Daniel Gilbert explains this preference in the following terms: 'We come into the world with a passion for control and we go out of the world the same way. And research suggests that, if we lose the ability to control things at any point between our entrance and our exit, we become unhappy, helpless, hopeless, and depressed.'[15] This 'passion for control' would come as no surprise to Dominic Cummings, the strategic mastermind behind the Vote Leave campaign, who made the supposed recovery of this lost national agency the heart of the battle for Brexit.

In the broadest terms, then, the challenge is to help the mind respond with less panic and reflexive symptoms to change or its prospects. In his book on happiness, Jonathan Haidt writes that '[a]daptation is, in part, just a property of neurons. Nerve cells respond vigorously to new stimuli, but gradually they "habituate", firing less to stimuli that they have become used to. It is change that contains vital information, not steady states'.[16]

Perhaps the most influential – and certainly the most flamboyant – writer on this subject in recent years has been Nassim Nicholas Taleb, the Lebanese-American essayist and statistician, best known for his 2007 book *The Black Swan* on unpredictable, high-consequence events and their significance. But it was a later book, *Antifragile*, that became required reading in Number Ten when David Cameron was prime minister and, later, in the circle of Trump's chief strategist, Steve Bannon – and was even mentioned approvingly in an episode of the Showtime hedge fund drama, *Billions*.[17]

According to Taleb, it is positively desirable to be broken by adversity and misfortune – and to learn from it: 'Antifragility is beyond resilience or robustness. The resilient resists shocks and stays the same; the antifragile gets better.' We thrive as a species when we resist neurosis and yield to curiosity – which, Taleb writes, 'is antifragile, like an addiction, and is magnified by attempts to satisfy it – books have a secret mission and ability to multiply, as everyone who has wall-to-wall bookshelves knows well.'

His analysis is sometimes brilliant – on, for instance, what he calls the 'treadmilling techno-dissatisfaction' that drives us to buy new digital devices we probably don't really want – and his central thesis has some truth in it. There is much wisdom to be derived from failure, and, if we are lucky, greater strength. His contempt for those who still behave as if the safety nets of the old 20th-Century institutional life were still in place is absolutely justified: they are deluding themselves about the scope for such security in our times.

But Taleb's prescriptions – hard, in any case, to sift from his often-impenetrable prose – are, in my view, too pitilessly macho to be of much use except for those who are *already* tough enough to take the medicine of modern life but would like a manual to hone their techniques. Antifragility is a worthy objective, but no complex society that hoped to cohere, or claim itself decent, could use this book as a handbook.

Better, if we are to seek interdisciplinary help, to look at the work of psychologists and the lessons we can draw about adaptation to change. In particular, the school of 'systematic desensitisation' associated with Joseph Wolpe has much to teach those trying to address the anxieties of a society traumatised by change or its prospect.[18] Wolpe's core teaching was that adaptation took time and patience, and that, to replace avoidance techniques with active coping, patients needed to be given an infrastructure of reassurance that would enable them to evolve satisfactorily and without terror.

The celebrated French psychoanalyst and writer on trauma, Boris Cyrulnik – who himself survived the Nazi persecution of the Jews – notes that '[r]esilience has nothing to do with vulnerability or invulnerability, and is quite different from the psychoanalytic mechanism of resistance, which denies us access to the unconscious, but it may have something in common with the notion that the ego's defences have to be supported by something'.[19] Cyrulnik's world is one in which 'wounded winners' who discover resilience and the capacity to cope not 'inside ourselves or in our environment. It is something we find midway between the two, because our individual development is always linked to our social development'.[20]

The read-across from psychoanalysis to public policy is not straightforward, and must never be glib. But the present constellation of change that faces the world – and which seems, to some, so full of threat – is one that is not going to vanish in a puff of populist magical thinking. Its rigours must be addressed. We need a better way of dealing with innovation, disruption and upheaval because, whether we like it or not, they are coming our way, indefinitely. We need to think through our options with greater care, civility and social ambition. That is the purpose of this final section of the book.

CHAPTER 11

LEARNING TO LIVE WITH ROBOTS

We make angels – in the service of civilisation. Yes, there were bad angels once, I make good angels now. That is how I took us to nine new worlds. Nine – a child can count to nine on fingers. We should own the stars!
    Niander Wallace (Jared Leto), *Blade Runner 2049* (2017)

As so often, human imagination precedes the reach of technology: we have lived for thousands of years with fantasies, dreams and stories of automated superhumans, such as the Norse giant Mokkerkalfe, designed to take on Thor, and the servants built from gold by the god Hephaestus in the *Iliad*.[1] The robot has been a constant and morally ambiguous presence in movies: from the *Maschinenmensch* in Fritz Lang's *Metropolis* (1927), via the replicants in the *Blade Runner* franchise, to the David 8 android model played by Michael Fassbender in the *Alien* prequels and Alicia Vikander's Ava in Alex Garland's *Ex Machina* (2014). It is central to our hopes and fears that machines will both surpass and supplant us: mechanising most human labour and, in time, cerebration; but also threatening the primacy of carbon-based life forms.

In practice, of course, reality is carved from crooked timber, and the long-predicted rise of the robot has not followed a linear path.[2] In particular, the evolution of the artificial person has been thwarted by Moravec's Paradox, which was expressed thus in 1988 by the Austrian-Canadian technologist Hans Moravec: 'it is comparatively easy to make computers exhibit adult level

performance on intelligence tests or playing checkers, and difficult or impossible to give them the skills of a one-year-old when
it comes to perception and mobility'.[3]

What this means is that machines can beat a chess genius such
as Garry Kasparov but struggle to fold towels. In 2008, Bill Gates
famously predicted that there would soon be a robot in every
home, taking over most of the routine housework. True,
machines have made significant strides: in the past decade the
time it takes them to fold a towel has decreased from 25 minutes
to one. The robotic valet is now within sight. But not imminently
so. The advances made, for instance, by GPT-3 (generative pre-
trained transformer version three) technology by companies
such as OpenAI are mind-boggling: screenplays, poems, medical
advice, video games and guitar riffs all are now being generated
by computers that stand somewhere in the shadowland between
machine and mind.[4] But the machine that wrote you a poem
would still struggle to help you with your coat and show you to
the door.

Remember Roy Amara's rule from the last chapter: that people
tend to overestimate the impact of innovation in the short run,
but to underestimate it in the long run. The impact of automation on the job market may not be as sudden or overwhelming as
some have feared – though there is no doubt that its march has
been accelerated by the coronavirus pandemic, which has forced
companies to look for economies and cut labour costs and over-
heads wherever they can.[5] Panic is never a sound basis for public,
corporate and individual policy. But complacency can be even
worse.

As Brynjolfsson and McAfee warn, 'it's becoming harder and
harder to have confidence that any given task will be indefinitely
resistant to automation'.[6] A Brookings Institution report in 2019
concluded that about 36 million Americans hold jobs with 'high
exposure' to total replacement by machines – based on the calcu-
lation that 70 per cent of what they do could already be mechanised.[7] These conclusions were reached before the pandemic and
should be revised upwards in the light of the pressures to which
it has subjected all employers.

The extreme end of this debate is conjecture about the so-called 'singularity' – a hypothetical moment when AI becomes so sophisticated and powerful that it transcends and surpasses the human race (a school of prophecy most closely associated with the inventor and futurist Ray Kurzweil, who is excited about the prospective union of human and machine).[8] The principal intellectual objection to the notion of the singularity is that it is defined by its unpredictability.[9] Therefore, almost any speculation about it is, by definition, closer to science fiction than science: enjoyable but entirely speculative. It imports the tone and sometimes the content of theology to technological debate. As a consequence, it is an extremely unreliable guide to the measures that are needed to make individuals, companies and nations more resilient in the face of automation's advance.

To return to more measured forecasts: optimists argue that periods of productivity improvement brought about by technological change are initially disruptive to the workforce, but that this very improvement gives rise to investment in new enterprises that, in turn, create jobs for humans whose precise character is presently unknowable.[10] In 2017, a study by the International Federation of Robotics concluded:

> Used effectively, [robots] enable companies to become or remain competitive. This is particularly important for small-to-medium sized (SME) businesses that are the backbone of both developed and developing country economies. It also enables large companies to increase their competitiveness through faster product development and delivery. Increased use of robots is also enabling companies in high cost countries to 're-shore' or bring back to their domestic base parts of the supply chain that they have previously outsourced to sources of cheaper labour. Currently, the greatest threat to employment is not automation but an inability to remain competitive ... Automation has led overall to an increase in labour demand and positive impact on wages. Whilst middle-income / middle-skilled jobs have reduced as a proportion of overall contribution to

employment and earnings – leading to fears of increasing income inequality – the skills range within the middle-income bracket is large.[11]

The model pursued by optimists is one of 'mutual augmentation', where humans aspire to work alongside robots rather than in competition with them. The assumption underpinning this model is one that has proven safe to date but cannot, with honesty, be described as conceptually inviolable: namely, that there will always be aspects to work, involving, in particular, empathy, agreeableness, communicational nuance, personal care, compassion and an understanding of (for instance) humour, anger and anxiety, that machines cannot replicate. There may one day be machines that can empathise, or parry jokes, or comfort an anxious patient about to undergo surgery as effectively as an experienced nurse. What *can* be said is that such machines are not marching towards our places of work right now. So – as a bare minimum – we should plan for the arrival of the robots that we know *are* coming.

The late business guru Peter Drucker argued long before the digital revolution had begun in earnest that '[every] country, every industry, and every business will, in its decisions, have to take into serious consideration its competitive standing in the world economy and *the competitiveness of its knowledge competencies*' (my italics).[12] The challenge issued by Drucker is more important than ever, and is one that every employee, employer and government should take very seriously indeed. It is a staple of all such debates that businesses, aided by the state, should be devoting time, energy and resources to 'reskilling' or 'upskilling' their workers. But what does this actually mean?

In 2017, the Pew Research Center and Elon University surveyed 1,408 people engaged in technology and education to explore their expectations about the training of workers in the future. Two-thirds anticipated that new methods of schooling would emerge. But this broad optimism was balanced by a pessimism about detail and implementation. 'I have complete faith in the ability to identify job gaps and develop educational tools to address those gaps,' said Danah Boyd, a principal researcher at Microsoft Research and founder of Data and Society, a research institute. 'I have zero confidence in us having the political will to address the socio-economic factors that are underpinning skill training.'

Andrew Walls, managing vice president at Gartner, went further: 'Barring a neuroscience advance that enables us to embed knowledge and skills directly into brain tissue and muscle formation, there will be no quantum leap in our ability to "up-skill" people.' More immediately, there was the danger that retraining would become an elite activity rather than standard practice, as Beth Corzo-Duchardt, a media historian at Muhlenberg College, noted. 'The fact that a high degree of self-direction may be required in the new work force means that existing structures of inequality will be replicated in the future,' she said.[13]

There is no shortage of good intentions. In 2018, a report by McKinsey & Company found that 66 per cent of companies were 'addressing potential skills gaps related to automation/digitization' within their workforces as at least a 'top-ten priority.' Nearly 30 per cent put it in the top five. By a margin of nearly five to one, the executives surveyed saw retraining as the responsibility of companies themselves.[14]

Where the discussion blurs into platitude and fuzziness is when the question of specifics is broached. For decades, governments have declared themselves committed to 'lifelong learning'; companies often echo this sentiment. But what does this mean in practical terms? In truth, the programmes that have been launched in different countries to kick-start the process are patchy, inadequate and often wrapped in red tape. But from those that exist we can already extract the germ of best practice that *if massively proliferated* might make a difference to the employment prospects of this transitional generation:

- **Private–public partnerships**: examples include the Skill India Mission, a project to retrain millions of Indians, and the Singapore government's SkillsFuture programme, a national undertaking to provide citizens with career-long learning opportunities. The key to success is the sophistication of the liaison between government agencies, education organisations and businesses. The pandemic also inspired ingenious training collaborations between state and private sector: in Sweden, Scandinavian Airlines (SAS) worked with human resources experts and academics to prepare grounded cabin staff for work in health care. Other Swedish workers were fast-tracked into support roles in schools.[15]

- **Meaningful choice for school-leavers**: enhanced access to university education has had the unintended consequence of devaluing technical training. In Switzerland, in contrast, when students leave high school, they have a genuine choice between going to college or doing a two- or four-year employer-paid apprenticeship. Thereafter, they can enter the job market or continue their studies.
- **Individual learning accounts**: co-financed accounts, in which employers, employees and the state deposit funds, can give structure to in-work education. In France, private-sector workers are given a personal training account with their first job and can spend it on approved courses until retirement.
- **Tax breaks:** Finnish companies can write off spending on training that enables workers to keep their jobs, and individual taxpayers can deduct expenses in excess of a set annual amount incurred to acquire professional or vocational skills.
- **Retraining as investment**: in 2019, the World Economic Forum calculated that, with an investment of $19.9 billion, the US government could reskill 77 per cent of those workers expected to be supplanted by machines for new jobs, while generating a net positive return in the form of a greater tax take and lower welfare spending.[16]

As the Boston Consulting Group's Henderson Institute argued in November 2019, state intervention of this sort needs to be matched by corporate urgency: 'Companies should run strategic workforce demand-and-supply simulations to quantify mid- and long-term talent gaps. They should complement this by classifying current skills needed for different jobs and mapping them against future needs on a regular basis. Doing this will allow them to assess what kind of upskilling they might need to do and how best to target their efforts. To create a database of employee skills, companies can use emerging tools such as game-based assessments of skills and behaviors or collect data on skills from social media sites'.[17]

Such coherence is unusual and involves sheer stamina, cultural commitment and heavy lifting as much as acute business strategy. In 2018, for example, Dentsply Sirona, a global manufacturer of dental products and technology, undertook a root-and-branch skills overhaul of this sort, involving 15,000 employees in 40 countries. This involved training in digital skills, fresh emphasis upon customer (ahead of product) and an intensive 20-hour webinar course for a new cohort of 'clinical development managers'. The company's dental academy went on to train 470,000 dental professionals in 97 countries.

Likewise, Walmart, the US retail giant, established its own training academy in 200 stores in 2017 and also phased in an online-learning platform for its 1.4 million employees in America. Much of this involved the acquisition of digital skills in partnership with IBM and other partner companies. The notion of 'de-learning' is gaining traction – the difficult task of persuading seasoned employees to ditch tried-and-tested procedures in order to prepare them for hybrid work patterns where they will increasingly be interacting with machines and robots (as well as – where applicable – working from home).[18]

Such case studies in good practice are not as commonplace as they need to be. According to Mercer's *Global Talent Trends 2020* survey, many employers report 'time poverty' as an obstacle to change – which is another way of saying that they are not ready to release their workforce for the hours involved for reskilling (training for new jobs) or upskilling (training for existing jobs that require new skills). According to the Mercer's study, only 45 per cent of employers believed that their workers could adapt to the new demands facing them. Yet 77 per cent of employees expressed a readiness for such training.[19] Herein lies the all-important decision facing companies in the next decade: whether to bite the bullet and commit resources to retraining on a grand scale or to haemorrhage money on redundancy packages and rehiring.

There is no one-size-fits-all answer to this dilemma.[20] But the extent to which workers, employers and governments collaborate successfully to retrain employees – iteratively, in many cases – will have huge social consequences. The recessionary impact of the pandemic is already driving up unemployment. Automation will certainly compound the problem: the question is by how much. Action now, of an imaginative and determined character, will at least mitigate the problem, and spare millions of people from the trauma of the sack and the risk of long-term exclusion from the labour market with all its well-established collateral effects upon mental health, social cohesion and public confidence (not to mention the colossal cost to the taxpayer of unemployment benefits).

Parallel to this germinal discussion – can we prepare the workforce for the coming storm? – runs an older one, which has acquired fresh and vivid significance. The case for a universal basic income (UBI) – or versions of it – has a venerable pedigree. In his 1797 pamphlet *Agrarian Justice*, Thomas Paine argued that everyone should be given a lump sum upon reaching adulthood to compensate for the accidents of birth. Martin Luther King declared himself 'convinced that the simplest approach will prove to be the most effective – the solution to poverty is to abolish it directly by a now widely discussed measure: the guaranteed income'.[21]

To an intriguing extent, the idea has attracted support across the political spectrum: not only embracing progressives but Friedrich Hayek and Milton Friedman, the philosopher-kings of the 20th-Century New Right, and President Richard Nixon. Friedman's version was a 'negative income tax' which would have involved a wage cut-off point below which the government would have paid the worker a notional rebate per dollar (say, for instance, 50 per cent of every dollar below $20,000 – a credit of $10,000).

Amongst contemporary thinkers, Rutger Bregman argues that 'we should give free money to everyone' while Martin Ford is more circumspect in describing a guaranteed income as, on balance, 'the best overall solution to the rise of automation technology'.[22] Though UBI or variants upon it have been tried in pilot form at many places and times around the world, the idea has fallen foul of the embedded capitalist notion that handing out money is a disincentive to work (which it often is).[23]

But what if the supply of work was radically diminished by the advance of machines? How would any society ensure that its citizens had at least a minimum income to prevent them slipping into absolute poverty? And might not such a safety net also act as a launch pad for enterprise and creativity, giving people the basic security they required to take risks and look for value that machines could not provide?

Even as automation has loomed over the global labour market, resistance to UBI has remained powerful. But the storm of the pandemic overturned the old orthodoxy that such payments were inevitably damaging to the operations of the labour market and incentives to work. In the UK, Chancellor Rishi Sunak's huge 'furloughing' scheme pumped public funds into the bank accounts of inactive workers (via their employers) to maximise the survival chances of their jobs and the businesses they worked for.

In the US, individuals earning less than $99,000 per annum received an initial $1,200 'stimulus cheque' (and more for those with children under 18).[24] Though these were temporary schemes designed to build a bridge between a frozen economy and prospective recovery, they normalised at a stroke the notion that even right-wing governments could reach deep into the public purse to hand over significant payments to *individuals* facing economic stress.

In a matter of weeks, an idea that had been confined to seminars and think tanks – the realm of hypothesis – was forced by epidemiological horror into the political mainstream.[25] The arguments for and against UBI are as they were pre-coronavirus. The difference is that the notion now sits within the realm of the possible. It remains doubtful that a full-blown version of UBI will be adopted by an advanced democracy in the near future. But the terms of trade have changed fundamentally; and it is all but certain that the multi-faceted response of our societies to the challenge of automation will include help from the state – and necessarily so. Resilience against robots cannot be nurtured by government fiat alone. Equally, the citizen will certainly need the active state at her side as we learn to live, work and prosper with the machines. In this, as in so many other respects, the old order changeth.

CHAPTER 12

CENTURY OF CENTURIES: THE CHALLENGE OF LIVING LONGER

The most testing time of our lives has shifted from the multiple perils of infancy and childhood to the long, sad, incremental shutdown of old age. The modern version of the workhouse is the nursing home.
A.A. Gill, *The Sunday Times*, 5 January 2014

One of the most unpopular newspaper columns I have ever written – for which I am still occasionally reprimanded on social media – appeared in the *Guardian* on Monday 22 May 2017. Its subject was the Conservative Party's manifesto for the snap election called by the then prime minister, Theresa May. She herself was not suited to the top job, and the campaign itself was a disaster – culminating on 8 June with the loss of the Tory Party's House of Commons majority (and a brief period thereafter of national Jeremy Corbyn-mania, in which the result was interpreted as a moral victory for the Labour Left).

All the same: the manifesto was a bold text, full of strong ideas and strategic proposals that, in different circumstances, would have kept an administration fruitfully busy for years. Its most important contention was that 'government can and should be a force for good – and its power should be put squarely at the service of this country's working people.' It proposed, in effect, an end to the Thatcherite inheritance of the Eighties, and a recognition that the 21st Century presented a series of challenges that could not simply be delegated to the invisible hand of the market. 'We do not believe in untrammelled free markets,' the manifesto declared. 'We reject the cult of selfish individualism. We abhor social division, injustice, unfairness and inequality. We see rigid dogma and ideology not just as needless but dangerous.'

Its sub-headings alone were unexpected in a Conservative Party document: 'the gender pay gap', 'the race gap', 'the mental health gap' and 'the disability gap'. Most audacious of all was its proposal that those with assets worth more than £100,000 would be expected to draw upon them to pay for their care when elderly (while not actually facing the risk of losing their homes during their lifetimes). It was hard, I wrote, 'to exaggerate what a shift this represents in the official Conservative attitude to wealth and its fiscal status.' As it turned out, almost none of the manifesto's promises would be enacted in the May government's dire final two years. But – at the time – it seemed right to acknowledge its significance as the 'most adventurous restatement of Conservatism since Margaret Thatcher and her allies smashed the . . . postwar consensus'.[1]

The speed and brutality with which the social care pledge unravelled during the campaign was extraordinary. As Nick Timothy, May's co-chief of staff, recalls in his book *Remaking One Nation*, the press quickly labelled the proposals a 'dementia tax'. The party's press officers briefed that the policy was to cap care costs at a maximum of £100,000, whereas the whole point was to impose a floor at that level below which nobody would have to pay for their care costs:

MPs and candidates struggled to explain the policy on the doorstep. Theresa herself failed to articulate it well: asked by the media how many people would have to sell their homes to pay for their care, she should have said, 'unlike now, nobody.' But she talked around the subject and failed to answer the question directly. After failing to fight back, or even to explain the policy properly, we all accepted we need to execute a U-turn.[2]

The substitute policy was messy, defensively presented ('Nothing has changed!' May insisted, when it patently had), and undermined the core promise of the campaign that she offered 'strong and stable' government. Such is the pitiless heat of a general election. But May's credibility and the Conservative Party's majority were not the only casualties of this fiasco. It hugely elevated the political radioactivity pulsing from a question that successive governments had simply failed to address: how to pay for the care of an ageing population and to ensure that that care was of a decent quality?

The failure of political will to resolve this question in the UK is little short of scandalous.[3] In 1999, the Labour-appointed Royal Commission on Long Term Care concluded that the present system, which starts to drain elderly residents' savings and income above a relatively low level, was untenable and that 'long-term care is a risk that is best covered by some kind of risk pooling.' Nothing came of the commission's findings.

In July 2010, David Cameron established Andrew Dilnot's Commission on Funding of Care & Support, which reported a year later. It concluded that individuals should contribute the first £35,000 of their care if they had more than £100,000 in assets – after which, the government would shoulder the burden. A version of Dilnot's findings was enacted in the Care Act of 2014 – legislation that, to the dismay of those who had fought for it, was not implemented by the Cameron government after it was re-elected with a clear Tory majority in 2015. In Boris Johnson's first speech as prime minister in July 2019, he promised to 'fix the crisis in social care once and for all'. At the time of writing, there is no apparent prospect of such a solution.

The case study of the 2017 general election campaign is important in this dismal narrative because it encapsulates a greater truth about contemporary politics: what happens when complex reality collides with the human instinct not to engage with difficulty, or upheaval, or additional responsibility of one sort or another. Indeed, the question of how to fund social care properly and fairly as more and more people require such assistance is only one of many issues raised by what might be described as the *species innovation* of increased life expectancy. We need to see the new shape of a human life, its extended duration and what its different phases mean through new lenses. The longer we resist that all-important shift, the more trouble we shall be storing up for ourselves.

In this respect, political will lags far behind a school of thinkers and policymakers who are addressing this question not as a pathology – primarily a medical and fiscal problem – but as an exciting opportunity for humankind. In their books *The 100-Year Life* and *The New Long Life*, Andrew J. Scott and Lynda Gratton argue that '[w]hat is striking is the contrast between the magnitude of change that society will embark upon as people live longer, and the relatively limited response from corporations and governments. Even more remarkable is the general lack of awareness of the agenda and issues. Saying that corporates and governments are "behind the curve" doesn't even come close'.[4]

The paradigm used by businesses and governments, they write, is based upon seriously obsolete assumptions about a world in which life expectancy, medical breakthroughs, improved nutrition, shifting relationships between the generations and dramatic changes in working patterns are (or should be) transforming the terms of trade:

> Too much policy is based on the assumption of a three-stage and a seventy-year-long life; that the key assets of firms are physical capital, such as machinery and real estate; and that most careers are spent in full-time employment anchored to a specific firm. Government policy must instead address the reality of a multistaged hundred-year life . . . This will involve rewiring existing institutions, polices and regulations in order to minimise the potential bad outcomes and support good outcomes.[5]

It is remarkable to consider that there are now, for the first time ever, more people on the planet aged over 65 than under five. In the last century, average life expectancy increased by 30 years in most developed nations (top of the table are men born in Switzerland, who have an average life expectancy at birth of 82, and Japanese women who live to around 87).[6] In the UK, between 1970 and 2011, life expectancy at 65 increased 20 times as fast as in the previous century. Progress is not uniformly linear – in February 2020 a review by Sir Michael Marmot found that life expectancy in England had stalled for the first time in more than 100 years – but the overall trend is clear enough.[7]

According to the Office for National Statistics, there are nearly 12 million people aged 65 and above in the UK, and 5.4 million over 75. The number of British centenarians has increased 85 per cent in the past 15 years. By 2030, there are expected to be more than 21,000 centenarians living in the UK. By 2066, seven per cent of the population is expected to be 85 or older.[8]

As Camilla Cavendish – former head of the Downing Street policy unit and now a member of House of Lords – points out in her own study of the ageing world, the possibilities and challenges of longevity should be considered in the round and as a broad spectrum of opportunity, rather than a grim inventory of therapeutic, remedial and palliative dilemmas. Indeed, the most pressing imperative is to persuade today's young and middle-aged to take nutrition seriously and to exercise – 'future-proofing' themselves as far as possible from ill health and a declining quality of later life. Cavendish is rightly open-minded about the potential of experimental medication to mitigate or suppress the effects of ageing but her emphasis upon regular exercise, buttressed by continued human interaction, and, increasingly, intergenerational living is also the right cultural backdrop against which such scientific advances need to be considered.

In this respect, the structure of care matters as much as the way in which it is financed – the highly humanised, non-profit *Buurtzorg* system in the Netherlands being an example of best practice. There is promise, too, in Germany's government-funded intergenerational households or *Mehrgenerationhauser*

– a means of combining economies of scale with the elixir of day-to-day human contact.[9]

Necessarily, this involves a redrawing of the intergenerational contract. And this is happening already. Around the world, millennial families are only half as likely to own a property as baby boomers were by the same age. In 1983, average older households were about eight times better off than younger families; by 2013, the multiple had risen to 20. Worse – in the present structure – the young face a future of paying ever greater taxes to subsidise the benefits and healthcare of their elders. As she writes, 'A basic principle must surely be that no generation should be asked to provide a higher level of support for the older generation than it can expect to receive'.[10]

I strongly suspect that this will involve a tax on disposable assets before too long. There are both strategic and tactical reasons why this is so. The first is that the notion of bricks and mortar as the fullest expression of the 'property-owning democracy' – a phrase coined by the Conservative MP Noel Skelton in the *Spectator* in 1923 – took as its silent assumption a much shorter lifespan: home owners paying off their mortgages, enjoying a relatively short retirement and then bequeathing to the next generation what remained of their estate after inheritance tax. Thus did Thatcher encourage the purchase of council houses by their occupiers, John Major envisage 'wealth cascading down the generations' and David Cameron insulate most home-owners with property worth £1m from any death duties.

Almost a century since Skelton wrote, however, we have a young generation that (in far too many cases) can only dream of owning a home, and ageing property-owners, who have benefited hugely from the housing market boom, paid off their mortgages and now literally inhabit, in their homes, the wealth that pure chance has bestowed upon them. They have also benefited from the so-called 'triple lock' introduced in 2010 which means that the state pension increases by the greatest of the following three measures: average earnings; prices, as measured by the Consumer Prices Index (CPI); and 2.5 per cent.

Politicians are habitually terrified of upsetting the so-called 'grey vote': older citizens who, proportionately, are more likely than their children and grandchildren to turn out on polling day. But the balance is shifting fast. In rational terms, the case for student fees and loans is strong: a degree increases an individual's earning potential, the debts are only payable after a certain salary level is reached by the graduate and the self-funding system has also enabled universities to admit more students (almost 33 per cent of all 18-year-olds in 2017).[11] Yet – to a remarkable extent – fees have become symbolic of a deeply felt sense of generational injustice: an anger that today's young people are paying for an experience that the older generation got for free in the 20th Century. Nick Clegg's U-turn on his Liberal Democrat pledge to vote against any increase in student fees was the emblematic cause of his party's electoral meltdown in the 2015 election.

This sense of generational imbalance meshes with a growing public alarm over the disproportionate extent to which the wealthy have gained from recent economic growth. This is a planetary phenomenon: according to the Credit Suisse Global Wealth report, the world's richest one per cent, now own 44 per cent of the world's wealth. Meanwhile, those with less than $10,000 in wealth make up 56.6 per cent of the world's population, but account for less than 2 per cent of global wealth.[12] In the UK, the top one per cent owns 21 per cent of total national wealth, while the top five per cent accounts for 40 per cent.

Such statistics help to explain why boastful rhetoric about aggregate GDP or declining levels of absolute poverty is such an inadequate response to the Left's concerns about deepening inequality and the populist Right's courting of those who feel 'left behind'. It is indisputably the case that, in relative terms, the majority is indeed being left ever further behind by a tiny group of the spectacularly wealthy. This is not a recipe for social cohesion, political trust or public optimism. It is also helping to remove the aura of partial inviolability from taxation that used to surround fixed assets, especially the home.

The polling evidence is unequivocal: the public now supports such taxation. In January 2020, a *Reuters*/Ipsos survey in the US found that 64 per cent agreed that 'the very rich should contribute an extra share of their total wealth each year to support public programs'.[13] In March of the same year, a BMG/ *Independent* poll in the UK reported strong support for wealth taxes: 63 per cent backed a 'mansion tax' on properties worth over £1m, while 62 per cent supported new higher-rate council tax bands for such assets. As a general proposition, almost half (49 per cent) backed a new wealth tax levied on the total value of an individual's assets, with less than a quarter (23 per cent) opposing the idea.[14]

To take the specific needs of social care for the elderly: the solution may not lie in general taxation on wealth. In Germany, under the mandatory long-term care insurance fund introduced in 1994, employees pay a compulsory levy which employers must top up. In Japan, workers over 40 have paid a national tax since 2000, leading to means-tested co-payments for specific services. A similar idea was floated in the UK without much success in the summer of 2020; an alternative under consideration is to fold social care costs into National Insurance payments, with top-ups paid for by equity release. There is no shortage of hybrid ideas in the Westminster ether, but none of them has yet captured the collective imagination of the political class.

This leads me to the tactical reasons why now is as good a moment as we may get to bite the bullet of wealth taxes. As Lord O'Donnell, the former head of the Civil Service and Cabinet Secretary, observed in July 2020, the nature of the debate has been transformed by Covid-19. The pandemic, he said, had created 'a clear burning platform' for tax reform. 'We know that Covid has a very unequal impact. The economic impact is particularly hard on the young, women and those on lower incomes – that is going to create a feeling of "it's not fair",' O'Donnell said. 'You've got a Conservative party and prime minister talking about the red/blue wall [formerly Labour seats which switched to the Tories in the 2019 election]. How to get to the forgotten man . . . One nation conservatism. Lots of different things suggest to me that there might be more of an appetite for [a wealth tax] than you might have thought politically from a Conservative government that came in with a manifesto that basically said no to all sorts of different tax changes'.[15]

The former Whitehall chief is right to imply that coronavirus is a horribly unwelcome disruption that may nonetheless provide political space for welcome reform – and make possible radical measures that were previously beyond the scope of practical politics, which would give the UK greater resilience in the face of long-term risks and challenges. And while I agree with those who say that we must look at longevity in the round – from personal conduct to macroeconomic trends – it is undeniable that the pandemic has lifted the lid on the horror of many care facilities and added fresh urgency to the ending of this national disgrace.

As the epigraph to this chapter by the late and much-missed A.A. Gill makes clear, the condition in which all too many care home residents live is not really a secret – rather, it is a matter of collective shame to which most have been unwilling to draw too much attention. When the light floods in, the picture is grim indeed. Here is Alan Bennett describing, in 2005, the 'gaunt pile' in Weston-super-Mare where his mother Lilian was living:

> The turnover of residents is quite rapid since whoever is quartered in this room is generally in the later stages of dementia. But that is not what they die of. None of these lost women can feed herself and to feed them properly, to spoon in sufficient mince and mashed carrot topped off with rhubarb and custard to keep them going, demands the personal attention of a helper, in effect one helper per person. Lacking such one-to-one care, these helpless creatures slowly and quite respectably starve to death. This is not something anybody acknowledges, not the matron or the relatives (if, as is rare, they visit) and not the doctor who makes out the death certificates. But it is so.[16]

As coronavirus tore through residential care homes in the spring and early summer of 2020, a humbling new version of Bennett's tableau from 15 years before was suddenly blasted across the political panorama. Elderly people were dying in their thousands, in isolation, segregated from their relatives, spoken to only by medical staff and carers in whatever protective equipment their facilities could afford. All too many of these 'homes', it became clear, were barely worthy of the name: reduced to under-resourced, inhumane silos of death and despair. In one of the worst errors made by the government, elderly people with Covid-19 were discharged from hospital to care institutions, which quickly became charnel houses of infection. Between 2 March and 12 June, almost 66,000 care home residents died in England and Wales, compared to just under 37,000 deaths over the same period in 2019. Only 20,000 of the excess 30,000 were directly attributed to coronavirus – although there remains considerable doubt about the level of testing, especially in the early weeks, and (as a result) the extent to which doctors filling in death certificates were able to ascribe a death to the virus with confidence.[17]

In August 2020, the all-parliamentary group on coronavirus heard shaming evidence from charities that many care home residents were 'losing the will to live' in what felt to them like medicalised jails – still often unable to see their relatives, grieving in isolation for spouses or friends and able to interact much less than before with their fellow residents. In the words of Helen Wildbore, director of the Relatives and Residents Association: 'Sadly, many of the callers to our helpline have been telling us that the current situation in care homes is now very much like a prison, with such restricted visiting, residents unable to leave the grounds of the home, and limited interactions with other residents and staff.' This was having a 'really devastating impact' on the mental and physical well-being of residents – and those outside were 'seeing their relative slowly deteriorate' on video calls.[18]

This is not tolerable, and we have, so to speak, an opportunity not to tolerate it: a period in which the wounds of the pandemic will still be raw and it will be legitimate to expect government, corporations and civil society to respond with urgency to this problem (even as we look more broadly at the issues raised by increased life expectancy). There is no shortage of wealth in this country to be taxed – and, sooner or later, it will have to be taxed to address the growing needs of the National Health Service and the national care system that should now be established, with vigour and political courage, to make sure that this pandemic marks an end to an era of shame in the way in which we treated the elderly in this country. If the measure of a society is the way in which it treats its vulnerable members, then our collective mission could scarcely be clearer.

CHAPTER 13

MISINFORMATION – HOW TO BE RESILIENT IN THE AGE OF POST-TRUTH

I hold it, therefore, certain, that to open the doors of truth, and to fortify the habit of testing everything by reason, are the most effectual manacles we can rivet on the hands of our successors to prevent their manacling the people with their own consent.

Thomas Jefferson, Letter to Judge John Tyler
Washington, 28 June 1804

In 2017, I took part in more than 100 events around the world on fake news, digitised propaganda, conspiracy theories and misinformation. The problem had surged into popular consciousness after the Brexit vote and Donald Trump's election victory in 2016 – and Oxford Dictionaries had made 'post-truth' its word of the year, defining it as '. . . circumstances in which objective facts are less influential in shaping public opinion than appeals to emotion and personal belief'.[1]

There is nothing new, of course, about lying, a practice as old as communication itself. But the study of post-truth is not about lies; it is about their consumption. Less about the liars, more about those to whom they lie. We live in an age in which the collapse of trust in institutions, experts and hitherto-standard sources has transformed the way in which we consume information. Simultaneously, digital technology has weaponised the primacy of emotion over fact: it amplifies the shrill, rewards intensity with traffic and drives users algorithmically towards content that bolsters prejudices instead of challenging them. In this setting, truth is not determined by reasoned evaluation, assessment and conclusion. You pick your own truth, as if from a menu.

At the seminars, conferences and book events in which I took part, there was always a sense of anxiety that something had gone badly wrong, often matched by a scepticism that much could be done about it. A compulsive liar was in the White House; the UK's exit from the European Union had been secured on the basis of demonstrable falsehoods; social media was a cacophony of phoney news; Holocaust denial was on the rise once more; and pseudoscience and therapeutic snake oil were not only gaining in power, but, in some quarters, positively voguish. Who, or what, could possibly turn back this tide of fakery, mendacity and misrepresentation?

Most moving were my experiences in countries that had experienced autocracy in the relatively recent past – especially Slovenia and Chile. In Santiago, I was taken to see Morandé 80, the street address of a door on the east side of the presidential palace, the Palacio de la Moneda, from which President Salvador Allende's body was removed in the 1973 military coup. Chileans are not remotely sanguine about fake news, or the rise of the populist Right in the West, or the use of social media to propagate lies and whip up ugly emotion. They have seen – albeit in the analogue age – where such things lead, and they do not want to see them again. They watch with justified anxiety as democracies vote for autocrats, as societies that have not recently experienced tyranny flirt with its practices, as foreign powers intervene in electoral processes with apparent impunity.

Sadly, the situation is worse than it was in 2017. Trump may be gone, but the mendacious networks of Trumpism still fizz with falsehood. There is ever clearer evidence of disruptive practices by Russian-controlled agencies, promoting antagonism on social media between, for instance, United Muslims of America and the Army of Jesus; and Black Lives Matter and the pro-police Blue Lives Matter campaigns. Bots swirl through the system telling lies about electoral processes to encourage selective voter suppression. In polarised societies, small swings can make all the difference – so micro-targeting is potentially very effective. As Philip N. Howard describes this information ecosystem:

> Lie machines have a purpose. They deliberately misrepresent symbols. They appeal to emotions and prejudices and use our cognitive biases to bypass rational thought. They repeat big political lies to misinform some people and introduce doubt among even the most active and knowledgeable citizens . . . But they are all made up of the same core components: political actors producing the lies, social media firms doing the distribution, and paid consultants doing the marketing.[2]

As these machines do their work, we are witnessing a deeply troubling epistemological innovation: which is to say, the declining value of truth as society's reserve currency and the spread of dangerous relativism masquerading as legitimate scepticism. Yes, there is greater consciousness than there was of fake news and digital fraudulence, and a measure of political pressure to do something about it. But the number of politicians who truly understand what is happening and how to address it is alarmingly small. One such is the Conservative MP Damian Collins, who, as chair of the Commons Digital, Culture, Media and Sport Select Committee, was the driving force behind its report on disinformation and fake news in February 2019 – arguably the best blueprint for action yet produced.[3] In any rational democracy, Collins would be a senior minister. Under Boris Johnson's populist leadership of the Conservative Party, he is no longer even chair of the Select Committee: make of that what you will.

Most politicians, however, are embarrassingly illiterate on the question of digital misinformation and its infrastructure. On the day that I appeared before the select committee alongside Carole Cadwalladr (the formidable *Observer* journalist who had done more than any other reporter to reveal the extent of digital manipulation of information and electoral procedures), one MP asked me what, exactly, an 'app' was.[4] This, let us say, did not inspire confidence.

In the US, meanwhile, the figureheads of big tech companies such as Facebook's Mark Zuckerberg have run rings around their supposed interrogators in a series of congressional hearings. As Rana Foroohar remarks in her book on the tech industry: 'their vague promises to "do better" and spurious claims that they simply can't police activity on their own platforms, just underscore the need for a cohesive regulatory framework around private companies that have amassed too much power'.[5]

The pandemic raised understandable hopes that the daily firestorm of lies would be counterbalanced by a renewed inclination to listen to scientists who knew what they were talking about and, if heeded, could help the public take action to save lives. In the US, especially, Dr Anthony Fauci, the long-time director of the National Institute of Allergy and Infectious Diseases, became something of a media hero as he calmly urged Americans at White House briefings to behave responsibly and be guided by science rather than whim, impatience or prejudice.[6] But – as the campaign to control the spread of the virus became a front in the culture wars – Fauci received death threats and, with incredulity, was forced to take security measures to protect himself and his family. As he said in August 2020: 'I wouldn't have imagined in my wildest dreams that people who object to things that are pure public health principles are so set against it and don't like what you and I say, namely in the world of science, that they actually threaten you'.[7]

As early as March 2020, Tortoise Media, working with the Bruno Kessler Foundation in Italy, compiled a report on the new contagion of untruths during the pandemic, identifying 275,000 Twitter accounts that had already posted 1.7 million links to unreliable information about coronavirus. The most viral claims included, allegations that Chinese scientists had covertly manufactured the pathogen; that drinking bleach could cure Covid-19; that Pope Francis had tested positive; and that new 5G technology caused the sickness.[8] By August, these falsehoods were joined by posts about harmful ingredients found in potential vaccines; and – especially – by conspiracy theories about the origins and alleged beneficiaries of the coronavirus pandemic, such as the bizarre contention that Bill Gates had masterminded the plague in order to plant microchips in us all.[9]

Most depressing of all, perhaps, was to observe these preposterous claims lead to harmful action. In the 18 hours after Trump suggested that injecting bleach might indeed be a treatment for coronavirus, New York City's Poison Control Center dealt with 30 cases of exposure to the cleaning agent.[10] So much impact did the lies about 5G have that a series of physical attacks were made on the mobile phone masts – including, unbelievably, one that served a Nightingale Hospital for coronavirus patients, isolated and totally dependent upon FaceTime and phone conversations to maintain even minimal contact with their loved ones. Deplorably, a number of BT engineers were assaulted because of their supposed involvement in this non-existent conspiracy.

In April, a lie previously confined to social media migrated to mainstream television, on ITV's *This Morning* show. Eamonn Holmes – notionally, the epitome of middle-market common sense – took issue with his colleague Alice Beer who, quite correctly, had dismissed the claims as 'ridiculous' and 'incredibly stupid'. In response, Holmes declared that 'what I don't accept is mainstream media immediately slapping [the 5G theory] down as not true, when they don't know it's not true. No one should attack or damage or do anything like that – but it's very easy to say it is not true because it suits the state narrative'.

Holmes duly retracted his statements on 5G and was reprimanded by the regulator Ofcom. More worrying was the fact that so experienced and prominent a broadcaster should have spouted such nonsense at all. Why do conspiracy theories

– however absurd – gain such traction and, all too frequently, a degree of respectability? Because, in the words of the academic psychologist Rob Brotherton, they 'pave over messy, bewildering, ambiguous reality with a simple explanation'.[11]

Faced with a global peril as frightening as Covid-19, some will always be drawn to the (limited) consolation of culpability and causality – someone is to blame for all this – which may be easier to handle psychologically than the cruelty and caprice of pandemic reality. Such fictitious claims are as old as anti-Semitism and witch-hunts. The difference is that that, today, they are turbo-charged to an unprecedented extent by social media – and often batter their way on to traditional channels, too. Yet again, in our networked world, the distinction between mainstream and fringe is blurred to the point of non-existence.

Though the alarm was initially triggered by post-truth in politics, the surge in pseudoscience is no less worrying. My own trade – journalism – has been far too indulgent in its breathless coverage of celebrity-endorsed snake oil and fashionable 'complementary medicine'. In September 2018, Gwyneth Paltrow's lifestyle company, Goop, was fined $145,000 in California over bogus claims that its vaginal eggs 'balance hormones, regulate menstrual cycles, prevent uterine prolapse, and increase bladder control'.

In the UK the following month, Goop was referred to National Trading Standards and the Advertising Standards Authority, over 113 alleged breaches of advertising law. But such complaints did nothing to dissuade Paltrow's followers from paying £1,000 a ticket to attend Goop's 'Wellness Summit' in London in June 2019.

Celebrity now poses a dangerous challenge to medical expertise. It is a key principle of the scientific revolution that, in healthcare, the only treatments and medications that should be deployed are those that have been subjected to randomised, double-blind, placebo-controlled testing. Of course, such trials are time-consuming and costly.

In contrast, the cheerleaders of alternative therapies tell tales of miracle cures brought about, they claim, by the right mix of detoxifying juices, the ingestion of charcoal or the rebalancing of chakras. Such stories often draw (supposedly) on the wisdom of the East, but are aimed squarely at the impatience of the West. More importantly, correlation is not causation; and the plural of anecdote is not data. What is generally cited as 'evidence' by the advocates of complementary medicine is no such thing.

Nor is the growing use of such pseudo-medication harmless: far from it. According to a landmark survey published in 2018 in the academic journal *JAMA Oncology*, collating evidence from around 1,300 patients, those who used complementary treatments were more than twice as likely to die at any point during the nine-year study – usually because they declined to complete courses of conventional therapy.[12] This is especially sad at a time when advances in oncology – especially in immunotherapy and algorithmically designed protocols for specific tumours – mean that, by mid-century, cancer should be, at worst, a chronic condition.

Unfortunately, the medical profession has not been spared the decline in trust in institutions and expertise. The notion that healthcare systems are in league with Big Pharma against the interests of patients has proved especially toxic – and has meant that disgraced individuals such as Andrew Wakefield, struck off for his discredited claim that there is a potential link between the measles, mumps and rubella vaccine and the rising incidence of diagnosed autism, have acquired a completely undeserved aura of heroism. Alongside the bogus new status enjoyed by Wakefield and his allies, there is the delusion that expertise has migrated to the informed amateur Internet from the special interest groups of the medical profession and the pharmaceutical industry.

Again, this has led to measurable social harms, and – in particular – the return of measles as a serious threat to public health in Western countries.[13] Indeed, so powerful has the 'anti-vaxx' movement become that – even in the middle of a pandemic that had, by then, claimed more than 750,000 lives worldwide – a study in August 2020 by Ipsos Mori and King's College London found that only half of Britons said they would definitely have a vaccination to protect them against Covid-19, if one were developed and marketed. Which is to say: for the other half, suspicion of vaccinations in general or of this particular inoculation (not yet available at the time of the poll) was so great that, at least in principle, it trumped their desire to get back to life, business and recreation as normal.[14] One could ask for no more vivid illustration of the grotesque power of pseudoscience, misinformation and post-truth in our times.

The question, then, is what to do about it. Samuel Woolley, a professor at the University of Texas in Austin, has argued that we require 'a kind of cognitive immunity' to fight off these new strains of viral misinformation.[15] This is an astute way of approaching the problem – and Woolley is also right that 'Band-Aid approaches focused on triaging help for the most egregious issues and oversights associated with the infrastructure of Web 2.0' will not be sufficient.[16] A systemic, multi-faceted response is needed – comparable, as he puts it, to the resilience measures in place to prepare for earthquakes and natural disasters. We should be tracking digital deception as we do seismic shifts and menacing weather.

Of all the green shoots to emerge, one of the most impressive is the fact-checking industry – especially Full Fact, whose chief executive, Will Moy, has transformed this independent charity into a formidable force for good, chasing misinformation in real time and holding liars and frauds to account.[17] There are now ever-more sophisticated applications that detect bots and photo-fakery, such as BotCheck, SurfSafe, Botometer and FotoForensics. The Hamilton 2.0 dashboard produced by the Alliance for Securing Democracy at the German Marshall Fund of the United States is a remarkable tool for the interception of misinformation by Russian, Chinese or Iranian state actors.[18]

As for content moderation by the main tech platforms, there has been some progress, especially in territories – such as Germany – where there is a genuine risk of prosecution or serious reputational damage. But the improvements remain slow. After the slaughter of 50 Muslim worshippers in two mosques in

Christchurch, New Zealand, in March 2019, the livestreamed video was seen millions of times on Facebook and YouTube. As Jacinda Ardern, New Zealand's prime minister, said, the horrific episode made clear that there was a fundamental moral principle at stake: 'We cannot simply sit back and accept that these platforms just exist and that what is said on them is not the responsibility of the place where they are published. They are the publisher, not just the postman. It cannot be a case of all profit, no responsibility'.[19]

It is endlessly pointed out by the main tech companies that the sheer volume of content uploaded every day makes the task of real-time moderation impossible. Certainly, the scale of material is beyond anything that has ever faced courts, regulators, in-house censors or other arbiters of taste and human decency. As *Forbes* reported in March 2018, 2.5 quintillion bytes of data are created every day; 90 per cent of the data in the world had been generated in the *two previous years*.[20] In this information ecosphere, it is patently incorrect to treat Facebook, Twitter and Google as if they were publishers in the traditional sense. Nor, however, can they get away with describing themselves – as they did for many years – as 'neutral platforms'. What is needed is a new jurisprudence that delineates in detail what has been called 'the third category': a way of apprehending tech giants as legal entities that makes them considerably more responsible for the content that they carry than they presently are, with sanctions that hurt as part of the new social contract (which is to say, more than fines that companies of their size can budget for as a relatively minor operating cost).

They also, at a minimum, should be required to archive all ads that they post in their micro-targeting of users. This is particularly urgent for political advertising: in most jurisdictions, online political ads are subject to much less regulation and scrutiny than all other forms of paid promotion – which means, in effect, that huge swathes of political discourse are unseen by anyone except their recipients. This is an intolerable violation of the principle of transparency upon which we insist in every other sphere of electioneering or referendum campaigning.

There is also a strong case for Facebook, at least, to be broken up using antitrust legislation – a case that was given fresh focus when Chris Hughes, one of the company's co-founders, advanced it in a *New York Times* article in May 2019. As Hughes wrote: 'the biggest winners would be the American people. Imagine a competitive market in which they could choose among one network that offered higher privacy standards, another that cost a fee to join but had little advertising and another that would allow users to customize and tweak their feeds as they saw fit. No one knows exactly what Facebook's competitors would offer to differentiate themselves. That's exactly the point'.[21]

That said, even the dismantling of Facebook would not address the two core issues that bedevil all efforts to bring big tech into line with the needs of a functioning liberal democracy. The first is the global trade in personal data – the most precious commodity in the world – which has spawned what Shoshana Zuboff calls 'the age of surveillance capitalism'.[22] It is not only the tech giants that trade in what they know about us. As the Internet of Things becomes a reality, every domestic device, vehicle, light switch, thermostat and surveillance mechanism will capture inconceivable quantities of information about us that will then be marketed.

Yet the companies that already profit – and will profit much more in the future – from our data do not even have to declare its value on their financial statements. As Peter Pomerantsev has reflected, it is disconcerting 'that "they" know something about me which I hadn't realised myself, that I'm not who I think I am – one's complete dissipation into data now being manipulated by someone else'.[23]

The tech companies protest that the deal they strike, implicitly or otherwise, is clear enough: we get to use their extraordinary digital tools for free, in return for access to our data. And everything, they continue, is set out in the terms and conditions to which we sign up. Leaving aside the utterly impenetrable language in which most T&C agreements are written, that is not, ethically, the end of the matter. The right to harvest our data does not, or should not, absolve them from saying what they do with it, and to whom they pass it on. The global defence trade is held together – albeit shakily – by the 'end-user certificate'. So who are the end users of my data and what do they do with it? No social media platform or device manufacturer that is unwilling to be transparent about this deserves your attention or your custom. It is the difference between legitimate data transfer and what amounts to data trafficking. We must learn to spot the difference.

The second great area of contention is the digital 'black box' of the algorithm. To date, tech companies have guarded their algorithms with furious jealousy as utterly sacred intellectual property. That is simply not sustainable in a free society that depends upon basic rights, essential dignities and checks and balances to cohere. Drug companies, the financial sector, manufacturing companies, mainstream media: all have to disclose reams of confidential information to regulators as part of their routine licensing. It is a measure of how bedazzled we have been by the first generation of Internet capitalism that we ever tolerated such secrecy.

At present, confidential computer code directs our newsfeeds, regulates our access to key services, selects options for us on streaming and retail sites, chooses the ads that appear on our screens, and, in many cases, embeds prejudice.[24] The case for algorithmic audit is now simply unanswerable: as Howard writes, 'There is no other domain of business in which a company can design and build something, release it onto the market, and change the product only when people complain'.[25]

Instead of resigning ourselves to the status quo, we should expect precisely the opposite: algorithms that are written within a clear ethical framework. In her book *Girl Decoded*, Rana el Kaliouby, CEO of Affectiva, an AI start-up, explains how this principle might be put into practice:

Algorithmic bias is a reflection of a larger issue: Humanity itself is inherently biased. As a starting point, we need to strive for AI to be less biased than people are. With some effort, a company can eliminate bias, or at least significantly reduce it, by being mindful of how it acquires its data, how it trains and validates its models, and most of all, by building diversity into its teams ... Even with good intentions, people in a group developing algorithms fall into a similar demographic and come from similar backgrounds, and may unwittingly introduce bias. That's why companies need teams that are diverse in age, cultural background, ethnicity, life experiences, education, and other factors.[26]

This turns the usual debate about algorithms on its head. Instead of treating them with deference as the *sanctum sanctorum* of tech religion, el Kaliouby describes them accurately – as no more or less than tools whose purpose is to enhance the lot of humanity and the world. Algorithms succeed or fail to the extent that they meet this standard (the examinations debacle in the summer of 2020 was a perfect case study of failure – precisely because Ofqual's coders had failed, to a quite remarkable extent, to consider the wreckage that their formulae might inflict upon individual lives). This marks a refreshing change of attitude, and one that the tech companies would do well to take seriously.

To be fully empowered citizens in the 21st Century we require a level of digital literacy that most people have not yet achieved. This is different from computer programming or other technical expertise: it is the capacity to navigate our way through the online universe, to understand which sources are reliable and which are not, to exercise due diligence, to see digital pseudoscience for the garbage it is and to raise our concerns when we discover falsehood, or conspiracy theories, or incitement to hate. It is the difference between being able to design a car and having the skills to drive it safely.

It is hard to overstate the importance of this objective. Just as a child is (or should be) taught how to understand a printed text, so she should be taught, from a very early age, how to make her way through the digital thickets that will surround her for the rest of her life. This is a matter of urgent social responsibility, a binding collective duty: for government, for schools, for charities, for tech companies themselves, and, of course, for families. No form of resilience is more important to the citizens of tomorrow. Fail in this, and we fail in all else.

CONCLUSION
THE WORLD OF
THE THREE 'I's

PRIOR: *We can't just stop. We're not rocks. Progress, migration, motion is . . . modernity. It's animate. It's what living things do.*

> Tony Kushner, *Angels in America* (1992)

All of our days are numbered. We cannot afford to be idle.

> Nick Cave, *20,000 Days on Earth* (2014)

For those struggling to survive coronavirus, and for the millions on the front line who worked round the clock to treat them, the pandemic that erupted in 2020 will always be remembered as a time of unrelenting freneticism. Yet the flipside of this freneticism was just the opposite: whole populations under what amounted to global house arrest, sequestered from their loved ones, wondering what the future held for them and for their livelihoods as the great economies of the world languished in something like an induced coma.

To call this period of suffering, disaggregation and surrealism a pause for thought would be a stretch: it was too burdened by grief, anxiety and apprehension to be framed as some sort of philosophical experience. But it indisputably posed a series of questions that will linger for many years to come. Was it ever really reasonable, or historically literate, to expect life to resume as normal? Will the world that emerges from the pandemic be one of melted orthodoxies, rekindled imagination and resourceful quests for new solutions? Or one of fortified walls, tightened borders, snarling nativism and (doomed) strategies for national self-sufficiency?

This book took as its premise the inadequacy of immigration (and its proxies) as a basis for modern politics. Instead, I have offered an alternative – intended as a stimulus to fresh debate, rather than as a comprehensive manual – rooted in the three 'I's: *Identity, Ignorance and Innovation*. As we rebuild the house where we live, they should be among the main joists of reconstruction.

The blueprint of that house is still being drafted and fought over. In his great book *The Roman Revolution*, Ronald Syme observed that '[i]n all ages, whatever the name and form of government, be it monarchy, republic, or democracy, an oligarchy lurks behind the façade'.[1] The oligarchic character of politics in our era is especially profound: its latest manifestation, in many countries, is the populist regime that claims to be speaking on behalf of 'the People', but spends more time rewarding its own members, insulating itself from scrutiny and vilifying the institutions – judiciary, media, legislatures – that are tasked with holding it to account.

Looming over contemporary oligarchy stands the spectre of 'ochlocracy' – that is, rule by the mob (the bloody reality of which was horribly illustrated by the storming of the US Capitol in January 2021). Today's crowds are furthermore as likely to impose their own form of rough justice online as in the street, piling in on social media, destroying lives and careers with their own destructive power and menace. If this is, as some claim, what passes for 'accountability' today, it is nothing to be proud of.

What risks being lost in this pincer movement is true democracy: not simple majoritarianism or the intermittent practice of casting a vote, but the richer culture that operates every day in the spirit of community, rule of law, respect for and protection of rights, and expectations governing personal and social responsibility. It is for this reason that I have called for a liberalism that learns lessons from identity politics, embraces its energy and heeds its grievances. The stakes are too high for progressives to waste a decade arguing about speech codes and cancel culture. A truce and then an alliance are needed, without delay.

A radically new approach to education is also required to raise young citizens as more than fodder for grade factories; as a generation for whom a hinterland of knowledge is a civil right. We need to recognise afresh the absolute modernity of what used to be called the 'liberal arts' and the value of 'right-side' brain capacity in a world of ever-greater automation. We have to remind ourselves how to read, and not settle for a lifetime of scrolling, hopping from one digital instant to the next.

Part of that endeavour is breaking down the ramparts that still separate the humanities from basic scientific literacy. The active citizen of the 21st Century should be able to navigate the high seas of digital technology and do so with understanding, vigilant always to the threat of fake news, pseudoscience and post-truth. We must not only be *willing* to keep learning after we leave school or university, but enthusiastically seek out opportunities to do so.

The notion of 'lifelong learning' has been promoted from political cliché to a collective social imperative. With increased life expectancy comes the responsibility to prepare for more than a single-profession career. Ambition in the 21st Century will more closely resemble agile mutation than a climb up a ladder. We shall all need the resilience, imagination and courage to be shape-shifters – and should expect, and demand, help from our employers and governments as, like Time Lords, we regenerate serially from cradle to grave. Innovation, then, is not only an economic and social mission. It is a way of life.

In which context: one of the many problems with modern populism is the shoddy inertia at its heart. Its rhetorical bluster is matched by a lack of statesmanlike ambition. It points guns at dinghies full of refugees, deploys heated language and offers bread and circuses. But it is a terrible framework within which to address the kinds of deep-seated social, economic and cultural issues described in this book. Populists love to talk – that is what they do – but they are not good at *getting stuff done*. In general, their talents are confined to pointing the finger, stirring up sentiment, unsettling people and taking pot shots at the better angels of our nature, lest they take flight. Populism is a response to our times. But it is not equal to them.

The world is destined to become more fractious, not less; not because human beings are inherently wicked, but because complexity is the modern condition. Even as we struggle to find new forms of what Theodore Roosevelt called 'fellow-feeling, sympathy in the broadest sense' we are structurally bound to encounter new conflicts, new abrasions, new competitions between competing rights and responsibilities. And this is precisely what we should expect from a society defined by hyperpluralism and heterogeneity.

The nativist movements that have emerged in recent years will not give up easily, but their prescriptions are hopelessly distant from reality – and will drift further from that shore as the years pass. The problems that they evade with noise, division and distraction will be left for others to solve. The paradox of the task that awaits the problem-solvers is that they will need the patience to accept that real reform is only accomplished over the long haul; but that it is never accomplished without a spirit of urgency, the infusion of short-term politics with a sense of the seriousness of what is at stake.

This is what the US commentator George F. Will meant when he famously wrote of 'statecraft as soulcraft'.[2] Reform is what we make of it, and change bears the imprint that we choose. There is no direction to history – ideological or divine. There is no teleology, or hidden purpose, in what we do and what is done to us. There is only human agency.

For those ready to accept the challenge, this should be a cause of great optimism. In *Angels in America* – written in the shadow of another pandemic – Tony Kushner has his central character, Prior (who is living with AIDs), end the play with a monologue in New York's Central Park: 'The world only spins forward. We will be citizens. The time has come . . . *More Life*. The Great Work Begins'.[3]

And so it does. This is a moment of extraordinary peril, promise and potential, waiting only for a generation with the courage to seize the opportunity and embrace the glorious uncertainties of what lies ahead.

NOTES

INTRODUCTION: THE THREE 'I's

1 I addressed this in *Post-Truth: The New War on Truth and How to Fight Back* (2017). See also (for instance) Philippe Legrain, *Immigrants: Your Country Needs Them* (2007), and my column in *The Guardian*, 3 December 2018, 'Let's be honest about what's really driving Brexit: bigotry'

2 https://www.politicshome.com/news/article/priti-patel-wants-to-send-in-the-navy-amid-channel-migrant-crossings-76366

3 Afua Hirsch, *BRIT(ish): On Race, Identity and Belonging* (2018), p272

4 Popularised by Renaud Camus' ridiculous book *Le Grand Remplacement* (2011)

5 See Erik Brynjolfsson and Andrew McAfee, *The Second Machine Age: Work, Progress and Prosperity In a Time of Brilliant Technologies* (pb 2016), p222 for the positive impact of immigration in the US and elsewhere

6 On the threat to democracy, see especially: Yascha Mounk, *The People vs Democracy: Why Our Freedom Is in Danger and How to Save It* (2018); Timothy Snyder, *The Road to Unfreedom: Russia, Europe, America* (2018); Ece Temelkuran, *How to Lose a Country: The 7 Steps from Democracy to Dictatorship* (2019); and, for a chilling historical precedent, Milton Mayer, *They Thought They Were Free: The Germans 1933–45* (2017 edition)

7 See Didier Eribon, *Returning to Reims* (tr. 2013); Arlie Russell Hochschild, *Strangers In Their Own Land: Anger and Mourning on the American Right* (2016); Jonathan M. Metzl, *Dying of Whiteness: How the Politics of Racial Resentment is Killing America's Heartland* (2019)

8 See, for instance: https://www.thesun.co.uk/fabulous/5726692/selfish-lazy-victims-who-take-offence-at-everything-why-i-hate-being-part-of-generation-z/ ; https://www.dailymail.co.uk/sciencetech/article-7033111/Millennials-Gen-Z-really-snowflakes.html

9 https://www.theguardian.com/environment/2019/sep/02/greta-thunberg-responds-to-aspergers-critics-its-a-superpower

10 https://adespresso.com/blog/instagram-statistics/

11 https://www.prnewswire.com/news-releases/americans-check-their-phones-96-times-a-day-300962643.html

12 Karl R. Popper, *The Poverty of Historicism* (1957)

13 Yuval Noah Harari, *Homo Deus: A Brief History of Tomorrow* (tr. 2016)

CHAPTER 1: THE RISE OF IDENTITY POLITICS

1   https://www.bristolpost.co.uk/news/bristol-news/artist-blm-sculpture-colstons-plinth-4347511

2   See Keeanga-Yamahtta Taylor, *How We Get Free: Black Feminism and the Combahee River Collective* (2017)

3   https://americanstudies.yale.edu/sites/default/files/files/Keyword%20Coalition_Readings.pdf;

4   David Lammy, *Tribes: How Our Need to Belong Can Make or Break the Good Society* (2020), p166

5   Erik H. Erikson, *Identity: Youth and Crisis* (pb 1994), p232ff

6   Erikson op. cit. p303

7   See David Eagleman: What makes us empathetic? IQ2 Talks (2012) https://www.youtube.com/watch?v=TDjWryXdVdo

8   Jonathan Sacks, *Morality: Restoring the Common Good in Divided Times* (2020), p132

9   See A.J. Gurevich, *Categories of Medieval Culture* (tr 1985)

10 Francis Fukuyama, *Identity: The Demand For Dignity and the Politics of Resentment* (2018), p115

11 Mark Lilla, *The Once and Future Liberal: After Identity Politics* (2017), pp10–12

12 Greg Lukianoff and Jonathan Haidt, *The Coddling of the American Mind: How Good Intentions and Bad Ideas are Setting Up a Generation for Failure* (2018). See also Jonathan Rauch, *Kindly Inquisitors: The New Attacks on Free Thought* (expanded edition, 2013) and Bradley Campbell and Jason Manning, *The Rise of Victimhood Culture: Microaggressions, Safe Spaces and the New Culture Wars* (2018)

13 Lukianoff and Haidt op. cit. p10

14 See Jean M. Twenge, *iGen: Why Today's Super-Connected Kids Are Growing Up Less Rebellious, More Tolerant, Less Happy – and Completely Unprepared for Adulthood* (2017)

15 https://www.telegraph.co.uk/politics/2020/03/06/government-looks-strengthen-free-speech-campus-oxfords-no-platforming/

16 Lukianoff and Haidt op. cit. p43

17 Lukianoff and Haidt op. cit. p60

18 See Matthew d'Ancona, *Post-Truth: The New War on Truth and How to Fight Back* (2017), pp49–51; and Henry Farrell, 'The consequences of the Internet for politics', *Annual Review of Political Science* (2012). For an ingenious analysis of the role that empathy plays in bolstering tribalism, see Rutger Bregman, *Humankind: A Hopeful History* (2020), pp201–21

19 See, for instance, Stephen Shames and Bobby Seale, *Power to the People: The World of the Black Panthers* (2016); Huey P. Newton, *Revolutionary Suicide* (1973); ed. Stephen Drury Smith and Catherine Ellis, *Free All Along: The Robert Penn Warren Civil Rights Interviews* (2019)

20 See Jodi Kantor and Megan Twohey, *She Said: Breaking the Sexual Harassment Story that Helped Ignite a Movement* (2019)

21 Philip N. Howard, *Pax Technica: How the Internet of Things May Set Us Free or*

Lock Us Up (2015). On network politics, see Matthew d'Ancona, 'Bannon's Britain', *Tortoise*, 28 September, 2019 https://members.tortoisemedia.com/2019/09/28/bannons-britain/content.html

22 Douglas Murray, *The Madness of Crowds: Gender, Race and Identity* (2019), p2

23 Murray, op. cit. p102

24 See James Kirkup, 'Why are women who discuss gender getting bomb threats?', *Spectator Coffee House*, 21 June 2018 https://www.spectator.co.uk/article/why-are-women-who-discuss-gender-getting-bomb-threats-

25 Murray op. cit. p6

26 Lammy op. cit. p172

27 Hirsch op. cit. p243

28 https://www.theguardian.com/world/2020/may/01/british-bame-covid-19-death-rate-more-than-twice-that-of-whites

29 https://www.independent.co.uk/news/uk/home-news/racism-uk-inequality-black-lives-matter-wealth-economic-health-a9567461.html

30 https://bylinetimes.com/2020/06/08/black-lives-dont-matter-in-britain/

31 https://www.accountancydaily.co/11-ftse-100-board-directors-are-bame

32 https://www.thisismoney.co.uk/money/markets/article-8445083/FTSE-100-firms-missing-BAME-director-target.html

33 https://www.theguardian.com/world/2019/oct/15/metoo-justice-system-complaints-up-convictions-down

34 https://www.womensaid.org.uk/information-support/what-is-domestic-abuse/how-common-is-domestic-abuse/

35 https://www.statista.com/statistics/1096724/workplace-sexual-harassment-uk/

36 https://www.independent.co.uk/news/uk/home-news/sexual-harassment-work-place-scared-sacked-study-metoo-a9155466.html

37 https://www.bbc.co.uk/news/uk-england-london-51049336

38 https://www.pinknews.co.uk/2020/05/26/trans-non-binary-young-people-suicide-mental-health-study-trevor-project/

39 The definitive book on this new insecurity is James Bloodworth, *Hired: Undercover in Low-Wage Britain* (2018). See also Jeremias Prassl, *Humans as a Service: The Promise and Perils of Work in the Gig Economy* (2018)

40 See Robert B. Reich, *The System: Who Rigged It, How We Fix It* (2020)

41 https://www.reuters.com/article/us-davos-meeting-trust/capitalism-seen-doing-more-harm-than-good-in-global-survey-idUSKBN1ZJ0CW

42 See, for instance: Thomas Piketty, *Capital in the Twenty-First Century* (2013) and *Capital and Ideology* (2019); Anand Giridharadas, *Winners Take All: The Elite Charade of Changing the World* (2018); Rutger Bregman, *Utopia for Realists* (2017); Kate Raworth, *Doughnut Economics: Seven Ways to Think Like a 21st-Century Economist* (2017); and David Pilling, *The Growth Delusion: The Wealth and Well-Being of Nations* (2018)

43 George A. Akerlof and Rachel E. Kranton, *Identity Economics: How Our Identities Shape Our Work, Wages, and Well-Being* (2010), p16

44 Akerlof and Kranton op. cit. p87

45 Akerlof and Kranton op. cit. p98–9

46 See, for instance: Ashley Jardina, *White Identity Politics* (2019); José Pedro Zuqete, *The Identitarians: The Movement Against Globalism and Islam in*

Europe (2018); David Neiwert, *Alt-America: The Rise of the Radical Right in the Age of Trump* (2017); Cas Mudde, *The Far Right Today* (2019); and Julia Ebner, *Going Dark: The Secret Social Lives of Extremists* (2020)

CHAPTER 2: LIBERALISM AT THE CROSSROADS – THE CHALLENGE OF IDENTITY POLITICS

1   *Financial Times*, 28 June 2019

2   See Matthew d'Ancona, 'The software of a decent society', *Tortoise*, 24 September 2019   https://members.tortoisemedia.com/2019/09/24/constitutional-crisis-matt-dancona/content.html

3   https://members.tortoisemedia.com/2020/07/10/200710-editors-voicemail/content.html

4   Mark Lilla, *The Once and Future Liberal: After Identity Politics* (2017), pp 95, 105, 111

5   Lilla, op. cit. p117

6   John Rawls, *A Theory of Justice* (revised edition, 1999), p11

7   Akala, *Natives: Race & Class in the Ruins of Empire* (pb, 2019), p171

8   Akala, op. cit. p205

9   Afua Hirsch, *BRIT(ish): On Race, Identity and Belonging* (2018), pp23, 316

10 Hirsch, op. cit. p317. See also Renni Eddo-Lodge, *Why I'm No Longer Talking to White People About Race* (2017)

11 https://www.nytimes.com/2017/08/15/world/europe/london-inequality-grenfell-tower-fire.html

12 https://www.bbc.co.uk/news/uk-53320082

13 See Amelia Gentleman, *The Windrush Betrayal: Exposing the Hostile Environment* (2019) and Maya Goodfellow, *Hostile Environment: How Immigrants Became Scapegoats* (2019)

14 David Lammy, *Tribes: How Our Need to Belong Can Make or Break the Good Society* (2020)

15 Ta-Nehisi Coates, *Between the World and Me* (2015), p9

16 https://www.bbc.co.uk/news/av/uk-53048748/boris-johnson-announces-inquiry-into-racial-inequality

17 https://www.standard.co.uk/comment/comment/tackling-racial-injustice-action-matthew-dancona-a4471621.html

18 https://www.racialequitytools.org/resourcefiles/mcintosh.pdf

19 https://www.newyorker.com/books/page-turner/the-origins-of-privilege

20 For a useful collection of McIntosh's studies, see https://nationalseedproject.org/about-us/white-privilege; for a magnificent exploration of the deepest roots of racism, see Isabel Wilkerson, *Caste: The Lies That Divide Us* (2020)

21 See, for instance, the Canadian psychologist Jordan Peterson on white privilege: https://www.youtube.com/watch?v=JEESNpAu1EU or the American conservative polemicist Ben Shapiro https://www.youtube.com/watch?v=fxDO7_C8gyo

22 Douglas Murray, *The Madness of Crowds: Gender, Race and Identity* (2019), p87

23 Lammy, op. cit. p161

24 Robin DiAngelo, *White Fragility: Why It's So Hard for White People to Talk About Racism* (2018); another notable bestseller in the fraught summer of 2020 was Ibram X. Kendi, *How To Be An Antiracist* (2019)

25 DiAngelo, op. cit. pp3, 9, 20, 22

26 http://libjournal.uncg.edu/ijcp/article/view/249

27 DiAngelo, op. cit. p109

28 See also Eduardo Bonilla-Silva, *Racism Without Racists: Color-Blind Racism & Racial Inequality in Contemporary America* (third ed, 2010)

29 https://www.theatlantic.com/ideas/archive/2020/07/dehumanizing-condescension-white-fragility/614146/

30 DiAngelo, op. cit. pp84–5

31 DiAngelo, op. cit. pxv

CHAPTER 3: WHERE IDENTITY POLITICS GOES WRONG

1 https://policyexchange.org.uk/wp-content/uploads/2019/11/Academic-freedom-in-the-UK.pdf

2 https://campaignforfreespeech.org/wp-content/uploads/2019/10/Free-Speech-Survey-Standard-Banners.pdf

3 https://members.tortoisemedia.com/2019/05/28/life-of-brian/content.html?sig=VSWXkZ4gPwJpQOLk5d_060DGJSx1g5tSUDc_ijakmlw

4 https://www.thetimes.co.uk/article/millennials-have-been-scarred-by-free-speech-mvmblpmfj

5 On this generation's response to digital overload, see Jean M. Twenge, *iGen: Why Today's Super-Connected Kids Are Growing Up Less Rebellious, More Tolerant, Less Happy – and Completely Unprepared for Adulthood* (2017)

6 Greg Lukianoff and Jonathan Haidt, *The Coddling of the American Mind: How Good Intentions and Bad Ideas are Setting Up a Generation for Failure* (2018)

7 https://www.theatlantic.com/politics/archive/2016/05/the-peril-of-writing-a-provocative-email-at-yale/484418/

8 Captured on video: https://www.youtube.com/watch?v=9IEFD_JVYdo&feature=youtu.be

9 Lukianoff and Haidt, p56

10 Lukianoff and Haidt, pp114–20

11 https://www.youtube.com/watch?v=bO1agIlLlhg

12 For audio of the meeting and edited transcript, see https://nationalpost.com/news/canada/heres-the-full-recording-of-wilfrid-laurier-reprimanding-lindsay-shepherd-for-showing-a-jordan-peterson-video

13 https://www.youtube.com/watch?v=Qpg6P1PNWR8

14 https://www.telegraph.co.uk/education/2019/02/02/universities-allowing-free-speech-curtailed-favour-rule-mob/

15 See Robert Paul Wolff, Barrington Moore, Jr., and Herbert Marcuse, *A Critique*

of *Pure Tolerance* (1969), pp. 95-137, or https://www.marcuse.org/herbert/publications/1960s/1965-repressive-tolerance-fulltext.html

16 See Robert Paul Wolff, Barrington Moore, Jr., and Herbert Marcuse, *A Critique of Pure Tolerance* (1969), pp. 95-137, or https://www.marcuse.org/herbert/publications/1960s/1965-repressive-tolerance-fulltext.html

17 https://mclaughlinonline.com/2017/10/11/nro-new-college-student-survey-yes-speech-can-be-violence/

18 See Mari J. Matsuda, Charles R. Lawrence III, Richard Delgado and Kimberle Williams Crenshaw, *Words That Wound: Critical Race Theory, Assaultive Speech, and the First Amendment* (1993)

19 https://www.nytimes.com/2017/07/14/opinion/sunday/when-is-speech-violence.html

20 https://www.theatlantic.com/education/archive/2017/07/why-its-a-bad-idea-to-tell-students-words-are-violence/533970/. See also Strossen, op. cit. pp123–4

21 See William Davies, *Nervous States: How Feeling Took Over the World* (2018); Peter Pomerantsev, *Nothing Is True and Everything Is Possible* (pb 2016) and *This Is Not Propaganda: Adventures in the War Against Reality* (2019); Matthew d'Ancona, *Post-Truth: The New War on Truth and How To Fight Back* (2017)

22 Cited in Nadine Strossen, *Hate: Why We Should Resist It with Free Speech, Not Censorship* (2018) pp1–2

23 Timothy Garton Ash, *Free Speech: Ten Principles for a Connected World* (2016), p90

24 https://www.newstatesman.com/2019/12/t-trans-movement-ongoing-struggle-tiny-vulnerable-minority See also ed. Christine Burns, *Trans Britain: Our Journey from the Shadows* (2018)

25 https://www.telegraph.co.uk/news/2019/10/08/next-census-will-allow-trans-people-choose-gender-bill-passes/

26 https://www.theguardian.com/society/2020/jul/17/trans-people-twice-as-likely-to-be-victims-of-in-england-and-wales

27 https://www.stonewall.org.uk/sites/default/files/trans_stats.pdf

28 https://www.jkrowling.com/opinions/j-k-rowling-writes-about-her-reasons-for-speaking-out-on-sex-and-gender-issues/

29 https://www.independent.co.uk/arts-entertainment/books/news/jk-rowling-harry-potter-fan-sites-trans-views-mugglenet-leaky-cauldron-a9601231.html

30 https://harpers.org/a-letter-on-justice-and-open-debate/

31 https://www.washingtonpost.com/nation/2020/07/08/letter-harpers-free-speech/

32 https://www.theguardian.com/commentisfree/2020/jul/10/free-speech-young-people

33 https://www.newstatesman.com/science-tech/2020/07/cancel-culture-does-not-exist

34 https://www.independent.co.uk/news/uk/home-news/maya-forstater-transgender-test-case-equalities-act-employment-tribunal-a9253211.html

35 Article in *The Times* newspaper, 27th October 2019

36 https://www.lawgazette.co.uk/news/barrister-raises-60k-to-sue-chambers-and-charity-/5104809.article

37 https://www.heraldscotland.com/news/18564550.scots-author-gillian-philip-dumped-backing-jk-rowling-transgender-row/

38 Strossen op. cit. pp75–6

39 Strossen op. cit. p136–8
40 https://www.chronicle.com/article/Racism-Was-Served-by-Silence/238667
41 Quoted in Strossen, op. cit. p40
42 See Robert Cohen, *Freedom's Orator: Mario Savio and the Radical Legacy of the 1960s* (2009); ed. Robert Cohen and Reginald E. Zelnik, *The Free Speech Movement: Reflections on Berkeley in the 1960s* (2002). And ed. Robert Cohen, *The Essential Mario Savio: Speeches and Writings that Changed America* (2014)
43 See Cohen op. cit. pp179–93
44 Quoted in Cohen and Zelnik, op. cit. pii
45 https://edition.cnn.com/2017/02/01/us/milo-yiannopoulos-berkeley/index.html
46 Jonathan Rauch, *Kindly Inquisitors: The New Attacks on Free Thought* (expanded edition, 2013), p177
47 There are times when such restrictions are obviously sensible. I supported a campaign in July 2020 to ban the rapper Wiley from social media after a series of viciously anti-Semitic posts that were (in my view) a clear incitement to racial hatred https://www.bbc.co.uk/news/technology-53553573
48 https://www.telegraph.co.uk/technology/2020/06/13/alt-right-using-covid-19-cover-spread-propaganda/
49 Rauch, op. cit. p180
50 See Anne Applebaum, *Twilight of Democracy: The Failure of Politics and The Parting of Friends* (2020)
51 https://theintercept.com/2017/08/29/in-europe-hate-speech-laws-are-often-used-to-suppress-and-punish-left-wing-viewpoints/
52 https://members.tortoisemedia.com/2019/07/17/the-take-free-speech/content.html?sig=hX56QeZPrkG_ak7UvUN7uyrYmKE9JgPaC7bdUrQHqhw
53 Quoted in Strossen, op. cit. p34

CHAPTER 4: IDENTITY POLITICS IS HERE TO STAY – AND THAT'S A GOOD THING

1 William Deresiewicz, *Excellent Sheep: The Miseducation of the American Elite & The Way to a Meaningful Life* (pb, 2015), p220
2 For the origin of the admonition, 'stay in your lane', see https://www.merriam-webster.com/words-at-play/stay-in-your-lane-origin-phrase-history
3 See Alberto Manguel, *Curiosity* (2015) and Ian Leslie, *Curious: The Desire to Know and Why Your Future Depends on it* (2014)
4 https://www.nybooks.com/articles/2019/10/24/zadie-smith-in-defense-of-fiction/
5 See John Gray, *Two Faces of Liberalism* (2000), p34
6 Afua Hirsch, *BRIT(ish): On Race, Identity and Belonging* (2018); Akala, *Natives: Race & Class in the Ruins of Empire* (pb, 2019); David Olusoga: *Black and British: A Forgotten History* (2016)
7 https://www.runnymedetrust.org/uploads/publications/pdfs/TIDERunnymedeTeachingMigrationReport.pdf

8   https://www.ourmigrationstory.org.uk/. See also https://www.theguardian.com/commentisfree/2019/dec/05/britain-colonial-history-curriculum-racism-migration

9   https://www.standard.co.uk/comment/comment/quote-churchill-at-your-peril-woke-ideologues-have-rewritten-history-a3958396.html

10 https://www.theguardian.com/politics/2020/jul/22/home-office-urged-to-correct-false-slavery-information-in-citizenship-test

11 https://www.nytimes.com/2016/01/29/opinion/must-rhodes-fall.html

12 https://www.theguardian.com/commentisfree/2020/jun/08/edward-colston-statue-history-slave-trader-bristol-protest

13 See Arlie Russell Hochschild, *Strangers in Their Own Land: Anger and Mourning on the American Right* (2016), Chapter 9; Robin DiAngelo, *White Fragility: Why It's So Hard for White People to Talk About Racism* (2018), pp91ff

14 Melvin I. Urofsky, *The Affirmative Action Puzzle: A Living History from Reconstruction to Today* (2020), pp358–9. For a useful comparison of the UK and US systems, see Rachel Herron's Durham University MJur thesis (2010) http://etheses.dur.ac.uk/662/1/Rachel_Herron.pdf?DDD19+

15 Quoted in Urofsky, op. cit. p419

16 https://www.credit-suisse.com/about-us-news/en/articles/media-releases/42035-201207.html

17 https://hbr.org/2019/09/research-when-women-are-on-boards-male-ceos-are-less-overconfident

18 https://www.cipd.co.uk/Images/ftse-100-executive-pay-report-2019_tcm18-62886.pdf

19 https://www.theguardian.com/education/2020/jun/23/bame-students-make-up-one-fifth-of-new-oxford-undergraduates

20 https://www.thetimes.co.uk/article/white-male-and-elite-why-arent-judges-moving-on-pqhhqdrr2

21 https://www.resolutionfoundation.org/publications/opportunities-knocked-exploring-pay-penalties-among-the-uks-ethnic-minorities/

22 Urofsky, op. cit. p306

23 https://www.hrmagazine.co.uk/article-details/lammy-uk-needs-heavy-dose-of-affirmative-action-on-race

24 See, in particular, Richard H. Thaler and Cass R. Sunstein, *Nudge: Improving Decisions About Health, Wealth and Happiness* (2008) and Robert B. Cialdini, *Influence: The Psychology of Persuasion* (2007)

25 Linda Hirshman, *Reckoning: The Epic Battle Against Sexual Abuse And Harassment* (2019), p254. See also Jodi Kantor and Megan Twohey, *She Said: Breaking The Sexual Harassment Story That Helped Ignite a Movement* (2019)

26 https://www.theguardian.com/world/2020/mar/11/harvey-weinstein-sentencing-rape-conviction

27 http://www.thesecondsource.co.uk/wp-content/uploads/2017/10/second_source_press_release.pdf; see also https://www.standard.co.uk/lifestyle/london-life/female-journalists-set-up-network-to-fight-sexual-harassment-a3675716.html

28 https://www.theguardian.com/world/2019/oct/15/metoo-justice-system-complaints-up-convictions-down

29 https://www.theguardian.com/society/2020/jul/14/we-are-facing-the-decriminali-sation-of-warns-victims-commissioner

30 https://www.theguardian.com/society/2020/aug/09/downing-street-to-set-rape-prosecution-targets-police-and-cps

31 https://www.theatlantic.com/magazine/archive/2014/06/the-case-for-reparations/361631/

32 https://www.theguardian.com/commentisfree/2020/jul/09/british-slavery-repara-tions-economy-compensation

33 http://anthropos-lab.net/wp/wp-content/uploads/2011/12/Weber-Politics-as-a-Vocation.pdf

34 Helen Lewis, *Difficult Women: A History of Feminism in 11 Fights* (2020)

35 Mark Lilla, *The Once and Future Liberal: After Identity Politics* (2017), p12

36 https://www.foreignaffairs.com/articles/2019-02-01/stacey-abrams-response-to-francis-fukuyama-identity-politics-article?amp&__twitter_impression=true

37 https://plato.stanford.edu/entries/berlin/#BerlDefiValuPlur

38 https://www.theguardian.com/uk-news/2019/may/26/birmingham-anderton-park-primary-muslim-protests-lgbt-teaching-rights

39 https://www.spectator.co.uk/article/is-it-a-crime-to-say-women-don-t-have-penises-19-august-2018

40 Lilla, op. cit. p130

41 Lilla, op. cit. p133

42 David Lammy, *Tribes: How Our Need to Belong Can Make or Break the Good Society* (2020), p201

43 https://www.orwellfoundation.com/the-orwell-foundation/orwell/essays-and-other-works/notes-on-nationalism/

44 See James S. Fishkin, *Democracy When The People Are Thinking: Revitalizing Our Politics Through Public Deliberation* (2018) and Anne Marie Jansen, *Liquid Democracy: Counteracting democratic deficits in German politics* (2013)

45 Lukianoff and Haidt, op. cit. p60

CHAPTER 5: BRILLIANT IGNORANCE

1 David Hare, *Asking Around: Background to the David Hare Trilogy* (1993), p3

2 William Deresiewicz, *Excellent Sheep: The Miseducation of The American Elite & The Way To A Meaningful Life* (pb 2015)

3 Jean M. Twenge, *iGen: Why Today's Super-Connected Kids Are Growing Up Less Rebellious, More Tolerant, Less Happy – and Completely Unprepared for Adulthood* (2017), pp59-65; also https://theconversation.com/why-it-matters-that-teens-are-reading-less-99281#:~:text=There%20was%20a%20study%20from,more%20books%20than%20older%20people.&text=When%20we%20look%20at%20pleasure,markedly%20less%20than%20previous%20generations.

4 https://www.theguardian.com/education/2020/feb/29/children-reading-less-says-new-research. See also https://www.newyorker.com/culture/cultural-comment/why-we-dont-read-revisited

5 Harold Bloom, *How To Read And Why* (2000), p21
6 https://www.brainpickings.org/2016/08/03/neil-gaiman-view-from-the-cheap-seats-reading/
7 https://www.nybooks.com/articles/1986/10/09/why-read-the-classics/
8 Gretchen McCulloch, *Because Internet: Understanding the New Rules of Language* (2019),
9 https://pubmed.ncbi.nlm.nih.gov/18980888/
10 https://www.cleveland.com/metro/2015/10/college_students_say_it_is_eas.html
11 https://drugfree.org/newsroom/news-item/adderall-abuse-increases-among-high-school-students/
12 https://yougov.co.uk/topics/health/articles-reports/2019/04/23/one-seven-gcse-students-taking-black-market-study-
13 https://www.bbc.co.uk/news/health-46472308; see also https://www.theguardian.com/society/2018/feb/09/reduces-people-zombies-uk-readers-xanax-misuse
14 https://www.telegraph.co.uk/news/2020/02/21/doubling-number-young-people-needing-hospital-treatment-self/
15 https://www.theguardian.com/society/2019/sep/03/suicides-rates-in-uk-increase-to-highest-level-since-2002
16 https://www.washingtonpost.com/health/teen-suicides-increasing-at-alarming-pace-outstripping-all-other-age-groups/2019/10/16/e24194c6-f04a-11e9-8693-f487e46784aa_story.html
17 Twenge, op. cit. pp93–118

CHAPTER 6: UNINTENDED CONSEQUENCES – HOW EXAMS LOST THE PLOT

1 See Michael Barber, *Instruction to Deliver: Fighting to Transform Britain's Public Services* (2008) and Nicholas Timmins, *The Five Giants: A Biography of the Welfare State* (revised edition, 2017)
2 For the intellectual hinterland of reform, see Richard Cockett, *Thinking the Unthinkable: Think-Tanks and The Economic Counter-Revolution, 1931–1983* (1994)
3 Kenneth Baker, *The Turbulent Years: My Life in Politics* (1993), pp164–5
4 For Margaret Thatcher's criticisms of the Baker reforms see her first volume of memoirs, *The Downing Street Years* (1993), pp595–7
5 Ken Robinson and Lou Aronica, *Creative Schools: Revolutionizing Education From the Ground Up* (iBook, 2015), p46
6 Robinson and Aronica, op. cit. p48–9
7 Rebecca Allen and Sam Sims, *The Teacher Gap* (2018), p4
8 Allen and Sims, op. cit. p1
9 Allen and Sims, op. cit. pp2–3
10 https://publications.parliament.uk/pa/cm200708/cmselect/cmchilsch/1003/1003.pdf

11 https://www.tes.com/news/uk-among-worlds-worst-teaching-test-research-finds

12 https://www.bbc.co.uk/news/education-41580550

13 Interview, 13 April 2020

14 Interview . . .; see also https://thepsychologist.bps.org.uk/volume-33/march-2020/schools-out

15 Stanislas Dehaene, *How We Learn: The New Science of Education and the Brain* (2020), Chapter 9

16 https://www.etoncollege.com/userfiles/files/TLC_brochure_FAW_080618.pdf

17 Dehaene, op. cit. pp218–19

18 See, for example, the work undertaken by the Rethinking Assessment group: https://rethinkingassessment.com/rethinking-assessment-home/

19 https://www.thetimes.co.uk/article/lets-scrap-gcses-for-ever-not-just-this-year-5n2f9tmcs ; https://www.telegraph.co.uk/education-and-careers/2020/04/21/exams-cancelled-year-time-scrap-gcses-altogether/

20 See, in particular, Lucy Crehan, *Cleverlands: The secrets behind the success of the world's education superpowers* (2016); also https://www.theguardian.com/education/2016/sep/20/grammar-schools-play-europe-top-education-system-finland-daycare

21 http://www.eurydice.si/publikacije/National-testing-of-pupils-in-Europe_Objectives%2C-organisation-and-use-of-results-EN-HI.pdf?_t=1569928954

22 https://www.thelocal.se/20191203/how-do-swedens-pisa-school-results-compare-to-other-countries ; https://www.simplylearningtuition.co.uk/advice-for-parents/everything-you-need-to-know-about-the-swedish-education-system/

23 https://factsmaps.com/pisa-2018-worldwide-ranking-average-score-of-mathematics-science-reading/

24 https://www.ccsu.edu/wmln/ ; see also https://www.theguardian.com/books/2016/mar/11/finland-ranked-worlds-most-literate-nation

25 Crehan, op. cit. p16

26 https://www.economist.com/international/2019/12/05/pisa-results-can-lead-policymakers-astray

CHAPTER 7: POINTLESS PERFECTION: HOW THE MERITOCRACY MYTH KILLS KNOWLEDGE AND LEARNING

1 William Deresiewicz, *Excellent Sheep: The Miseducation of The American Elite & The Way to a Meaningful Life* (pb 2015), p3; see also Frank Bruni, *Where You Go Is Not Who'll You'll Be: An Antidote to The College Admissions Mania* (pb 2016)

2 Deresiewicz, op. cit. pp10–11

3 In his 2015 book, *The Road to Character*, David Brooks draws a relevant distinction between 'résumé virtues' (wealth, status, accomplishments) and 'eulogy virtues' (kindness, humility, courage)

4 Deresiewicz, op. cit. p22

5 Greg Lukianoff and Jonathan Haidt, *The Coddling of the American Mind: How Good Intentions and Bad Ideas are Setting Up a Generation for Failure* (2018), pp186ff

6 Lukianoff and Haidt, op. cit. p189

7 This subject, amongst much else, is explored in Nick Timothy's excellent book, *Remaking One Nation: The Future of Conservatism* (2020)

8 For Young's late reflections see: https://www.theguardian.com/politics/2001/jun/29/comment

9 Daniel Markovits, *The Meritocracy Trap* (2019), p300, quoting the *Guardian*, 22 October 2015. See also Michael J. Sandel, *The Tyranny of Merit: What's Become of the Common Good?* (2020)

10 See Deresiewicz, op. cit. p206. See also Walter Benn Michaels, *The Trouble With Diversity: How We Learned to Love Identity and Ignore Inequality* (2006) for the failure of modern public service systems to address the socio-economic core of social injustice

11 Quoted in Jerry Z. Muller, *The Tyranny of Metrics* (pb 2019), p31. See also https://towardsdatascience.com/on-the-tyranny-of-metrics-and-metric-fixation-b4c1d44b5f6c See also ed. R.H. Super, Matthew Arnold, *Democratic Education* (1962), pp212–43

12 Quoted in Muller, op. cit. pp32–3

13 On this cultural descent, see Carl T. Bergstrom and Jevin D. West, *Calling Bullshit: The Art of Scepticism in a Data-Driven World* (2020)

14 Douglas Kinnard, *The War Managers* (1977)

15 See Viktor Mayer Schönberger and Kenneth Cukier, *Big Data: The Essential Guide to Work, Life and Learning in the Age of Insight* (2017 edn, p166).

16 Quoted in Muller, op. cit. p19

17 Muller, op. cit. p86

18 https://www.telegraph.co.uk/news/2020/06/23/unemployment-rates-new-graduates-highest-among-law-computer/#:~:text=Overall%2C%20nearly%20one%20in%20ten,months%20after%20leaving%20higher%20education

19 https://www.tuc.org.uk/sites/default/files/BlackQualifiedandunemployed.pdf

20 https://www.forbes.com/sites/jackkelly/2019/11/14/recent-college-graduates-have-the-highest-unemployment-rate-in-decadesheres-why-universities-are-to-blame/#2a24bebb320b

21 Deresiewicz, op. cit. p39

22 https://www.investors.com/politics/editorials/millennials-patriotic-survey/

23 https://www.washingtonpost.com/news/acts-of-faith/wp/2018/04/12/two-thirds-of-millennials-dont-know-what-auschwitz-is-according-to-study-of-fading-holocaust-knowledge/

24 https://forward.com/opinion/438652/young-people-are-staggeringly-ignorant-about-the-holocaust-its-dangerous/

25 See Matthew d'Ancona, *Post-Truth: The New War on Truth and How to Fight Back* (2017), pp76–83

26 https://www.shoutoutuk.org/2017/07/07/the-age-of-ignorance/

27 https://www.democraticaudit.com/2017/04/27/who-dont-young-people-vote-self-confessed-ignorance-and-dislike-of-the-mainstream/

28 Denise Clark Pope, *'Doing School': How We Are Creating a Generation of Stressed Out, Materialistic, and Miseducated Students* (2001), ppxi–xii

29 Pope, op. cit. p11–12, 15

30 Pope, op. cit. p32, 34, 37

31 Pope, op. cit. p155

CHAPTER 8: THE DIGITAL INSTANT

1 The most intelligent such argument is to be found in Nicholas Carr, *The Shallows: What the Internet is Doing To Our Brains* (10th anniversary ed, 2020). See also Larry Rosen, *iDisorder: Understanding Our Obsession With Technology and Overcoming Its Hold on Us* (2013)

2 https://qz.com/1367506/pew-research-teens-worried-they-spend-too-much-time-on-phones/#:~:text = According % 20to % 20Common % 20Sense % 20 Media,kids % 20between % 200 % 20and % 20eight.

3 Jean M. Twenge, *iGen: Why Today's Super-Connected Kids Are Growing Up Less Rebellious, More Tolerant, Less Happy – and Completely Unprepared for Adulthood* (2017), p51

4 Rosen, op. cit. p65 (iBook edition)

5 Mark Bauerlein, *The Dumbest Generation: How The Digital Age Stupefies Young Americans and Jeopardizes Our Future (Or, Don't Trust Anyone Under 30)* (pb 2009), p236

6 Gretchen McCulloch, *Because Internet: Understanding the New Rules of Language* (2019), p274

7 Team led by Dr Joseph Firth, Senior Research Fellow at NICM Health Research Institute, Western Sydney University. The "online brain": how the Internet may be changing our cognition. *World Psychiatry*, 2019; 18 (2): 119 DOI: http://dx.doi.org/10.1002/wps.20617

8 https://www.theguardian.com/society/2019/apr/16/got-a-minute-global-attention-span-is-narrowing-study-reveals. See also L.E. Levine, B.M. Waite, L.L. Bowman, 'Electronic media use, reading, and academic distractability in college youth', *CyberPsychology & Behavior*, 10(4), pp560–6

9 K. Purcell, L. Rainie, A. Heaps et al. *How teens do research in the digital world.* Pew Research Center, 1 November 2012

10 See Mary Aiken, *The Cyber Effect: A Pioneering Cyberpsychologist Explains How Human Behaviour Changes Online* (pb 2017), pp110–3; Nicholas Kardaras, *Glow Kids: How Screen Addiction Is Hijacking Our Kids – and How to Break the Trance* (2016) and Adam Alter, *Irresistible: Why we can't stop checking, scrolling, clicking and watching* (2017)

11 https://www.opencolleges.edu.au/informed/features/5-ways-digital-media-impacts-brain/

12 See https://academic.oup.com/jcmc/article/11/2/522/4617731 and https://www.verywellmind.com/the-recency-effect-4685058

13 Rosen, op. cit. p380 (iBook ed)

14 https://neurosciencenews.com/memory-internet-cognition-4854/

15 https://news.columbia.edu/news/study-finds-memory-works-differently-age
    -google

16 See, for instance, Mark O'Connell, *To Be a Machine: Adventures Among
    Cyborgs, Utopians, Hackers and the Futurists Solving the Modest Problem of
    Death* (2017)

17 Mark Edmundson, *Why Read?* (pb 2005), p15

18 G, Dong, M.N. Potenza, 'Behavioural and brain responses related to Internet
    search and memory'. *Eur J Neurosci* 2015

19 https://www.dartmouth.edu/press-releases/digital-media-change-050816.html

20 William Poundstone, *Head in the Cloud: Dispatches from a Post-Fact World* (pb,
    2017), p266. For recent reports on the scale of the problem, see Philip N. Howard,
    *Lie Machines: How to Save Democracy from Troll Armies, Deceitful Robots,
    Junk News Operations, and Political Operatives* (2020); and Michiko Kakutani,
    The Death of Truth (2018)

21 Poundstone, op. cit. 267–8

22 See Matthew d'Ancona, *Post-Truth: The New War on Truth and How to Fight
    Back* (2017), pp23–34

23 http://sitn.hms.harvard.edu/flash/2018/dopamine-smartphones-battle-time/

24 Eric S. Raymond, *The Cathedral and the Bazaar: Musings On Linux and Open
    Source by an Accidental Revolutionary* (1999)

25 Clay Shirky, *Here Comes Everybody: The Power of Organizing Without
    Organizations* (2008)

26 See Tim Wu, *The Attention Merchants: From the Daily Newspaper to Social
    Media, How Our Time and Attention is Harvested and Sold* (2016)

CHAPTER 9: NEWS THAT STAYS NEWS

1 The best primer on the different schools of analysis is still Terry Eagleton, *Literary
   Theory: An Introduction* (1983). See also Ed Paul Rabinow, *The Foucault Reader:
   An Introduction to Foucault's Thought* (1991); Jacques Derrida, *Writing and
   Difference* (2001); Jean Baudrillard, *Simulacra and Simulation* (1994). For a bril-
   liant satire of the new campus culture, see Malcolm Bradbury, *The History Man*
   (1975)

2 Harold Bloom, *The Western Canon: The Books and School of The Ages* (1994)
   Allan Bloom, *The Closing of the American Mind: How Higher Education Has
   Failed Democracy and Impoverished the Souls of Today's Students* (1987)

3 Allan Bloom, op. cit. p382

4 https://www.ft.com/content/bfe61952-be91-11e7-9836-b25f8adaa111

5 Quoted in Fareed Zakaria, *In Defense of a Liberal Education* (2015), p19

6 https://www.oprah.com/omagazine/toni-morrison-on-reading/all

7 https://www.brainpickings.org/2014/02/10/the-project-of-literature-susan-sontag
   -92y/

8 Richard Hoggart, *The Uses of Literacy* (1957); see also Jonathan Rose, *The
   Intellectual Life of the British Working Classes* (2001)

9 http://s-f-walker.org.uk/pubsebooks/2cultures/Rede-lecture-2-cultures.pdf

10 https://www.independent.co.uk/news/education/education-news/education-secretary-nicky-morgan-tells-teenagers-if-you-want-job-drop-humanities-9852316.html

11 http://s-f-walker.org.uk/pubsebooks/2cultures/Rede-lecture-2-cultures.pdf

12 https://www.bbc.co.uk/news/world-us-canada-42170100. See also https://www.bankofengland.co.uk/knowledgebank/will-a-robot-takeover-my-job

13 https://www.nature.com/articles/d41586-019-02874-0

14 https://www.bbc.co.uk/news/technology-41829534

15 https://www.forbes.com/sites/cognitiveworld/2020/04/05/why-ai-is-transforming-the-banking-industry/#41e8b0bf7dd6

16 http://news.mit.edu/2019/toward-artificial-intelligence-that-learns-to-write-code-0614

17 Daniel H. Pink, *A Whole New Mind: How to thrive in the new conceptual age* (2005), p1

18 Quoted in Pink, op. cit. p53

19 https://www.forbes.com/sites/georgeanders/2015/07/29/liberal-arts-degree-tech/#6412648a745d ; see also George Anders, *You Can Do Anything: The Surprising Power of 'Useless' Liberal Arts Education* (2017)

20 Scott Hartley, *The Fuzzy and the Techie: Why the Liberal Arts Will Rule the Digital World* (2017)

21 Quoted in Zakaria, op. cit. p90

22 Quoted in Zakaria, op. cit. p79

23 http://www.fields.utoronto.ca/talks/What-does-stand-STEAM

24 See Robert Elliott Smith, *Rage Inside the Machine: The Prejudice of Algorithms, and How to Stop the Internet Making Bigots of Us All* (2019). See also https://theconversation.com/steam-not-stem-why-scientists-need-arts-training-89788

25 Quoted in Zakaria, op. cit. p82

26 See Zakaria, op. cit. p67

27 Quoted in Erik Brynjolfsson and Andrew McAfee, *The Second Machine Age: Work, Progress and Prosperity In a Time of Brilliant Technologies* (pb 2016), pp195–6

28 https://www.theguardian.com/commentisfree/2018/dec/28/silver-linings-2018-world-cup-summer

29 Mark Edmundson, *Why Read?* (pb 2005), p28

30 Edmundson, op. cit. p16

31 https://readabilityguidelines.co.uk/clear-language/low-literacy-users/#:~:text=1%20in%206%20adults%20in,challenges%20because%20of%20low%20literacy.

32 See for instance https://booksinthemedia.thebookseller.com/articles/black-lives-matter-an-anti-racist-reading-list

33 https://www.jordanbpeterson.com/great-books/

34 https://www.fables.co.za/hundred_best.html

35 https://bigthink.com/mind-brain/philosophy-books?rebelltitem=9#rebelltitem9

36 https://bookriot.com/50-books-to-read-if-you-love-medicine/

37 https://quantumphysicsmadesimple.com/best-quantum-physics-books-for-beginners/

38 https://www.nytimes.com/interactive/2020/climate/climate-change-books.html

39 https://www.oxfamamerica.org/explore/stories/19-books-help-you-better-under-stand-poverty/
40 https://bookauthority.org/books/best-art-books
41 http://www.hiphopshakespeare.com/
42 https://www.booktrust.org.uk/
43 https://childrens.poetryarchive.org/
44 Edmundson, op. cit. p34

CHAPTER 10: THE AGE OF METATHESIOPHOBIA: OR HOW FEAR OF CHANGE HAS CHANGED EVERYTHING

1 Matt Ridley, *How Innovation Works* (2020), pp2, 4. For the global nature of the battle to innovate see Alexandre Lazarow, *Out-Innovate: How Global Entrepreneurs from Delhi to Detroit Are Rewriting the Rules of Silicon Valley* (2020); see also Clayton M. Christensen, *The Innovator's Dilemma* (1997)

2 Ridley, op. cit. p261

3 Ridley, op. cit. p10

4 https://www.bbc.co.uk/news/uk-53065306

5 https://www.bushcenter.org/catalyst/immigration/what-are-we-so-afraid-of.html

6 Quoted in Robert Hughes, *The Shock of the New: Art and The Century of Change* (2019 edition), p9

7 Hughes, op. cit. p15

8 See Christopher Booker, *The Neophiliacs: A Study of the Revolution in English Life in the Fifties and Sixties* (1969)

9 Michael Lewis, *The New New Thing: How Some Man You've Never Heard of Just Changed Your Life* (1999)

10 John P. Kotter, *Leading Change* (1996), p40; see also Peter Drucker, *Managing in a Time of Great Change* (Kindle edition, 2011)

11 Kotter, op. cit. p36

12 Kotter, op. cit. p162

13 https://psychtimes.com/metathesiophobia-fear-of-change/

14 https://liberationist.org/this-is-the-reason-why-people-resist-change/

15 https://www.cse.iitk.ac.in/users/amit/books/gilbert-2006-stumbling-on-happi-ness.html; see also Daniel Gilbert, *Stumbling on Happiness* (2006)

16 Jonathan Haidt, *The Happiness Hypothesis: Putting Ancient Wisdom and Philosophy to the Test of Modern Science* (2006)

17 Nassim Nicholas Taleb, *Antifragile: Things that Gain from Disorder* (2012)

18 See, for example, Joseph Wolpe and David Wolpe, *Life Without Fear: Anxiety and Its Cure* (1988) and Joseph Wolpe, *The Practice of Behavior Therapy* (2nd edition, 1973)

19 Boris Cyrulnik, *Resilience: How Your Inner Strength Can Set You Free From the Past* (2009 edition), p284

20 Cyrulnik, op. cit. pp 287, 284

CHAPTER 11: LEARNING TO LIVE WITH ROBOTS

1 See Erik Brynjolfsson and Andrew McAfee, *The Second Machine Age: Work, Progress and Prosperity in a Time of Brilliant Technologies* (pb 2016), p250

2 See Martin Ford, *The Rise of the Robots: Technology and the Threat of Mass Unemployment* (pb 2016)

3 Hans Moravec, *Mind Children* (1988), p15

4 https://www.ft.com/content/51f1bb71-ce93-4529-9486-fec96ab3dc4d

5 https://www.forbes.com/sites/simonchandler/2020/05/12/coronavirus-is-forcing-companies-to-speed-up-automation-for-better-and-for-worse/#4e3adc555906

6 Brynjolfsson and McAfee, op. cit. p203

7 https://www.workitdaily.com/career-advice-workplace-automation/always-be-aware-of-where-your-job-stands

8 See Ray Kurzweil, *The Singularity is Near: When Humans Transcend Biology* (2018 edition)

9 https://www.technologyreview.com/2011/10/12/190773/paul-allen-the-singularity-isnt-near/

10 See Thomas H. Davenport & Julia Kirby, *Only Humans Need Apply: Winners & Losers in the Age of Smart Machines* (2016), p226–7; and https://knowledge.wharton.upenn.edu/article/the-network-revolution-creating-value-through-platforms-people-and-digital-technology/

11 https://ifr.org/downloads/papers/IFR_The_Impact_of_Robots_on_Employment_Positioning_Paper_updated_version_2018.pdf

12 Peter Drucker, *Managing in a Time of Great Change* (Kindle edition, 2011), pp227–8

13 https://www.nytimes.com/2017/05/03/upshot/how-to-prepare-for-an-automated-future.html

14 https://www.mckinsey.com/featured-insights/future-of-work/retraining-and-reskilling-workers-in-the-age-of-automation

15 https://hbr.org/2020/06/how-reskilling-can-soften-the-economic-blow-of-covid-19

16 https://www.weforum.org/whitepapers/towards-a-reskilling-revolution-industry-led-action-for-the-future-of-work

17 https://www.bcg.com/en-gb/publications/2019/decoding-global-trends-upskilling-reskilling

18 https://hrexecutive.com/reskilling-a-matter-of-survival/

19 https://www.mercer.com/our-thinking/career/global-talent-hr-trends.html

20 See, for instance, https://www2.deloitte.com/us/en/insights/focus/human-capital-trends/2020/reskilling-the-workforce-to-be-resilient.html

21 Brynjolfsson and McAfee, op. cit. p233

22 See Rutger Bregman, *Utopia for Realists* (pb 2018), Chapter Two; Ford, op. cit. pp263ff

23 https://www.vox.com/future-perfect/2020/2/19/21112570/universal-basic-income-ubi-map

24 https://www.cnbc.com/2020/07/20/will-there-be-a-second-1200-stimulus-check-heres-what-we-know.html

25 https://www.thersa.org/discover/publications-and-articles/rsa-blogs/2020/05/ubi-basic-income-covid

CHAPTER 12: CENTURY OF CENTURIES: THE CHALLENGE OF LIVING LONGER

1 https://www.theguardian.com/commentisfree/2017/may/21/politics-audacity-may-manifesto

2 Nick Timothy, *Remaking One Nation: The Future of Conservatism* (2020)

3 https://commonslibrary.parliament.uk/home-affairs/communities/paying-for-social-care-20-years-of-inaction/

4 Lynda Gratton and Andrew J. Scott, *The 100-Year Life: Living and Working in an Age of Longevity* (2016) and *The New Long Life: A Framework for Flourishing in a Changing World* (2020). See also their website: http://www.100yearlife.com/

5 Scott and Gratton, *The New Long Life*, p183

6 See Camilla Cavendish, *Extra Time: 10 Lessons for an Ageing World* (2019), p9

7 https://www.theguardian.com/society/2020/feb/24/austerity-blamed-for-life-expectancy-stalling-for-first-time-in-century. Life expectancy rebounded in 2019 https://www.theguardian.com/society/2020/mar/03/life-expectancy-in-england-rebounds-after-years-of-stagnation

8 https://www.ageuk.org.uk/globalassets/age-uk/documents/reports-and-publications/later_life_uk_factsheet.pdf

9 On the possibilities of increased longevity, see also Carl Honoré, *Bolder: Making the Most of Our Longer Lives* (2018)

10 Cavendish, op. cit. p215. See also Joseph C. Sternberg, *The Theft of a Decade: How the Baby Boomers Stole the Millennials' Economic Future* (2019) and David Willetts *The Pinch: How the Baby Boomers Took Their Children's Future – And Why They Should Give It Back* (updated edition 2019)

11 https://www.ucas.com/corporate/news-and-key-documents/news/largest-ever-proportion-uks-18-year-olds-entered-higher-education-2017-ucas-data-reveals

12 https://www.credit-suisse.com/about-us/en/reports-research/global-wealth-report.html

13 https://uk.reuters.com/article/us-usa-election-inequality-poll/majority-of-americans-favor-wealth-tax-on-very-rich-reuters-ipsos-poll-idUKKBN1Z9141

14 https://www.independent.co.uk/news/uk/politics/budget-mansion-tax-rishi-sunak-nhs-social-care-climate-change-a9384861.html

15 https://www.ft.com/content/68800d9b-1a78-41a0-b63e-18b447fcc6e6

16 Alan Bennett, *Untold Stories* (2006 pb), pp114–15

17 https://www.bbc.co.uk/news/uk-53280011. On the disgraceful financial structures that underpin the care industry, see Ian Birrell's award-winning investigations https://members.tortoisemedia.com/2020/05/18/coronavirus-care-homes-ian-birrell/content.html

18 https://www.theguardian.com/society/2020/aug/12/care-home-residents-losing-will-to-live-amid-covid-restrictions-in-england

CHAPTER 13: MISINFORMATION – HOW TO BE RESILIENT IN THE AGE OF POST-TRUTH

1　See Matthew d'Ancona, *Post-Truth: The New War on Truth and How to Fight Back* (2017), pp8–9

2　See Philip N. Howard, *Lie Machines: How to Save Democracy from Troll Armies, Deceitful Robots, Junk News Operations, and Political Operatives* (2020), p137

3　https://publications.parliament.uk/pa/cm201719/cmselect/cmcumeds/1791/1791. pdf

4　See Cadwalladr's 2019 TED talk https://www.ted.com/talks/carole_cadwalladr_ facebook_s_role_in_brexit_and_the_threat_to_democracy?language=en; Jehane Noujaim and Karim Amer's Netflix documentary *The Great Hack* (2019); and Christopher Wylie, *Mindf*ck: Inside Cambridge Analytica's Plot to Break the World* (2019)

5　See Rana Foroohar, *Don't be Evil: The Case Against Big Tech* (2019), p272

6　https://www.newyorker.com/magazine/2020/04/20/how-anthony-fauci-became-americas-doctor

7　https://www.theguardian.com/world/2020/aug/06/anthony-fauci-death-threats-coronavirus

8　https://members.tortoisemedia.com/2020/03/23/the-infodemic-fake-news-coronavirus/content.html

9　https://members.tortoisemedia.com/2020/08/04/rise-of-the-super-spreaders-infodemic/content.html

10　https://www.independent.co.uk/news/world/americas/us-politics/coronavirus-trump-treatment-disinfectant-bleach-new-york-a9483786.html

11　See Rob Brotherton, *Suspicious Minds: Why We Believe Conspiracy Theories* (2016), p121

12　https://jamanetwork.com/journals/jamaoncology/fullarticle/2687972

13　https://www.theatlantic.com/magazine/archive/2019/08/measles-as-metaphor/ 592756/; for ethnographic insights into the anti-vaxx movement, see Jennifer A. Reich, *Calling the Shots: Why Parents Reject Vaccines* (pb 2018). See also ed. Massimo Pigliucci and Maarten Boudry, *Philosophy of Pseudoscience: Reconsidering the Demarcation Problem* (2013) and Jean-Pierre Changeux, *The Physiology of Truth: Neuroscience and Human Knowledge* (tr. 2009)

14　https://www.theguardian.com/world/2020/aug/09/only-half-of-britons-would-definitely-have-covid-19-vaccination

15　See Samuel Woolley, *The Reality Game: How the next wave of technology will break the truth and what we can do about it* (2020), p177

16　Woolley, op. cit. p174

17　https://fullfact.org/

18　https://securingdemocracy.gmfus.org/hamilton-dashboard/

19　Quoted Foroohar op. cit. p273

20　https://www.forbes.com/sites/bernardmarr/2018/05/21/how-much-data-do-we-create-every-day-the-mind-blowing-stats-everyone-should-read/#1a3d2c1860ba

21　https://www.nytimes.com/2019/05/09/opinion/sunday/chris-hughes-facebook-zuckerberg.html

22 Shoshana Zuboff, *The Age of Surveillance Capitalism: The Fight for a Human Future at the New Frontier of Power* (2019)

23 See Peter Pomerantsev, *This Is Not Propaganda: Adventures in the War Against Reality* (2019), p234

24 See Robert Elliott Smith, *Rage Inside the Machine: The Prejudice of Algorithms, and How to Stop the Internet Making Bigots of Us All* (2019)

25 Howard, op. cit. p166

26 Rana el Kaliouby (with Carol Colman), *Girl Decoded: My Quest to Make Technology Emotionally Intelligent – and Change the Way We Interact Forever* (2020)

CONCLUSION: THE WORLD OF THE THREE 'I's

1 Ronald Syme, *The Roman Revolution* (1939), p7

2 George F. Will, *Statecraft as Soulcraft: What Government Does* (1983)

3 Tony Kushner, *Angels in America* (2017 pb), p290

ACKNOWLEDGEMENTS

This book was mostly written in the shadow of the pandemic, in a strange season that oscillated between solidarity and isolation.

I heard it said more than once that lockdown must be good for authors – what more could we ask for, after all? – but I take leave to differ. Writing, however personal a process it may be at the sharp end, is ultimately a social pursuit: the consequence of a thousand conversations, reading recommendations, face-to-face interviews, acts of guidance, chatter over coffee, and, above all, friendship.

So, more than ever, I want to thank the people who helped me. At Hodder, Rupert Lancaster was a sensationally good editor, always on hand to clarify and sharpen an idea and engage intellectually with the task. His colleagues Cameron Myers, Eleni Lawrence and Michael Ridge were hugely professional, as was our hawkeyed copy-editor Sophie Bristow.

My incomparable agent, Caroline Michel, was, as ever, an inspiration, friend, and source of wisdom. I thank her from the bottom of my heart.

In Emma Irving, I was amazingly fortunate to find a brilliant researcher who is an accomplished journalist in her own right and an editor of the future. I only hope she will give me a job one day.

At Tortoise Media – as should be clear from these pages – I have been extraordinarily lucky to work with a group of remarkable people engaged in an equally remarkable start-up news project.

To the co-founders, James Harding and Katie Vanneck-

Smith, I owe a profound debt of gratitude: they were supremely supportive of the book and encouraged me at every stage. They are both remarkably gifted people, formidable champions of a new way of doing journalism, and it is an honour to be on their team.

Particular thanks, too, to my colleagues Liz Moseley, Alexandra Mousavizadeh, Paul Caruana-Galizia, Chris Cook, Merope Mills, Giles Whittell, Liv Leigh, Annabel Shepherd-Barron, Emily Benn, and Keith Blackmore. All kept my spirits up and my brain ticking over in more Zoom calls than any of us would care to mention.

One of the best professional decisions I ever took was to hire the absurdly talented Pete Hoskin when I was editing *The Spectator*, and he is now Executive Editor at Tortoise. I am proud to count him as a great friend and creative partner in crime.

So many friends and mentors helped me to write this book, directly and indirectly. None of them is responsible for the content of these pages, but each and every one has supported and inspired me in all sorts of ways. So a big thank you to: D-J Collins; Suzie Norton; Tony Hall; Emily Maitlis; Julia Pasaron; Ciro Romano; Young Kim; Professor Tim Bale; Sarah Sands; Harriet Marsden; Jane Miles; Sarah and Johnnie Standing; Julia Hobsbawm; David Yelland; Professor Philip Bobbitt; Jack Kessler; Rafael Behr; Lara Spirit; Rosamund Urwin; Suzanne Moore; and Sir Ian Blatchford.

Two intellectual giants whom I was honoured to know died in the months of this book's preparation: Rabbi Lord Jonathan Sacks and Sir Roger Scruton. The world is a lesser place without them, though their respective legacies are colossal. Selfishly, I was sorry not to be able to send them the manuscript – seeking, as ever, their wisdom, guidance and erudition, always bestowed with such generosity.

Another sadness: this is the first of my books that I shall not be able to discuss with either of my parents, following the death of my beloved father in June 2019. I miss them both every day and try to honour their memory in all that I do. RIP.

This book is for their two eldest grandchildren, my sons, Zac and Teddy, with all my love. They are my world, and make the world seem better every day.

Matthew d'Ancona
London
January 2021

An invitation from the publisher

Join us at www.hodder.co.uk, or follow us
on Twitter @hodderbooks to be a part of
our community of people who love the very
best in books and reading.

Whether you want to discover more about a book
or an author, watch trailers and interviews, have the
chance to win early limited editions, or simply browse
our expert readers' selection of the very best books,
we think you'll find what you're looking for.

And if you don't, that's the place to tell us what's missing.

We love what we do, and we'd love you to be a part of it.

www.hodder.co.uk

@hodderbooks

HodderBooks

HodderBooks